LICENSE *to* DEAL

LICENSE *to* DEAL

A SEASON ON THE RUN WITH A MAVERICK BASEBALL AGENT

JERRY CRASNICK

RODALE

Book design by Drew Frantzen

Library of Congress Cataloging-in-Publication Data

Crasnick, Jerry.
    License to deal : a season on the run with a maverick baseball agent / Jerry Crasnick.
        p.   cm.
    Includes index.
    ISBN-13 978–1–59486–024–9 hardcover
    ISBN-10 1–59486–024–6 hardcover
    1. Sosnick, Matt.   2. Sports agents—United States—Biography.   3. Baseball players—
United States.   4. Major League Baseball (Organization)   I. Title.
GV734.5.C73   2005
796.357'092—dc22   2005003845

Distributed to the trade by Holtzbrinck Publishers

2   4   6   8   10   9   7   5   3   1   hardcover

To my late parents, Max and Rose Crasnick,
who built a home with love and always put their children first.

CONTENTS

Chapter
ONE

The road was dry, the sky was clear, and Dontrelle Willis hadn't had a drop of alcohol the day he should have died.

He'd just finished lunch and was headed north up Route 101 near Palo Alto, California, when he heard a *bang* coming from the right rear of his Ford Mustang. About a half-mile south of the Stanford University exit, Dontrelle felt his car drifting toward the right lane and instinctively yanked the steering wheel to the left to avoid a collision. But the fleeting instant for adjustment had already passed. The Mustang skidded northbound while facing west, then toppled on its side and flipped counterclockwise once, twice, three times before coming to rest beside the center divider, facing the oncoming traffic.

As a minor-league pitcher with the Florida Marlins, Dontrelle was accustomed to setting events in motion. Now, a random and inexplicable occurrence was hurling him down the highway at 65 mph. Buckled in his seat, he felt a sense of horror: His fate was out of his hands. He kept his eyes open through each flip, watched the front windshield shatter, and raised his arms and braced them against the roof of the car.

I don't want to die like this, he told himself. He felt a wet sensation on the back of his neck and later surmised that the radiator had sprung a leak. The scene unfolded with a sickening, slow-motion feel, yet it happened so quickly that there was barely time to pray.

The accident photographs are both grotesque and surreal. They show a green mass of metal propped on its side, so mangled you can barely discern that it's a car, much less a Ford Mustang. As Dontrelle shimmied out the busted back window onto the asphalt, he looked at his vehicle. The hood was gone and the windshield was but a memory. Traffic was passing by so quickly on Route 101 that another car nearly struck him on the highway's shoulder. His blue-and-white polo shirt was stained with some sort of fluid. He later chose to keep the shirt as a memento, to remind him of how lucky he had been.

Dontrelle took a quick inventory, thanked God that he was in one piece, then pulled out his cellular phone. Who to call? His mother was at work, and she'd freak, he knew. So he dialed his agent's number.

"Dude, I've been in a bad accident," he said to Matt Sosnick. "Come get me."

Matt knew it was bad when he called the dispatcher and she told him that several motorists had already reported the accident. He jumped in his Jaguar and reached the scene in 20 minutes, only to find the off-ramp closed. So he drove down the embankment through the bushes, into a place no Jaguar XJ8 had gone before. Then he crossed several lanes onto the shoulder and wedged his way behind a parked police car.

Matt glanced at the traffic and saw passers-by making the sign of the cross. A California Highway Patrol officer later described the accident as "gnarly." Dontrelle was 100 percent, Grade A fine. But he emerged from his car in an almost trancelike state. He approached Matt with tears on his face, and they hugged each other so hard it hurt.

The baseball agent exists to negotiate contracts and provide round-the-clock babysitting services for millionaire big leaguers in need. He frets over your salary arbitration case and talks the hotel manager back to Earth after you've skipped out on the bill. The agent exudes an air of mystery: His profession is a marriage of romance and sleaze, and he's either a detail man, an opportunist, or both, depending on your vantage point. He works ridiculously long hours looking out for the best interests of his clients, or risks sleep deprivation hatching schemes to screw management out of every buck. Who knows what motivations race through his head behind that gelled hair and those designer shades? The agent is a riddle wrapped in an enigma, cloaked in a tailored Italian suit.

Matt Sosnick, who runs a growing baseball agency in suburban San Francisco, bats about .500 on stereotypes. "There are four things you need to know about me right away," he'll say, once he opens the passenger door to his Jaguar and you're ensconced in leather. "I live for the Dave Matthews Band. I've taped every *Simpsons* episode ever made. I don't have a crumb of food in my house. And I only sleep on sheets with a really high thread count."

Matt also owns several top-of-the-line suits that he buys from the Hong Kong tailors who pass through town every few weeks for private fittings. The suits are worth $3,000 apiece, but he purchases them for $800 to $900 each. He's proud of the price and quick to reveal the inner lining, where his name is stitched in fancy script. The suits help him look sharp on frequent trips to the heartland, where he sweeps in like a Texas twister to romance prospects who have 95-mph fastballs and personal relationships with the Lord Jesus Christ.

After all, a man has to make a nice first impression if he wants to make a living.

Matt seems perfectly tailored for his profession, with his flair for shrewd snap judgments and pathological need for action. He talks frequently and he talks fast, with a 10-item-or-less-checkout-line urgency more suited to, say, midtown Manhattan than his native northern California. But the glamour and money aren't what drive him, despite what his competitors say. Matt already has more money than your average bachelor around town would ever need. He's in the agent business for the sense of family it provides, and for the opportunity to play mother hen and surrogate father to a bunch of kids in need of guidance.

Matt and his partner, Paul Cobbe, determined several years ago that the barriers to entry in their profession required them to do more than negotiate draft bonuses and supply batting gloves and spikes to players. *The competitive advantage,* Paul calls it. Bigger, more established agencies could print slick brochures and crow about multimillion-dollar deals struck on behalf of marquee free agents. Mom-and-pop shops need a more personal touch. So Sosnick and Cobbe decided they wouldn't represent players as much as adopt them. They invest emotionally in their clients and are available for counsel on everything from money worries to girlfriend problems, regardless of the time of day. Their welcome mats are always out—and extraordinarily worn.

Every now and then, the guest stays a while. In October 2002, Matt handed over a spare key to his duplex apartment to a minor-league pitcher named Dontrelle Willis. Four years into an improbable friendship, Matt and Dontrelle shared a 1,700-square-foot space and a life for several months. They broke down enough societal and generational barriers to bridge the gap from affluent Burlingame to hardscrabble west Alameda.

In the summer and fall of 2003, Dontrelle would make an All-Star team, win the National League Rookie of the Year award, and become a national sensation as a pitcher for the world champion Florida Marlins. Only a handful of starters in the majors are black; even fewer big leaguers wear their caps askew and play the game with a sense of joy so pronounced, it's palpable. Dontrelle approaches life in a headfirst-slide sort of way, and his pitching motion is so contorted, it looks like a kinesiology experiment gone awry. No wonder fans were lining up for his autograph and a chance to be near him.

There weren't any cameras or reporters waiting to chronicle the event when Dontrelle, an aspiring Carolina Mudcat, moved into the spare room of Matt's $775,000 duplex near the airport in the fall of 2002. Logic would say that a 33-year-old Caucasian wheeler-dealer and a 20-year-old African-American male with street smarts and a gangsta vocabulary had no business cohabiting or bonding with any sense of permanence. Yet bond they did.

In his own way, Matt helped Dontrelle prepare for the season. He jostled the kid at 7:00 A.M. each day for training runs. They'd drive 10 minutes to the Crystal Springs reservoir, and if Matt found a parking place within three spots of the front gate, he knew it was destined to be a good day. The Sawyer Camp Trail is postcard pretty, enveloped in thick groves of oak, and every twist and turn can bring a surprise in the form of a rabbit or perhaps a deer crossing the path. Matt and Dontrelle would begin their runs beneath a blanket of fog, before the sun sliced through the chilly morning air, and they'd feel their hearts race to the accompaniment of heavy breathing. At 6'4" and 235 pounds, Dontrelle was too thick in the legs for serious distance running, but he was dogged enough to keep pace with his agent, who ran with a fervor bordering on desperation.

On many of the runs, Matt talked about world events and misery and strife in far-flung locations. One time, Dontrelle returned to his old neighborhood in Alameda and began rambling on about Pol Pot and the horrors of the Khmer Rouge in Cambodia. His "people," as he likes to call them, looked at him as if he'd grown a second head.

Agent and player rubbed off on each other in ways you wouldn't expect. Dontrelle took things in stride and approached life with a sense of balance and perspective. He felt strongly that there was a time and place for work and a corresponding time and place for fun. He'd tilt his head with an admonishing look as Matt spent hour after hour on the cell phone doing business.

"He's crazy," Dontrelle says. "He doesn't stop working. He works until he sleeps. There's no leisure time. A lot of times I'd say, 'Hey, you gotta relax, dude.' He's a very important man. His M.O. is to be in control of everything because he's a smart guy. He's a very intelligent guy. He makes good decisions. Therefore, he feels responsible for everyone.

He feels accountable for everyone. And it doesn't work like that. But you can't fault a man for that trait. That's a good trait. It's the same trait I have. I think that's why we connect."

The competitive advantage. Matt invited Dontrelle to his grandmother's house for Thanksgiving dinner and took his client to parties full of thirtysomething Jewish singles. Dontrelle would listen quietly and absorb as Matt's crowd discussed the hunt for Osama bin Laden or debated whether the term *homicide bomber* was preferable to *suicide bomber*. Then he'd chime in with a few opinions of his own.

Matt's sister, Alisa Law, gave birth to twin girls that fall: Sophia and Olivia. The babies were a month premature and confined to a special-care nursery. Both had jaundice and one suffered from sleep apnea, so visitation was restricted to immediate family. Then Matt stopped by with Dontrelle one day and sweet-talked them both past the nurses' station. "My brother," he said, pointing to his friend.

Matt has a photograph from a Halloween party that reflects his off-beat sense of humor. In the picture, he's wearing a Randy Moss jersey, several gold chains, a wave cap, and jeans so spacious they keep sliding off his hips. Beside him is Dontrelle, clad in a bar mitzvah suit, yarmulke, and prayer shawl. Duddy Kravitz, say hello to P. Diddy. "It was absolutely hilarious," Dontrelle says. "It was one of the greatest nights of my life."

In the winter of 2002 to 2003, Dontrelle became fast friends with Matt's English bulldog, Griffey, who routinely wandered into the spare bedroom upstairs and hopped onto the mattress beside him. Many a morning, Dontrelle awoke to an ugly mug and the blast of hot bulldog breath in his face. Sometimes the dog would fall asleep on his right arm and pin it to the mattress, and Dontrelle would grab the TV remote with his left hand and watch *SportsCenter* until the moment arrived for both of them to rise and face the world.

Dontrelle looked unassuming in his baggy jeans and throwback jerseys, but he was making an impression with the Florida brass. In his first three professional seasons, he posted a 23–5 record and was anointed an up-and-comer. Baseball America's *Prospect Handbook*, the Kelley Blue Book of minor-league talent, rated him the fourth best player in the Marlins' farm system. His progress was particularly distressing to the Chicago Cubs, who had been prescient enough to select him in the eighth round of the 2000 amateur draft, only to send him to the Marlins in a six-player trade 2 years later.

"Willis creates excellent deception with an unorthodox delivery he says he learned from his mother as a child," read the scouting report on Dontrelle. "After opening eyes throughout his new organization, Willis figures to return to high Class A to start 2003."

Maybe so, but Dontrelle had already received the prize in the Cracker Jack box: a letter from the Marlins telling him he'd been invited to big-league camp. It meant he was no longer relegated to the back fields at spring training, where he'd be forced to practice mundane chores like covering first base on bunt plays with other young hopefuls. Through this latest stroke of good fortune, Dontrelle would tackle the mundane, mind-numbing chores of PFP—pitchers' fielding practice—on the main fields with A. J. Burnett, Brad Penny, and other established Marlins.

Dontrelle was at his mother's house playing PlayStation 2 when his invitation arrived in the mail. He spent most of that night lying in bed staring at this little sheet of paper, reluctant to sleep because it might force him to relinquish the sweet sense of accomplishment for only a few hours. "Dude, I'm going to be the kid that changes the game," he told Matt, out of a can-do spirit rather than a sense of boastfulness.

The winter was an emotional ordeal for Sosnick in many respects. He'd been banging away at this agent business for more than 5 years—always in the red—only to discover that each step forward was accompanied by two steps back. Matt and Paul had hustled up an impressive stable of players through the annual June draft. But as the kids progressed through the minors and got close enough to glimpse life in The Show, they began leaving for more established agencies, often suddenly or with little explanation.

Sometimes players would break the news by phone, and other times with a failure to return calls. Sometimes, notification would come in the mailbox, in a missive known among agents as a "fire letter." A fire letter makes the knot in your gut twist exponentially as you open the envelope.

Nothing personal, the letter would say. *It's just business.*

"The dark side of the business was something Matt and I didn't know about," says Paul, the calmer, analytical half of Sosnick-Cobbe Sports, Inc. "The stealing and paying and that sort of stuff. We haven't made any mistakes on the business side. Our mistake—and it's an evolving thing—is understanding what it really means to maintain relationships with guys. To this day, we tend to take stuff way too personally. It's been a big problem for us."

Each departure fed Matt's insecurity and made him more cynical and fatalistic about the future of his enterprise. He was so conflicted that when his players succeeded, he wondered if it merely increased the odds that they would bolt. "I hate my job," Matt would say, with the doomed look of a man who loved his job so much he had no choice but to endure.

Dontrelle, the pragmatist, ultimately cut to the chase. You say players are leaving and that loyalty is fleeting? You say this business stinks? Well, let's roll up our sleeves—or one sleeve, at least—and make a statement.

How about I get your agency logo tattooed onto my arm?

That October, as is his custom, Matt invited several new clients to San Francisco for a weekend of hanging out and fraternal bonding. The group attended a Rolling Stones concert on a Saturday night—fourth-row center seats—and a 49ers game on Sunday before collapsing in front of the big-screen TV in Sosnick's living room.

Dontrelle's plan arose in conversation in a can-you-believe-this-craziness sort of way, and it might have died if not for the enthusiasm of Jason Pridie, an aggressive young outfielder in the Tampa Bay Devil Rays chain. Jason stands 6'1", weighs 180 pounds, and first attracted the attention of scouts for his feistiness as much as for his raw ability. If a famous player embodies his outlook on life and baseball, it's probably Lenny Dykstra, the former Mets and Phillies outfielder who never came home clean or conserved a shred of energy. Dykstra was known as "Nails" because he was too relentless to succumb to failure.

Jason's biggest problem, long before his arrival in pro ball, was keeping track of body parts. He survived pneumonia when he was 5 years old, then a bike wreck, then a broken collarbone while swinging a bat as a high school freshman. During one game, Jason was filling in at shortstop when he moved his glove prematurely on an attempted steal and the throw from the catcher caught him between the eyes. He suffered a fractured frontal sinus and emerged with a scar that bridged his temples and a titanium plate in his forehead. He collected scars the way some people collect miniature bottles of hotel shampoo.

Jason already sported a pair of tattoos—one of a Celtic tribe and another with his middle name. His zest for adventure was exceeded only by his pain threshold. What was the big deal about a few more pin pricks?

"I'll get one too," he said.

Matt laughed. "When?" he said.

"Right now."

Should Matt, a good dozen years older than these kids, have snipped the insanity before the momentum built? Probably. But the boys were already too far gone. They approached the stunt with the sense of exhilaration that comes with hatching a plan to steal your college rival's mascot and knowing that if you wait, someone's better judgment will take hold and you'll reconsider.

The biggest challenge was finding a tattoo parlor open on Sundays. Matt leafed through the Yellow Pages, made several calls, and finally found an establishment just a short drive up El Camino in the town of San Bruno. Wayne's Tattoo Studio is located amidst a mind-numbingly endless string of nail parlors and shares a 100-foot patch of suburban turf with a dentist's office, a dry cleaner, a tuxedo rental place, a Karate Kung Fu establishment, and Madame Dora's Psychic Readings—where palmistry is a specialty.

Appointment made, Sosnick and his players piled into two cars for a field trip of the bizarre. Dontrelle and Jason were resolute in their conviction. Matt and four other minor leaguers—Zach Hammes, Brandon Weeden, Blair Johnson, and Adam Donachie—showed up for moral support.

The tattoo joint was run by a Chinese man and woman, apparently husband and wife, whose politeness was surpassed only by their dexterity. It was comfortingly clean, with a wall full of samples and a fuchsia couch where patrons could relax and flip through books filled with colors and assorted patterns.

The proprietors studied the logo on a Sosnick-Cobbe business card, duplicated it on a piece of paper, then got down to business. Dontrelle settled into one chair and Jason, who wanted his in color, plopped down in the other. "It doesn't really hurt," Jason says. "After 5 to 10 minutes, your arm goes numb." And after an hour, you rise from the chair, watch your agent pay the artists $200 for each tattoo, and realize you have a serpentlike *S* on your biceps for eternity.

When Dontrelle went home to Alameda and showed his mother his new adornment, she rolled her eyes in displeasure. Joyce Guy-Harris had made it clear that tattoos with women's names weren't permissible, but her son sure had a flair for inventiveness. He came home one year with a tattoo that said "Proven Point," then another with the inscription "Mr. Willis," as if he might forget his own name. But pledging allegiance to your agent? How can anyone be so sure of a relationship in a world where money speaks volumes and so many actions are based on mutual convenience?

"The Sosnick-Cobbe sports logo, I think that was a bit much," Joyce says, "because you never know. . . ."

Or maybe you do. In the spring of 2003, Jason Pridie's brother Jon, a pitcher in the Minnesota Twins chain, became the third Sosnick-Cobbe player to get emblazoned. He remembers the event vividly because of the timing. Just as Jon was settling into the chair, someone rushed into the tattoo parlor with news that U.S. troops had bombed Iraq.

As word of the tattoo escapade traversed the agent grapevine, Matt

Sosnick became something of a curiosity in an insular, backbiting world. In December 2000, agent Jeff Moorad achieved a special brand of notoriety by inviting an ESPN camera to tag along for outfielder Manny Ramirez's negotiations with Boston and the New York Yankees. Scott Boras, the Bill Gates of baseball agents, guaranteed his place in baseball history that same year by forging a record 10-year, $252-million deal for Alex Rodriguez with the Texas Rangers, then charming Lesley Stahl into submission in a *60 Minutes* interview.

Matt Sosnick, who hopes to attain their level of prominence one day while staying true to his principles as a self-proclaimed "peace and love" guy, is known as the weird, reclusive Californian who's fighting to keep his lunch money in a schoolyard filled with bullies. The players who stay with him care about him enough to turn themselves into human billboards.

"It's a loyalty thing," says Jason Pridie. "I'll stick with Soz even if I'm his last guy. If he dies, I'll go down with him."

Dontrelle Willis, on the verge of much bigger things, concurs.

"Even in the minor leagues, you have to keep in mind that everybody promises something," Dontrelle says. "And you have to keep in mind the people back home. This guy has done a good job for me thus far. I've been with Matt since I signed out of high school, so I don't want to feel like I'm switching now just because I'm having success. We've had the same relationship since I was in Rookie Ball. That goes a long way."

They lingered at the accident scene for maybe a half-hour, talking to the patrol officer as he jotted down information. When Matt looked at Dontrelle—incredulous that he had crawled out of that mess intact—he wondered how he would have felt if the kid had been lying motionless in the car instead of standing in front of him, looking frightened but perfectly fine.

"We were so close, I just thought if he had died, how it would have changed my life," Matt says.

He called Dontrelle's mom, who rushed over from her job as a welder at the San Mateo Bridge project and met up with them at Matt's Burlingame apartment. When Joyce saw Dontrelle without a scratch, she burst into tears and praised Jesus. Then she saw the photographs and was rendered speechless.

But the photos had nothing on seeing the car up close, in all its decimated splendor. A day after the accident, Joyce went to retrieve Dontrelle's baseball equipment from the trunk of the Mustang. "Your son must have an angel," the guy from the tow truck company told her as they surveyed the damage.

"It was like death," Joyce says. The Mustang was so far gone, Dontrelle's baseball equipment would never see the light of day. The only item that could be retrieved from the vehicle was a Bible in the backseat.

Images of the accident haunted Joyce's sleep for the next four nights. She had nightmares about her baby losing an arm, or a finger, or an eye, or crushing his skull. She stayed home from work for 2 days to squire him around town just in case he lacked the nerve to get behind the wheel again. But Dontrelle was young, resilient, and naturally unflappable, and he recovered quickly. Mazonie Franklin, Dontrelle's best friend from the old neighborhood in Alameda, theorizes that he handles setbacks better than most because of his astrological sign.

"Capricorns are mellow and they go with the flow," Mazonie says. "I tell Dontrelle, 'It's because you're a Capricorn, dude,' and he's like, 'Whatever.'"

Joyce walked into Matt Sosnick's living room after the accident and found Dontrelle in a state of shock, but not hysterical, as might have been expected from someone who had just flipped his car on Highway 101. Her baby was sitting on the sofa and staring at his foot. "Hey, I scratched my tennis shoe!" Dontrelle said, sounding more than slightly annoyed.

The evening was devoted to quiet reflection at the Sosnick duplex. Dontrelle's girlfriend, Kim, and Mazonie came over, along with Matt's father. Ron Sosnick is a tall, friendly man with a business mind and a tendency to get emotional with friends and loved ones on special occasions. He burst through the duplex door, headed straight to Dontrelle, wrapped him in a bear hug and kissed him on the cheek.

"Is that the first man who's ever kissed you?" Matt later asked his friend.

"Besides you," Dontrelle said.

Chapter
TWO

Matt finds pennies unnerving. His irritation goes beyond garden-variety annoyance with a piece of currency so trivial in the world of modern commerce. Pennies weigh him down as they jingle in his pocket, and by Pavlovian reflex he tosses them to the curb, in hopes that a lucky penny might brighten someone else's day, rather than disrupt his own.

Green is his favorite color, and paper his vehicle of expression. He disdains credit cards for the immediacy of cash—preferably with U. S. Grant or Benjamin Franklin's likeness on the front—and routinely carries a $2,000 wad under the theory that he should be ready when the next opportunity comes along. Seems they always do.

If cellular phones cause cancer, as some studies suggest, there's a bed in an oncology ward with Matt's name on it. When a 2,300-minute-a-month mobile plan failed to suit his needs, he topped it with another 2,300-minute plan, and then another. He stacks cell phone plans like sandbags, in a one-man effort to halt the flood of roaming charges.

Matt's phone, like Matt, has no "power off" button. Maybe it's a

prospect in the South
lift, or a San Francisco
this weekend's game,
Dontrelle-related prop
bring Matt's life into foc
storm. The words spill o
the salad, pecked half
deliberating whether to
berry torte.

He prefers a certain ty
accomplished, petite, an
assembly-line regularity—s
as a form of spectator sport.
princess? In the movie vers
for the role of love interest. ....unu his lifestyle exciting at
first, then exasperating, then impossible. Before long, his quirkiness will
be the subject of another conversation at another dinner table—with a
new boyfriend—who has the capacity to turn off the mobile phone and
pay attention for more than 10-minute installments.

Matt aches for a lifetime partner and soulmate, but he's commitment-
phobic, even with cars. The silver Jaguar he drove last February has
been replaced by a maroon Jaguar, which will be replaced by a Jaguar of
a different color soon enough. Spin enough concert tickets, catch a ride
aboard a few hot stocks, and make some prudent moves with your venture
capital, he's learned, and it gives you the freedom to travel in style.

In matters of appearance, Matt picks nits out of self-consciousness
more than narcissism. He gets a haircut once a week and shaves every
36 hours, up and down, side to side, until 30 minutes have elapsed and
his skin is bleeding and chafed. The Sistine chapel, in comparison, was
a blow-off. He works out rigorously, wears shirts that complement his
athletic frame, and rarely drinks anything stronger than a Coke.

Creature comforts are important to Matt. He's partial to Egyptian
cotton towels and knows his way around a Bed Bath & Beyond. A
comfortable mattress and powerful showerhead rank first and second in

e water pressure isn't strong enough
...ack wall, it's substandard.

...run toward Counting Crows and Simon &
...ve Matthews. Although he plays no instruments,
...rendition of Jean Stapleton as Edith Bunker singing
...he Days." It never ceases to crack up his family and

...collects unread books by the dozen because he lacks the pa-
...ce and attention span to finish them. But he devoured *Tuesdays with
Morrie* and found its live-for-today message so inspiring that he bought
220 copies and sent them to his clients, his closest friends, and *their*
closest friends as gifts. Then he e-mailed the author, Mitch Albom, and
offered his heartfelt thanks. Matt's favorite artist is Alexandra Nechita,
a Romanian prodigy who was hailed as the "Petite Picasso" at age 8.
Matt bought a dozen of her paintings, hung several on the walls of his
duplex, and gave away several more as gifts, because he's convinced that
a work of art enjoyed is even more beautiful when shared.

He's ardently pro-Israel in his politics, and he is active in both Jewish
causes and the social scene. A few years ago, Matt organized a singles'
trip to Israel and was dismayed to find that the ratio of women to men
was out of whack (from the women's perspective, at least). So he put the
hard sell on a male friend, telling him the trip was a wonderful opportunity to return to his roots and expand his cultural horizons.

"Plus," Matt assured the friend, "you're guaranteed to get laid."

He is generous beyond belief to friends and loved ones, who receive
bottles of Dom Pérignon or autographed Salvador Dalí lithographs as
gifts for birthdays or anniversaries or for no reason at all. And his
largesse extends to people he's never met and probably will never see
again. Each Christmas morning, he arises early, buys $500 worth of
sandwiches, and hands them out to San Francisco's homeless. He gives
concert tickets to strangers, sends cash to homeless shelters (anony-
mously), and performs a "random act of kindness" every day. No one is
immune. Like Mike, the Lebanese immigrant who owns the corner
store. Matt pops into the Adeline Market routinely with free 49ers

tickets, but he won't take a soda from the shelf without paying for it. "He's a very kind, good-hearted man," Mike says of Matt. "And he never expects anything in return."

He stockpiles knowledge as a form of currency to trade. Who else scours the World Wide Web to learn the names of third-world dictators and Moroccan soccer stars so he'll have conversational common ground with foreign-born taxi drivers?

Matt, hopping into a cab in L.A.: What country are you from?

Driver: I lived in Germany 15 years, but I'm from Iran.

Matt: What year did you come over here?

Driver: In '84.

Matt: Oh, you came here after the revolution. Did that cost your family a lot of money?

Driver: Yeah, the people who left before got out with all their money.

Matt, with a touch of sympathy: Yeah, Beverly Hills High School is all Persian now.

Matt keeps a diary of strange life experiences, memorable bumper stickers, song lyrics, and off-beat, George Carlin or Steven Wright–like observations that resonate with him. He's also a whiz at trivia. He can tell you that a pig's orgasm lasts 30 minutes, a twit is a pregnant goldfish, a dork is a whale's penis, the glue on Israeli postage stamps is kosher, and that Adolf Hitler was *Time* magazine's Man of the Year in 1938. "I'd be very good at Jeopardy," he says.

He has a slew of friends who drift in and out of his existence, and a small inner circle that he relies upon and trusts implicitly. It consists of Eric Polis, a property manager who lives in Las Vegas; Pat O'Brien, a former high school classmate who's now a golf pro in Texas; Eric Karp, an MGM studio executive in Los Angeles and the husband of Matt's college friend Chelsea; and Paul Cobbe, his boyhood pal, emotional anchor, and business partner.

The Big Four have ready access to the psychic and emotional mechanisms, cogs, and springs that make Matt tick. Take another step, to the next concentric ring, and Matt has to pick and choose carefully. There are only so many hours in a day—even his day.

"Matt is constantly running an inventory of the valuable things in his life, so he perpetually refers to the people who are important to him," Eric Karp says. "It's a reassuring thing—like patting your pocket to make sure your wallet is there."

And of course, there's business. In 2002, Matt and Paul were spending so much money on seats to rock concerts and sporting events as a means of entertaining clients that they bought a ticket brokerage to gain access to its inventory. Naturally, the San Francisco Giants made the World Series that October, and the demand for seats at Pac Bell Park was so relentless, they made a killing.

Matt typically awakes at 5:00 or 6:00 A.M. each day and writes a list of 15 vital things to do on a small index card, then methodically checks off each task when it's addressed. When he isn't tending to his Bay Tickets enterprise, calling his stockbroker, sinking some cash into a friend's "ab-shocker" business, or exploring the possibility of pooling money with Paul to invest in a dozen Asian-fusion restaurants, he spends 12 to 14 hours a day on a far less lucrative venture: obsessing over dozens of kids who play baseball for a living.

In 1997, Matt left his job running a Silicon Valley high-tech company to be a sports agent, against the advice of seasoned professionals who told him he was insane to try. He chose baseball because the game attracts the kind of suburban Wonder Bread types he could relate to best. Seven years later, he's compiled a client roster filled with Mormons from Utah and Baptists from Texas and Oklahoma, in the belief that they're morally grounded and family-oriented enough to resist sales pitches from other agencies who try to lure them.

The Sosnick-Cobbe agency has an eclectic mix of players. Matt and

Paul represent Rex Rundgren, a minor-league shortstop whose father, Todd, is the pioneering rock musician, and whose half-sister, actress Liv Tyler, is the daughter of Aerosmith frontman Steven Tyler. As a boy, Rex spurned drumming lessons for the lure of the ballfield, and it paid off when Florida selected him in the 11th round of the 2001 draft. He can "pick it," as scouts say of middle infielders with range, but has a troubling tendency to swing at everything inside or outside the strike zone.

Sosnick and Cobbe have a slew of "stealth" prospects who could either wash out or be very good if the planets properly align. Like Chad Qualls, a pitcher from Nevada-Reno who's plugging away in the Houston chain. Chad labors at times with mechanics and command, and he tends to nibble rather than just throw the ball over the plate and trust the natural movement on his pitches. But he's a load at 6'5" and 220 pounds, and he doesn't pitch scared. "He's a competitor," Houston farm director Tim Purpura says of Qualls. "If you're a hitter and he's on the mound, you know you're in for it."

Some prospects are much farther along. Brandon Lyon, a righty reliever with Arizona, has already pitched for three big-league clubs at age 24, and he routinely receives overtures from teammates and agents who say he should switch to a more established firm. But Brandon resists. He's unconcerned that Matt has never prepared an arbitration case or conducted a big-time contract negotiation.

"For me not to give him an opportunity because he's never been through something is totally against the way I feel," Brandon says. "Matt represented me when he'd never seen me go through anything, either. As long as I feel that trust and know he's going to do the best job he can, I'm very comfortable having him do it. Hopefully, I can pave the way for him to get other players."

The Sosnick-Cobbe agency is, in some respects, a family affair. Two years ago, Matt and Paul determined that they didn't have the time to tend to their existing clientele and spend weeks on the road signing up fresh talent for the June draft, the seminal event in the firm's year. So they hired a former college football recruiter named Toby Trotter to travel the backroads of Texas and Oklahoma in search of prospects.

Toby's brother-in-law, Montreal Expos pitcher Mike Hinckley, might be the best Sosnick-Cobbe player not named Dontrelle Willis. As a high school sophomore in Moore, Oklahoma, Mike stood 6 feet tall and 125 pounds, and his coach called him "One Pocket" because he was too skinny to have two pockets in his pants. But when Mike filled out and hit 93 mph on the radar gun as a senior, scouts began circling the backstop, and the Expos drafted him in the third round and paid him a $425,000 bonus. Mike treated himself to a Chevy Tahoe and a laptop computer, and helped his parents, both teachers, pay off the mortgage. "When I get to the big leagues and make a million-dollar contract, I want to put them in a retirement house," he says. "I know it's not too far down the road."

Mike Hinckley plays guitar in his church group, and he abstains from alcoholic beverages and other temptations that might present themselves to a young, good-looking athlete on the rise. He is also understated, yet fervent, in his devotion to Jesus Christ. "The Lord leads you to it," Mike says on his cell phone message. "He'll definitely bring you through it."

Most important, Mike Hinckley has the aptitude to make it. In the summer of 2003, he made the jump from Montreal's low Class A farm club, the Savannah Sand Gnats, to high Class A Brevard County, where he posted a 4–0 record with a 0.72 earned run average. In a Montreal organization that's short on funds and strapped for talent, he could rise in a hurry.

Which leads to a pressing question: Once he's on the cusp of making it, will Mike decide that he wants an agent who's been through the rigors of salary arbitration and free agency? Will he want a representative with a track record for schmoozing with Owner A or General Manager B? Will Matt walk to his mailbox one day soon and find a farewell letter with Mike Hinckley's signature at the bottom?

Mike seems resolute that it won't happen. "Yeah, I'm going to have more things happen as I get higher, especially this year," he says. "If I make the big leagues there will be people trying to get a piece, trying to be close. They'll tell me, 'Mike, I'll give you this and that.' I have to be really careful. Do I think I'd ever switch? No, I don't. I gave Matt my word that I'd never switch. My word is my bond."

Matt has faith that Mike Hinckley and Dontrelle Willis will never make a judgment call that bigger is better and leave the Sosnick-Cobbe group, as Bobby Jenks, Dennis Tankersley, Dan Haren, Travis Hafner, and so many other top prospects have done. He forces himself to believe it's true because the alternative is too painful to contemplate. "If Dontrelle ever left us, Matt would leave the business," Paul says.

But no matter how often you pat your pocket for your wallet, there's no accounting for holes. On a good day, Matt will have a genuine impact on a kid's life. Maybe it's escorting Oakland minor leaguer Mike Rouse to San Francisco's diamond district to shop for an engagement ring, because Matt's Israeli connection can get Rouse a great deal. Or maybe he's hopping a commuter flight to Los Angeles to see Steve Nelson, a lanky, Canadian-born Dodgers prospect who's having his right elbow reconstructed. Matt enters the Centinela Hospital prep room and encounters Nelson, pale with anxiety, wearing a hospital gown and waiting to get sliced. "I knew I'd see you in a dress one day," he says, and he and Steve share a laugh.

On a bad day, allegiances that Matt considered special or even sacred are discarded like candy wrappers. New York Mets outfield prospect Jeff Duncan will call and say he's leaving the Sosnick-Cobbe agency for the Levinson Brothers' firm in Brooklyn. Or Matt will check his mailbox and find a letter from a client who's just dropped him for one of the 300-pound gorillas, Scott Boras or Jeff Moorad or the Beverly Hills Sports Council or SFX.

The big agencies have a sense of entitlement that makes Matt's stomach turn, and the moxie to walk into his front yard and take what's rightfully his. Matt had seen it in the case of Jesse Foppert, a tall, slender, good-looking kid who went to school nearby at the University of San Francisco. Jesse had begun his college career as a first baseman—just an anonymous walk-on with no scholarship—until the Dons' coaching staff unearthed his true potential and converted him to a pitcher. In Jesse's junior year Matt met him in the school cafeteria. They instantly hit it off, and the Foppert family picked Matt to be Jesse's adviser for the 2001 draft. That's the disingenuous term that baseball uses —"adviser"—as part of an elaborate dance that allows amateur players to seek professional advice without jeopardizing their collegiate eligibility.

Jesse Foppert was a sleeper at the time, but when he went 8–4 with 112 strikeouts as a junior, the secret started to get out. In Foppert's final college game, Scott Boras walked in the gate with an associate or two, and it was apparent that he, too, was paying attention. Boras already represented Tagg Bozied, a college teammate of Foppert's and a big-time prospect. But as one scouting director in attendance recalled, "the Boras group was definitely scouting Jesse Foppert. They even had the radar gun on him."

Most small agents prefer to avoid run-ins with Scott Boras at all costs, under the theory that it's a fight you can't win. But the specter of losing Foppert struck such a nerve with Sosnick that he confronted Boras, quietly but firmly, away from the crowd behind the stands.

"I spend all my time trying to make this business work for me," Matt said. "When you steal a guy who's being treated well for no reason other than that you're able to wear him down, it doesn't add to the goodness or the kindness of the world."

The sermon did not have its desired effect. "I sleep like a baby every night," Boras said, before turning to walk away.

"That's the problem with your life," Matt replied. "You sleep like a baby every night."

There's nothing personal about it, Matt realizes. It's not as if he's going to pull a thorn out of Boras's paw one day and have a friend and a benefactor for life. "I have great players and not much of a track record, so I'm a prime guy for Boras to beat the shit out of," Matt says. "He'll do it because he can."

The Giants selected Jesse Foppert with the 74th overall pick in June of 2001. He signed for a $520,000 bonus, of which Sosnick and Cobbe received the obligatory 5 percent cut. But in the summer of 2002, Foppert cut the cord. He pitched in the Texas League in Shreveport and the

Pacific Coast League with Fresno, and began seeing one of Boras's field representatives, Jim McNamara, at ballpark after ballpark. McNamara took Jesse Foppert to dinner, and in the off-season Jesse visited the Scott Boras Corp. headquarters near Los Angeles and was smitten. He was impressed by Boras's longstanding relationships with baseball's front-office elite, and bowled over by the elaborate computer system and statistical data available at the click of a button. Boras asked questions and raised scenarios about issues that Sosnick, as a relative novice, had never addressed. And as a former ballplayer, Boras was known for arriving early at big-league parks to watch batting practice and take notes. When Jesse pitched, his new agent would sit behind the screen and pinpoint mechanical flaws. Matt Sosnick couldn't do *that* in a million years.

Just a year after changing agents, Jesse Foppert blew out his right elbow in San Francisco and underwent "Tommy John" surgery. Now he's looking to rediscover the promise he showed in 2002, when he was the Pacific Coast League's top prospect, and he's confident that Scott Boras will help guide him in the right direction.

"If my career was heading in the path I wanted, I figured I would switch eventually anyway," Jesse says. "I thought it was better to get it done early so there were less feelings involved. Nothing against Sosnick. He did everything I ever asked him for. I just felt Scott's agency had more to offer to me."

Each new breakup adds to the emotional carnage, and Matt recovers by unburdening himself to Jacob, his no-nonsense therapist. By his own estimate, Matt spends more than $10,000 a year on counseling for self-improvement. Part of it is coping with life in general, and the rest is dealing with the residual pain of his parents' divorce, which screwed him up royally for a time.

As someone who values "good karma," Matt is repulsed by the predatory nature of his profession. But he's learned to mix it up and rationalize. After the 2003 season, he romanced a promising Marlins minor-leaguer named Scott Olsen away from a Chicago agent named Bob Garber. Matt paid to fly Olsen and his girlfriend to San Francisco, where he wined and dined them for 2 days. Matt justified the initiative because he had lost a player to Garber a few years earlier. "After that, everything is open game," Matt says. Even when pressed, Matt can't recall who the player was. It's just so hard to keep track.

The ups and downs of the business can give you vertigo, while causing moral lines to blur. This is an important period in the evolution of Matt's agency, and he knows it. With more players on the verge of the big leagues, he and Paul will either get over the hump or become a bigger target for predators. Sosnick and Cobbe aren't worried about their money holding out, because of their financial stake and outside businesses. But can they hold up emotionally?

Some days, it's a chore for Matt just to get out of bed in the morning. And other days, when a relationship clicks and the adrenaline rush is almost palpable, he absolutely loves it. He loves it enough to forget the nauseating feeling in the pit of his stomach every time he's dumped.

"This is a business that's almost solely based on shame and humiliation," Matt says. "How much humiliation can you give to your competitors? That's the reason the Beverly Hills Sports Council, when they steal a guy, they write in the termination letter, 'I have decided to switch to Beverly Hills Sports.' They not only want to take the player from you. They want to humiliate you and basically say, 'Look, you can't stop us.'

"It's an unbelievable business. The dichotomy for me is, I've spent my life and a lot of money trying to promote my own self-esteem. And now I'm caught up in this business that tries to strip it from you."

Welcome to his world.

Gene Orza, the number 2 man at the Players Association, classifies agents in two categories. The first group has an appreciation for labor law and a desire to participate in what Orza calls the "ordering" of the relationship between players and owners. That ordering might include big-picture questions about scheduling, or the issue of whether players should be paid when injured. Scott Boras is naturally inquisitive in this manner. So are Randy and Alan Hendricks, numerous other veteran agents, and Peter Greenberg, a young agent who represents many top Venezuelan players.

Orza has barely heard of Matt Sosnick and Paul Cobbe, but he conveniently lumps them in with the dozens of agents that he characterizes as "hobbyists." Too many agents, in Orza's estimation, are simply jock-sniffers who think it's fun to hang around ballplayers and gloat about it at cocktail parties.

"How wonderful that these kids grow up today and say, 'I love baseball, so I want to work in baseball,' " Orza says. "Well, my father loved baseball too, but he was a dress cutter. Where did you get this notion that because you love baseball, you should be an agent? What qualifies you? Have you taken any negotiating classes? Have you taken any labor law classes? Have you read the basic agreement? What are you good at? You're good at schmoozing. This is a serious business we're in."

In reality, the 300-plus agents certified by the Players Association fit beneath a much broader umbrella, and they have a more human face if you care to discern it. Some of them pay the bills with modest legal practices while representing a player or two. One day, they're helping Joe Average wriggle out of a speeding violation. The next day, they're trying to find a home for a 6-year minor-league free agent.

Rob Plummer, a young Philadelphia agent, is taking the Matt Sosnick approach in Latin America. Several years ago, Plummer worked part-time for US Airways so he could fly free. He'd log 21 days in a row, then head off to Santo Domingo in search of talent. Plummer has a bachelor's degree from Haverford and a law degree from the University of Virginia, and he once camped out in the Appalachian Mountains in a tent for $8 a night while recruiting Willie Martinez, a pitcher in the Minnesota Twins' system.

"My feeling is, you have to be one step ahead of the competition, sometimes two," Plummer says. "You have to be a leader and not a follower." But even with his top-shelf education and unbridled ambition, he has to work like a demon to make inroads against the Scott Boras reps in Puerto Rico and the Dominican Republic.

Some aspiring Jerry Maguires are sitting in front of a computer screen. A company called Sports Management Worldwide, run by an NFL agent and Oregon college professor named Lynn Lashbrook, offers an 8-week online course on how to become an agent. Among the topics addressed are draft preparation, marketing and endorsements, and business ethics. Total cost of the program: $799.

At the opposite end of the scale are the massive conglomerates, agencies with names like Octagon, SFX, and IMG. Contract negotiations are a small part of what they do. With the onset of salary caps and standardized fees, agents in all sports have had to branch out and find alternate revenue sources. So now, the big groups have in-house divisions for marketing, endorsements, and public relations, and they arrange for medical consultations, tax planning, and post-career counseling. It's a vertically integrated wonderland of client service—all with a fee, of course.

Several of these entities are public companies, with earnings targets and profit reports and shareholders, and this, too, makes you wonder. Critics point to a spate of lawsuits and perceived conflicts as evidence that the big company, all-things-to-all-people model of representation is an unwelcome trend.

Big or small, there's no denying the impact that agents have had on baseball's economic picture. The first effect is monetary. The game's average salary was $51,501 in 1976. Then, free agency arrived, players could shop their services unfettered, and by 2004 the average salary was about $2.3 million. The agents were primarily facilitators, but they had influence in a variety of ways—by studying the market, drumming up interest, and exploiting schisms in the ownership ranks.

"I think the agents made a profound contribution to the escalation of salaries in the '80s and '90s," says Boston Red Sox president Larry Lucchino, who uses the word "contribution" loosely. "And the system contributed to it, to be sure—the sort of Rube Goldberg contraption we created through these successive collective bargaining agreements that gave players certain rights and benefits and opportunities."

Sometimes the biggest rubes wear the most expensive suits. Texas owner Tom Hicks chose to make Alex Rodriguez richer than Croesus even though the Atlanta Braves and Seattle Mariners, A-Rod's two other suitors, weren't in the same stratosphere as the Rangers' $252 million offer. In the eyes of the sporting press, the deal transformed Hicks from mover and shake to misguided boob. But then, he was hardly alone. When Scott Boras was looking for a big payout for Bernie Williams in 1998, he was smart enough to realize the best way to get George Steinbrenner's attention was to enlist the rival Boston Red Sox as a potential suitor. Williams, who had previously received a $60 million offer from New York, signed for 7 years and $87.5 million with the Yankees. It was a clinic in Button Pushing 101.

The image of the agent as hard-working facilitator or evil incarnate depends on your perspective. Baseball's new breed of young, Ivy League–educated general managers, like Boston's Theo Epstein or Paul DePodesta of the Los Angeles Dodgers, has grown up with the understanding that agents are an inevitable part of the process. And Cleveland's Mark Shapiro, a former Princeton football player, regards the profession from an even more personal vantage point. Mark's father, Ron, has represented dozens of major-league ballplayers since the 1970s, including Hall of Famers Brooks Robinson, Eddie Murray, Jim Palmer, and Kirby Puckett, and future Cooperstown inductee Cal Ripken Jr. When Mark was 16 years old, former Baltimore pitcher Mike Boddicker and his wife moved into the Shapiro family home for a year. And Mark still corresponds regularly with Willie Mays Aikens, a former Ron Shapiro client who went to prison in 1994 for selling crack cocaine to an undercover police officer.

Mark Shapiro firmly believes that since clubs and agents both want what's best for the player, there's no reason not to find common ground. "The best agent stories are the ones where you work together to help a player through adversity, and everybody benefits," Shapiro says.

That concept is harder to grasp for, say, Atlanta Braves general manager John Schuerholz, who broke into pro ball when agents were virtually nonexistent. In the late 1960s, Schuerholz was making $6,800 a year as a junior high school English teacher when he followed his heart and took a job in the Baltimore Orioles front office. All it took was courage and a willingness to accept a $2,100-a-year pay cut. He moved to Kansas City, developed the likes of George Brett and Frank White on the farm, and built a World Championship club in 1985 on a modest budget.

Schuerholz can remember when a baseball man with vision could really make a difference, and he equates agents with a bad rash. Several years ago, Schuerholz observed that agents should all be made to wear "chartreuse suits and big-brimmed hats with feathers in them," to distinguish themselves as the con men they were.

When Schuerholz joined the Braves in 1990, he found a kindred spirit in club president Stan Kasten, whose antipathy toward the fraternity was equally pronounced. Kasten, bald, brash, and brilliant, gives a stock speech on agents that skewers them inside, outside, and upside down. The Kasten doctrine holds that every single bad thing about professional sports—from greedy athletes to an absence of loyalty to rising ticket prices—is directly or indirectly traceable to the evolution of the agent business.

"I used to think they were a necessary evil in sports," Kasten says, pausing for effect. "Now I just think of them as evil." In 2000, the Sports Lawyers Association named Kasten its Man of the Year and invited him to speak at the group's convention in San Francisco. Agent Randy Hendricks, who represents Roger Clemens, Andy Pettitte, and several other prominent big leaguers, was so outraged he resigned his membership in protest.

In recent years, John Schuerholz has entrusted his assistant, Frank Wren, with the unsavory job of fielding phone calls from agents. "We have a very productive arrangement in our office," Schuerholz says. "Frank talks to the agents, and I talk to Frank."

Schuerholz has two particular objections to the role that agents play. First, he's convinced that they drive a wedge between players and teams as a buffer to communication. In the 1960s and '70s, if a player arrived at training camp overweight, you'd tell him to lose the beer gut. Under the new world order, teams deliver the message through an agent, and there's invariably some shading involved. When the club's sentiments are filtered, Schuerholz believes, the agent comes across as the player's ally, and the club is invariably perceived as the bad guy.

Agents are also an affront to Schuerholz's inherent sense of fairness. How is it, he wonders, that they're able to glom on to the system, contribute nothing, and take a cut in increments of 3 to 5 percent? The "system" decrees that players are eligible for salary arbitration after 2-plus years of service time, and free agency after 6. If a player sticks around long enough, he can make money with Bonzo the Chimp negotiating his deal.

"What better place to be an agent than in a system like this?" Schuerholz says. "If they're honest with you and they get behind closed doors and they're not out in public, they probably can't wipe the smile off their face."

When front-office officials aren't complaining about salaries, they blame agents for a rampant sense of self-entitlement among players. Baseball is a little boys' game at its core, and the men who play it reside in a world of make-believe that gets more surreal from Little League through the majors. They're perpetually catered to and fawned over, and the better they perform, the more likely the catering and fawning will persist.

To many executives, agents have helped cultivate a concierge mentality in the game. They're enablers for millionaires who can't - balance a checkbook, pay an electric bill, or make a plane reservation without help. Ballplayers, as a rule, are begging to be indulged, and many agents are quick to oblige.

Pat Gillick, a long-time front office executive, thinks agents intentionally foster dependency. "They don't want the players to be able to think for themselves," Gillick says. "It's sort of like an addiction to drugs. *You call me before you buy a car. You call me before you buy a house. You call me on the mortgage. You call me.* A lot of the things that normal people do in the course of life, they never experience because they have somebody doing it for them."

In the minor leagues, kids face such long odds to get to the majors and make so little money, it's a source of amazement to some that they actually *have* representation. One agent recalls standing at a minor-league field with Dick Tidrow, a former New York Yankees pitcher who's now an executive with the San Francisco Giants. Tidrow, who goes by the nickname "Dirt," is a tough-looking hombre with a thick mustache and a menacing stare, and he works for an organization that most agents consider hostile to their kind. "I saw Tidrow at a game and he was dropping F-bombs left and right," the agent says. "He was like, '98 percent of these kids will never see a big-league field, yet 80 percent of them have agents. I don't get it.'"

In an age where agent-hopping is a rite of passage for young players, the "dependency" cited by Pat Gillick has a fringe benefit: A player who's dependent on a particular agent is less likely to leave for someone else. But while team officials are largely detached from the agent infighting, they still perceive it as a problem.

"When a player jumps from one agent to the next, he's jumping based upon a set of promises that he's been given, or something he feels he's entitled to," says Colorado Rockies general manager Dan O'Dowd. "Now there's this attitude of, 'What's in it for me?' Or, 'How does this benefit me?' When you're trying to create a team environment based upon players having a selfless attitude, it's a force you're fighting on a continual basis."

Matt Sosnick has a problem with the Gene Orza ivory-tower theory—that just because he doesn't know the Basic Agreement backward and forward, he should expect to have his clientele pillaged. "If he went through that experience one time emotionally, I think he might be a little more empathetic," Matt says.

Mark Levin, a former New York investment banker and Mike Krzyzewski lookalike, is watching the story play out with interest. Several years ago, Levin and a partner started their own baseball agency in Virginia. They adhered to the same "bottom up" model that Matt and Paul have followed, recruiting players through the draft and bonding with them as they progressed through the minors.

But the model was ultimately flawed and was a recipe for stress. As bigger agencies raided his business, Levin saw his prospects for success grow dim. He concluded, with all reasonable objectivity, that he no longer controlled his own destiny. Optimism gave way to heartache, then resignation. In 2001, Levin left the sports agent business for a job in equity research.

"If you don't have the track record or the salary arbitration experience, it gets thrown in your face," Levin says. "I'm a competent statistics, numbers, and finance guy. But you're dealing with 20- to 25-year-old ballplayers who have one shot, and they want to make sure their financial interests are represented.

"I had players tell me we provided excellent client service, advice, and attention as an agency. But at the 11th hour, right before they attained prominence, the big guys would come in and sweep them away. And the worst part is, you don't know when that phone call will come."

Matt and Paul are leaving nothing to chance. They've already made plans to farm out salary arbitration cases to Rick Shapiro, a consultant with a raft of experience and high marks from the players' union. He's agreed to help them at a substantial price, but one that they feel is justified. They've also traveled to Southern California and spent time with Tom House, a freelance pitching coach of great renown, and they've arranged for him to work with some of their prospects. This, too, is a service they plan to provide that goes beyond the call of duty.

But no matter how detail-oriented they are, the odds are stacked against them, because success in the business is no longer based on hustle, hope, and a long-range plan. Many established agents who got their starts in the good old days—during the Carter and Reagan administrations—claim they could never survive as startups today because the industry is so carnivorous and cutthroat.

Mark Levin views Matt from a different sort of rearview mirror. He became friends with Sosnick several years ago when they were haggling over a client. The player owed Levin some money and planned to jump to Sosnick, but Matt refused to represent him until Levin's debt was repaid in full. Mark Levin saw something noble and honorable in Matt's stance.

After quitting because the business was too seamy for his tastes, Levin now looks on from a new job tracking stock quotes, and he roots vicariously for Matt to succeed.

"It's instructive to me, because I see how my business might have evolved if I had made the determination to stay in it," Levin says. "Matt's a really good person. I think he has the best intentions. I really want him to make it, because it'll prove that good guys who stick with it can make it happen."

Chapter
THREE

The morning of February 8, 2003, is important to
Matt in a self-validating way. Burlingame High School, his alma mater,
has invited him to speak to an antidrug, youth-empowerment program
called Know Limits. The initiative is tailored for good, ambitious kids
who are conscientious enough to surrender a Saturday morning to do
the right thing, and Sosnick is happy to take a chunk of his free time to
impart a few life lessons while they're still earnest enough to listen.

Burlingame, located 20 minutes south of San Francisco, is an affluent
community by most standards. Its population is 85 percent Caucasian
or Asian, and the median household income approached $70,000 in
2000. Now for the good or bad news, depending on whether you're a
buyer or a seller: A soaring real estate market had swelled the median
house value to $685,000 at the turn of the millennium. But that's
nothing in the overall scheme of things. A town away, in Hillsborough,
where Matt's father lives, fixer-uppers routinely go for more than $2
million. Bing Crosby's family owns property nearby, and newspaper
heiress Patty Hearst grew up in the town. Joe Montana, Dwight Clark,

and Barry Bonds are among the prominent Bay Area athletes who've called Hillsborough home through the years.

In the Burlingame High teachers' lounge, the sense of self-entitlement among students is the source of a running joke. "You can tell where we're parked," the teachers say, "because the teachers drive the old cars."

Matt drove a red Pontiac Fiero in high school, and he graduated from Burlingame in 1987 with a reputation as the class procurer of concert tickets, baseball cards, and Joe Montana and Jerry Rice memorabilia. The sports agent in popular culture is known through Tom Cruise's portrayal of Jerry Maguire or Robert Wuhl's *Arli$$* shtick on HBO. Sosnick, as a teenager, was Mike Damone scalping Van Halen seats in front of the mall at *Fast Times at Ridgemont High*, or Ferris Bueller, slipping the maître d' a bill and talking his way into a snooty French restaurant.

Had he channeled his energy and fertile imagination into his studies, an Ivy League education might have beckoned. But he was too preoccupied with making classmates and teachers take notice and laugh. How could they resist, when he arrived late for school one morning with a friend and handed his homeroom teacher a note from the manager of the neighborhood McDonald's?

"Please excuse Matt and Pat," the note read. "The Egg McMuffins weren't ready on time."

Pat O'Brien, Tom Spencer, and the 20 girls in ninth-grade Advanced Placement English will never forget the day Matt hired a stripper to perform for their teacher's 50th birthday. Mr. Umpleby was stoic and a bit uptight, but Matt liked him a lot. And hiring a cheesy dancer to perform in the classroom sure seemed like a good idea until Bubbles, or whatever her name was, walked through the door and Mr. Umpleby freaked out, threw his sport coat over her shoulders, and ushered her out of the room.

The school administrator in charge of discipline was not amused. After summoning Sosnick to his office, he closed the door for a heart-to-heart. First he lectured Matt on the impropriety of the stripper stunt and levied a suspension.

Then he put in a request. "Got any tickets to *Guys and Dolls*?" he said.

Some Burlingame teachers and students considered Matt too showy to be trusted, but John Devincenzi always had a soft spot for the kid. Where most people saw an operator, Devincenzi, a popular history teacher, found a lonely adolescent who papered over his self-doubt with bluster. In high school, fitting in with the crowd ranks second to breathing on the list of relevant survival skills. Matt was a good basketball player, but not good enough to make the varsity. He was smart, but lacked the focus and discipline to make National Honor Society. So he expanded his social circle and developed an identity as a master bull-shitter-in-training. Devincenzi, or "Devo," was one of the few adults able to cut through the façade and see the big-hearted kid yearning to break out.

"His self-esteem was in the crapper," Devo says.

Says Matt: "Outside of Fat Tony in *The Simpsons*, Devo is the most important Italian-American in my life."

Teacher and student had a running joke for several years. Devo teased Matt about his rather prominent nose, and Matt teased Devo about his weight. Then one day, Matt went off to the University of Southern California and got a nose job. He returned to Burlingame during vacation and headed straight to Devo's office.

"I just got my nose fixed," Matt told Devo. "And you're still fat."

In high school, Matt discovered a sense of purpose and self-awareness in Devo's leadership class, which challenged students to go beyond the classroom and design projects to benefit the community. Matt contacted a senior citizens' home two blocks from school and spent numerous afternoons bonding with the octogenarians. And when the Space Shuttle Challenger exploded, killing schoolteacher Christa McAuliffe and the six astronauts on board, Matt walked into Devo's classroom and they shared a good cry.

The relationship endures, even as Devo celebrates his 20th anniversary at the school and Matt is a man of the world. Once or twice a year, Devo invites Sosnick back to Burlingame High to acquaint a new generation of kids with life's harsh realities, and there's only one precondition.

"When Matt comes and talks to a class, I tell him he can only drop two F-bombs," Devo says.

Devo is here today, with Dontrelle, Matt's father, and Rochelle Eskenas, the Los Angeles psychologist that Matt's been dating, to see the speech. Matt, true to form, has prepared obsessively. He wants to warn the kids against the dangers of drugs and steer them onto a straight path without sounding like the moral police. He needs to be hip enough to relate to teens on their level while tapping into his life experiences. It's like walking a balance beam.

The kids break the ice with a series of 20 "warmer-uppers" on the main basketball court. "How many of you can tie a knot in a cherry stem with your tongue?" says the moderator, and a handful walk up and try. Other students stand before their peers and talk like Donald Duck, or do handstands or the Electric Slide.

Properly warmed up, the kids retire to a dank multipurpose room in the back to listen to the day's speakers. About 80 teens sit Indian-style on tumbling mats as Matt Sosnick, Burlingame grad turned sports agent, looks down at them from his stool.

"Who here has already heard me speak?" Matt says, asking for a show of hands. "I feel bad that you people have to listen to me one more time. Feel free to get up and walk away."

No one leaves, and while Matt lets it all hang out over the next half-hour, he comes in under Devo's limit. His speech includes the word "prick," two "craps," two "assholes," an "ass," a pair of "penises," one "shit," a "shitload," one "full of shit" and a solitary "fuck." It's like grazing at the profanity buffet.

The kids who've already heard Matt speak bear with him, and those unacquainted with his presentation are riveted. The room is adorned with posters bearing words like *Confidentiality* and *Trust,* and it's so quiet that when Matt speaks and one of the posters begins peeling off the wall, you can hear the tape detach from the cinder blocks.

Sosnick, a stickler for neatness and order, rises from his stool and reattaches the poster to the wall. Then he tells his story.

He was just a teenager like them once, he recalls, lugging around the obligatory baggage of adolescence. He felt overwhelmed by the demands of fitting in, plagued by self-doubt, and burdened by a sense of unhappiness that he could neither pinpoint nor explain. He compensated by showing off or bragging. And talking. And selling.

Matt Sosnick is an emotional hybrid in the truest sense, having inherited his business savvy and generosity from his father and his romanticism, imagination, and flair for the dramatic from his mother. As for his neuroses and personal baggage, they were a group effort, forged by Ron and Victoria's failure to turn a marriage into a productive long-term union.

Matt's parents met as students at UCLA in the mid-1960s, and the family history is dotted with baseball signposts. Ron Sosnick was sitting on the floor of the student union listening to the 1964 World Series when Victoria Zackheim, typically shy around men, spotted him and struck up a conversation. When she began discussing the merits of St. Louis shortstop Dick Groat, he was hooked.

They dated for 10 months and were married in Long Beach on August 22, 1965—the same day that San Francisco pitcher Juan Marichal clubbed Los Angeles catcher John Roseboro over the head with a bat during a famous baseball brawl. *Ron's going to be sorry he got married today,* Victoria thought, *because he could have been watching the game instead.*

Everything about Ron Sosnick's background smacked of industriousness and the American dream. His grandfather, Melvin Sosnick, emigrated to the United States from Russia as a child in the early 1900s, and he eventually started a distribution business that sold cigarettes and sundries to small grocery stores. Sosnick Co. generated $300 million a year in sales at its peak before a series of squabbles prompted the family members to sell to Core-Mark in 1997.

Victoria, Matt's mom, comes from a long line of Eastern European left-wingers, atheists, and crusaders for principle. Matt's grandfather, Sam

Zackheim, worked his way through college as a boxer under the name Buddy Lewis, and he took a job as a teacher in Nevada before marrying and taking his young bride to California. He ultimately made his mark as a racial healer and educator, winning awards for his work in the black community in the most downtrodden section of Los Angeles. As principal at Centennial High in Compton, Sam Zackheim was a father figure to future big-league ballplayers such as Roy White and Reggie Smith.

Matthew, the elder of Ron and Victoria's two children, was born on April 23, 1969, and he quickly established his precocity. At age 3, he developed a strange fascination with vacuum cleaners, rooting through peoples' closets during family visits and going straight for the Hoover. His parents called him the Vacuum Freak. At age 4, he was doing division and multiplication problems in his head and discovering the value in phrasing things *just so*. When his little sister Alisa arrived and they reached elementary school age, Matt would settle disputes by flipping a coin. "Heads, I win," he told his sister. "Tails, you lose." After a humiliating string of defeats, Alisa ran to her father and complained about the unfairness of the process.

The family's distribution business near San Jose was a source of endless bounty and opportunity. Matt routinely visited the warehouse and returned home with boxes of baseball, basketball, and football cards. With their colorful photos and biographical information on the back, the cards were a source of refuge. Matt hauled boxes into his room, memorized the statistics, and felt compelled to share.

"We were at a candy convention," says Matt's mother, "and one guy was kind of a braggart and didn't like the fact that an 8-year-old kid knew so much. So he told Matt, 'If you know so much about sports trivia, tell me the name of the basketball player who scored 100 points.' Matt laughed and he said, 'Wilt Chamberlain,' and he gave the date and the team they played against. Then Matt turned to the guy and said, 'Okay, now your turn: Which guy scored the second-most points for Wilt's team?" The braggart didn't know the answer (Al Attles, with 17 points). But Matt's parents took it as a sign that they needed to teach their boy some humility.

Matt's capitalistic bent was first evidenced by his hustle in washing cars and mowing lawns for a few bucks. By age 15, he graduated to bigger things, such as selling baseball tickets and scalping seats to concerts. When Madonna came to town, Matt would buy homeless people a sandwich and a cup of coffee and enlist them to stand in line for seats. Or his friends would sleep over at the Sosnick house, arise en masse at 4:00 or 5:00 A.M., and troop over to the mall. They'd line up at the Ticketmaster outlet next to the teddy bear store, buy four tickets each to the show, and hand them over to Matt, who'd spin them for a profit.

While other kids were bagging groceries or serving fries for spending money, Matt wangled a position with a local businessman named Walt Lembi at Continental Savings & Loan. In his first week on the job, Matt approved a $525,000 loan and pocketed a $2,700 commission. Then the bank discovered he was too young to be an agent for a financial institution—he was 16 at the time—and sent him home.

Even the media took notice. In 1987, an enterprising ticket broker advertised Bruce Springsteen seats in the *San Francisco Chronicle* for $1,000 a pop. In a subsequent Chronicle story, the broker identified himself as a high school student named Matt Smith. The broker was, in reality, Matt Sosnick, who told the reporter, "My dad would kill me if he knew I was doing this."

Here's something else Matt's parents were oblivious to: By his 18th birthday, he'd sold enough concert tickets, baseball cards, and NFL personal seat licenses to fill several shoe boxes with cash. Hundreds of thousands of dollars' worth.

The parents were different as different could be. Ron Sosnick was an open book, solid, dependable, and ambitious in a 15-hour-a-day sort of way. Victoria was the dreamer, the artist, the creative one. She wrote a novel, *The Bone Weaver*, chronicling a search for self-discovery by Miriam "Mimi" Zilber, a single, 40-year-old professor who comes to grips with her fear of intimacy by exploring her family's past. The book, while fictional, has a strong autobiographical tone. It's like a 264-page therapy session for Victoria Zackheim.

Ron and Victoria tried to make it work. But after 15 years of marriage and two children, they looked up and realized that they didn't belong together. A letter or two between lawyers, and just like that, it was over. Matt went to live with his dad at age 12, Alisa stayed with her mom, and it was hard to understand because there were never any screaming matches or kitchen utensils thrown in anger.

"My children were devastated by the divorce," Victoria Zackheim says. "Sometimes I think angry divorces are better because the kids can really see, 'My parents don't belong together and it's better if we're apart.' But his father and I remained friends for quite some time, and I think that was very confusing for the children."

Matt's mother was just trying to be protective, but in her self-absorption and transition to the world as a divorcée, she either lacked time or made snap judgments that came off as negative or hypercritical. Her voyage of self-discovery included room for only one passenger, and they never worked through the obstacles that mothers and sons typically work through.

Matt still remembers feeling mortified at Little League games when he asked his mother not to yell from the stands, and he could hear her voice resonating above all the others. Victoria was the type of mom who'd burst into song while carpooling, much to her children's embarrassment, or sing while the movie credits were rolling.

"My mom's very well intended," Matt says. "She loves her kids more than anything, and she's a brilliant person. But I've never really related to her socially or understood her very well. I think she's motivated at times by her own insecurities—just like I am."

During a trip to Israel in 1994, Matt met a girl named Jill Ornitz, who worked in Hollywood as an executive assistant to power broker Michael Ovitz and then to renowned director Francis Ford Coppola. They returned to California and began dating long-distance, and Jill spurned her mother's advice and left Los Angeles to move in with Matt for a year. She discovered many things in the process:

1. Matt has an awful lot of street smarts, even though he didn't spend much time on the streets.

2. He'd be successful whether he started out with a million dollars or nothing, simply because he's built that way.

3. He has the attention span of a 4-year-old.

4. Even though he has money, he likes to view himself as an underdog.

5. He's obsessive about being obsessive. Matt can't just *like* a band, Jill discovered. Before Dave Matthews, it was the Grateful Dead. And it was nothing for Matt to call home and say, "Hey, I just met a guy named Scott at the Dead concert. Is it okay if he sleeps on the couch?"

6. For all Matt's flaws, he's inherently likeable because he really wants to do the right thing. "It all comes from the right place," Jill says.

7. He has an amazing capacity for persuasion, of himself and others. "I mean this in the nicest of ways, although it doesn't sound very nice," says Jill. "But Matt believes his own shit."

Some people, Jill theorizes, need to have crises or problems to work through in life, as if they're characters in dramas of their own creation. Today, Matt's real-life drama is his attempt to build a successful sports agency against the odds. Ten years ago, it was a gambling problem that all but consumed him.

Compulsive gambling, as described by Gamblers Anonymous, is "an illness, progressive in its nature, which can never be cured but can be arrested." The GA 12-step recovery program, which has helped millions of problem gamblers overcome their affliction, is "fundamentally based on ancient spiritual principles and rooted in sound medical therapy."

Step 1 requires the problem gambler to admit that he's powerless and acknowledge that his life has become unmanageable. Matt Sosnick was 24 years old when he made the admission and sought help. But you didn't need to be psychic or have a transportation schedule to see this particular bus coming.

At age 10, Matt needed an outlet for his lawn-mowing and car-washing money, and shooting dice seemed like a cool way to have fun. When his mother caught wind of his preoccupation, she was determined to teach him a lesson. So she sat him down at the backgammon table with the objective of taking his gambling winnings. After several days at the board, Mother Sosnick was down $300 and becoming more agitated by the minute. "Give me $100," Matt said, "and we'll call a truce."

Matt was in the seventh grade when he placed his first real bet, on a day trip to Golden Gate Fields in Albany, near Oakland. His friend Paul's older brother took the kids to the racetrack and a Billy Joel concert. Matt approached the window, somehow managed to lay down $10 on a 10-to-1 shot, and the horse came in. "That was my downfall," he says. He was hooked.

A kid with a business mind, in an affluent community, has access to more high-powered toys than blue-collar teens who might be content to drink beer and read porn magazines. Matt was introduced to a local bookmaker by the older brother of a kid in school. By age 15, he was wagering on pro sports and feeling awfully important about it.

"I was bored with life and insecure, and I needed life to be superlife," Matt says. "If you've ever gambled and bet $1,000 on the Clippers and Hawks, you take two stupid, boring teams like that and it's the most exciting 2 or 3 hours of your day. That's the reason people do it."

His gambling jones followed him all the way to college. At the University of Southern California, Matt discovered Pai Gow poker, a hybrid of Chinese dominos and American poker at which he was particularly adept. He also met Brad Carmel, a worldly New Yorker who went by the nickname of Big Daddy, and whose father allegedly owned more real estate than Donald Trump.

They fed off each other in a spoiled rich-kid sort of way. On Saturday mornings in the fall, Matt and Brad would place their wagers and unwrap their Egg McMuffins in front of Matt's big-screen TV, and spend 16 hours watching college football. The day's activities began at 9:00 A.M. with Cornell vs. Yale on ESPN, and concluded at 1:00 A.M., when the final gun sounded on Hawaii vs. Brigham Young.

When standard wagers became boring, Matt and Brad pooled their imaginations. They'd spend $200 on 20 boxes of trading cards and play a game called basketball poker. "We'd open the pack and bet who could make the best hand," Matt says. "If you had the dream hand, you'd win an extra hundred bucks." The dream hand consisted of David Robinson or Hakeem Olajuwon at center, Michael Jordan and Magic Johnson at the guards, and Karl Malone and Larry Bird at forward.

They attended Los Angeles Clippers games, bet against the sad-sack franchise, and sat close enough to the court to heckle the players. On slow sports days, when action was scarce, they'd hang out at an inner-city park and bet on youth girls' soccer matches. Matt would take the Lavender Lady Bugs, Brad would settle for the squad in blue, and they'd lay odds and wager $500 on the result.

The showiness, the fast pace, the adrenaline rush . . . it all filled an emptiness in his life. Josh Rittenberg, now a doctor in Chicago, occasionally accompanied Matt to the local Bank of America at USC—the one that got robbed every other month—and laughed when Matt handed the teller $20 for instant access to his safety deposit box. It's the only time Josh had ever seen someone tip a bank teller.

The odds, of course, favored an unhappy ending. Matt estimates that he lost "close to a million bucks" before he got his gambling under control. As for the emotional toll, it was impossible to quantify. The thrill of winning a bet was negligible compared with the knot in his stomach and the dreams of games and numbers, numbers and games that invaded his sleep.

Matt was very good at the NFL and college basketball, but it didn't matter. "No one can manage their money well enough to win unless they're incredibly disciplined," he says. "Based on my personality—the fact that I was compulsive, idiosyncratic, and insecure—it didn't play well into betting three games a week at X amount. I needed the action to make my life more exciting than it was. To feel better about myself. To sort of be a big shot."

He continued to gamble after college, buying a handheld sports ticker for $500 to monitor the scores, and he'd click the device to the exclusion of human interaction and every other pursuit short of breathing. All the clicking eventually became too much for his girlfriend, Jill. They were driving to Napa one weekend, and she was talking and he was clicking (while driving, no less), and Jill grew so exasperated that she took the ticker from his hand, opened the window and threw it off a bridge into the drink. "Matt was like, 'Oh my God,'" Jill says. "Then he totally laughed. He was relieved, I think."

True to Jill's mother's premonition, the relationship failed to work out. She moved back to Los Angeles and married a plastic surgeon, while Matt devoted himself to being the best recovering gambler he could be. He climbed the 12 steps, kicked his addiction, and threw himself into other pursuits—such as compulsive work, compulsive dating, compulsive monitoring of stocks during the Internet bubble, and compulsively caring about players as a sports agent.

Funny thing, though. While Matt has sworn off gambling, he still checks the Vegas lines in the sports page and can't wait to let his friends know that the Cowboys are a lock to cover at home against the Saints. When friends tease Matt about his parade of girlfriends and failure to commit, he'll blurt out, "What odds will you give me that I'm married within 2 years?"

Two years ago, when Twins minor leaguer Jon Pridie got married in Bettendorf, Iowa, he asked Matt to be part of the wedding party. The ushers all visited the John Deere museum in nearby Moline, Illinois, for kicks, and Matt and another groomsman made a wager based on pride.

"I bet him I could bite, swallow, and eat 20 John Deere suckers in 90 seconds," Matt says. "He said it couldn't be done, so I told him statistically, he wasn't evaluating it carefully enough. I also told him I was probably the only Jew ever to set foot in the John Deere museum in Moline."

Matt has never operated under the illusion that he would find many friends or mentors in the agent business. For most of his life, he's regarded his father as his best friend and sagest counsel. Ron Sosnick is a gentle, big-hearted man who ingrained a sense of industriousness and obligation in his son. On the rare occasions when he showed anger, it was prompted by lapses in judgment or the abdication of responsibility.

Late in Matt's senior year at USC, he called his father and said that he was dropping accounting and wouldn't be graduating until the following semester. Ron Sosnick got as mad as his constitution allowed. "Here's what you're going to do," Ron told his son. "You're going back to USC and pay the tuition out of your pocket and you're going to graduate, and I don't even want to talk about it anymore."

Ron also believed that his boy should spend a year on his own before joining the company business, so Matt took a job selling fax machines for Lanier and wowing his customers with personal service. He knew that all the machines were basically the same, so customers would be inclined to buy from the salesman they liked the most. He took them to concerts and tended to their needs, and they overlooked the fact that his fax machine expertise began and ended with knowing how to plug one into the wall.

Matt's next step was running his uncle Howard's company, a Silicon Valley electronics firm called Allied Electronic Recovery that recycled used computer parts. He hated the job, felt antsy and bored, and knew he was destined for something more.

An escape route was ultimately provided by his mother, the novelist. Victoria Zackheim was living in France in the late 1990s when she befriended the brother of David Morway, a sports agent living in Utah. Victoria believed there was something cosmic about the link, and she passed along a phone number to her son under the assumption that he'd feel similarly.

Within days, Matt made an appointment with Morway and traveled to Utah, where he heard a tale that was both cautionary and uplifting.

David Morway had graduated from law school and worked in the San Diego Padres' front office in the mid-1980s before taking a blind leap into athlete representation. He built a client roster that included Junior Seau in football and Tony Clark and Esteban Loaiza in baseball, and he handled marketing deals for a number of golfers and volleyball players.

Morway gave Sosnick what he calls his "10-cent speech" on the hazards of the industry. He talked about client stealing and the risks inherent in the business model. If you sold pens for a living, Morway told Matt, you could recover from a bad stretch by working harder and selling more pens. If you were an agent and crapped out on the draft, you had to wait a whole year to try again. The only alternative was luring players from established agents, and good luck doing that.

The agent business was also an emotional grind. Agents, no matter how accomplished, had to kiss athletes' asses all the time. It was degrading when you made phone call after phone call on behalf of a player and still couldn't find him a job. And just try feeling like a hotshot when you are talking to the general manager and one of your players happens by and asks, "Have you picked up my dry cleaning?"

Morway's speech should have deterred Matt, but it only served to invigorate him. Determined to become a baseball agent, Matt rushed out and recruited his first client, a San Francisco–born infielder named Lou Lucca who'd been drafted by Florida in the 32nd round in 1992 and kicked around the minors for 6 years. When Matt spirited Lucca away from Reich, Katz and Landis, the firm's agents didn't care because they barely noticed.

David Morway has since left the agent business and is now a high-ranking official with the National Basketball Association's Indiana Pacers, and Matt calls him regularly with updates.

"I've had tons of people do what Matt did," Morway says. "I just try to give them an honest feeling about what they should expect—the risks and ramifications. He was the one guy who came back for more. He went after it and did it. That's the amazing thing. He actually did it."

The students at Know Limits sit stone silent as Matt Sosnick, Burlingame High grad turned sports agent, shares six revelations that have helped him come to grips with the world and live a more well-adjusted life. This is what he's come to tell the kids:

1. The desire to be perceived positively drives human behavior more than you'll ever know. So do yourself a favor and be true to yourself.

"People will lie, they'll kill each other, they'll cheat, they'll steal, they'll do whatever they can so that people will look at them in a way they want to be viewed," Matt tells the kids. "You guys all know people who reinvent themselves every year and are a different person when they come back to school. Very few people say, 'I'm a good person. I'm going to take myself as I am.'"

2. The world isn't black and white. As someone who's ardently pro-choice and pro-death penalty, Matt believes in seeing the value in someone else's opinion.

"I'm Jewish and I represent a lot of Christians and Mormons," he says. "A fundamentalist Christian—I totally respect that. That's somebody who will not vote for a candidate who is pro-choice because they believe so strongly in the right to life. A fanatical Christian is someone who kills an abortion doctor. There's a big difference between those two things."

3. Addiction has underlying causes wholly separate from the act itself.

"All of you know somebody who is anorexic, is bulimic, binge eats, gambles too much, is a habitual pot smoker, drinks, or is overly sexually active," he says. "Addiction is about not liking yourself and feeling an emptiness inside and understanding there's a hole you need to fill. When people cure the addiction, that's when there's a high suicide rate. All of a sudden, you've taught yourself not to do something. And now you have to deal with all the shit underneath that you've been covering up."

4. Don't take things too personally.

"Someone flips you off on the freeway—that person doesn't know you," Matt tells the kids. "Somebody tells you you're ugly or smart or you're never going to make it, it's just one asshole's opinion. I have AOL, and every morning when I log on, there's, like, 30 messages. If I took everything personally, every time I logged on, I'd think I needed to refinance my house or get a penis enlargement."

5. Collect people in your life who are meaningful and important.

"People who talk about other people, people who are negative, people who are afraid to say 'I love you' or are not supportive: They're not worth having," Matt says. "Live your life like you have 3 months left to live. If you had 3 months left to live, I promise you a lot of the people you hang out with now, you wouldn't."

6. Do something to change the world for the better.

"When an ambulance drives by, instead of thinking what a pain in the ass it is to pull over, think about the fact that there could be someone dying inside there, and say a prayer that the person is okay," Matt tells the kids. "Man a crisis hotline for teen kids. Take an hour a week. Step up and make a difference."

The list goes on. Help teach inner-city kids to read, Matt urges the group. Visit the elderly. Go to a local dry cleaner and volunteer to collect all the unclaimed clothing and bring it to a shelter for the homeless or a battered women's shelter. Give blood. Become an organ donor. Help build somebody a house for Habitat for Humanity. And if all else fails, at the very least, refrain from littering. Keep the world safe from stray candy wrappers.

He's learned from experience, Matt tells the kids. He was a mess himself as a teenager, all bluster, braggadocio, and insecurity, and that was *before* a gambling addiction nearly ruined his life. But with time, personal will, and a good therapist, there's a road to self-discovery.

"Do you want people to remember that you made a bunch of cash in high school, or do you want them to remember that you were there as a friend?" Matt says. "Write your obituary in your own mind, and think about what you want it to say."

The 80 kids in attendance, unaccustomed to being addressed so bluntly by an adult, break into a loud, extended round of applause when Matt concludes his speech. Although some of the Burlingame teachers were a bit unnerved by the salty language, they applaud as well. Matt wanted to make an impression, and he's clearly hit the mark.

Part of it is the earthiness of his tone and the gravity of the subject matter. Matt seems so in touch with his feelings—in a New Age, Oprah Winfrey sort of way. But the message also transcends words and taps into the lure of pop-culture stereotypes. The kids all regard sports agents as so mysterious and powerful. Maybe Matt Sosnick, Burlingame grad, doesn't have an Alex Rodriguez or Barry Bonds in his stable yet. But he walked these same halls 16 years ago, and now he's making it. Or at least he's on his way.

Andrea Glick, one of the teens in attendance, knows Matt better than most. She worked for him one summer at the Sosnick-Cobbe agency, doing errands, running odd jobs, and taking his bulldog for walks in the neighborhood. A day before Matt's speech, Andrea and another student followed Matt around on a job-shadowing assignment for a class. When he wasn't on the phone making deals, he was frantically pacing around his duplex thinking about making deals.

The guy is a walking reality show, Andrea concluded.

"Matt's life is very suspenseful," she says. "I keep wanting to know what else is going to happen."

Chapter
FOUR

Baseball's winter meetings were once renowned as a place for club executives to gather and conduct business over hard drinks and harder sells. No one personified the old horse-trading mentality more than Bill Veeck, the late Cleveland Indians and Chicago White Sox owner. The old-timers still talk wistfully about the meetings in Hollywood, Florida, when White Sox general manager Roland Hemond, with Veeck's blessing, set up a card table in the lobby with a sign reading "Open for Business," then watched his fellow executives line up and make offers. There was room for creativity and even a little fun in the good old days, when trades were driven purely by scouting judgments and mutual need.

Then came free agency, and escalating salaries, and agents, and a labyrinthine array of dates and deadlines. Baseball now holds its winter meetings over a 4-day stretch sometime between the December 7 arbitration offering deadline and the December 20 contract tender date, and general managers grouse that agents have become the de facto "stars"—

hijacking the agenda, holding press conferences in the lobby, and playing teams off against each other for talent.

Several years ago, Atlanta's John Schuerholz complained that the meetings had become a "feeding tank for agent sharks" with a facility for working the room. "There are more lies told in the lobby of a winter meeting than anywhere on the face of the Earth at any one time," Schuerholz said.

During the 2003–2004 free-agent signing season, the air is thick with collusion speculation. In 1990, a panel of arbitrators found that clubs had illegally conspired to hold down salaries from 1985 to 1987, and it awarded the players $280 million in damages. Now, in '03–'04, agents are once again invoking the "C" word, and the union is paying attention. In a letter just days before the December 2003 New Orleans meetings, union lawyer Michael Weiner tells agents to be on the lookout for suspicious behavior. If a fringe free agent receives the same $750,000 offer from six clubs, it might qualify as a tipoff. "Already this signing season we have received several reports of troubling conduct by club officials," Weiner says in his letter.

The slowdown is affecting players at all levels. While pitcher Bartolo Colón signed a four-year, $51 million contract with Anaheim before the meetings, Vladimir Guerrero, Miguel Tejada, and Pudge Rodriguez are among the high-profile names still on the market. And Texas is trying to trade Alex Rodriguez—the American League Most Valuable Player—after finishing in last place 3 straight years with the richest man in sports at short.

Everyone, it seems, is consumed by A-Rod rumors. Boston wants to trade for him, and outfielder Manny Ramirez could go to Texas as part of the deal. Ramirez is notoriously sensitive, and his pride is wounded when the Red Sox place him on waivers in hopes that someone might bite and assume the $100 million left on his 8-year, $160 million contract. Nobody bites.

If conflict and stagnation are the order of the day, there are worse places to endure it than New Orleans, where a bowl of gumbo and a cold draft beer are a short walk away on Bourbon Street and the piano bar in the Marriott lobby makes for a convenient thoroughfare. Reporters linger in search of team executives passing through, and everywhere you turn, another agent is holding court.

Over here is Tom Reich, patron of the Reich, Katz and Landis agency, projecting a distinguished *Lion in Winter* look with his great gray mane of hair and salt-and-pepper beard. Reich, a Pittsburgh lawyer, began representing ballplayers after he met Pirates pitcher Dock Ellis at a party in 1969. He felt a sense of outrage when Ellis told him that black major leaguers were paid inequitably based on race. Reich is well-connected in baseball ownership circles and inclined to rant about the evils of collusion or agent "terrorists" who pilfer from the competition. You never know whether he'll show up dressed in a conservative blue suit or a fishing vest.

Adam Katz, a Notre Dame law school graduate and Reich's younger partner, is tall and lean, maybe 6'3", with a perpetual five-o'clock shadow and a brusque manner that's alternately off-putting and entertaining. Katz was a basketball junkie as a kid and still fills it up from downtown during occasional games of HORSE, even though an achy back has hindered his mobility. He's a tenacious advocate for Chicago Cubs outfielder Sammy Sosa and his other clients, and he chafes at the notion that bigger-name, publicity-seeking agents somehow do a better job. If Katz ever leaves the profession, his dream job is running an NBA team as its general manager.

The "bad boys" of the agent ranks—Dan Lozano, Rick Thurman, Dan Horwits, and Jeff Borris of the Beverly Hills Sports Council—are ever-present with their Rolexes, black silk shirts, and matching menacing expressions. While the Beverly Hills boys strike fear into the hearts of competitors as relentless client-stalkers, team officials generally regard them as reasonable agents who know how to strike a deal. J. P. Ricciardi, Toronto Blue Jays general manager, affectionately refers to the Sports Council foursome as the "Sopranos."

And no assemblage of agents would be complete without Tommy Tanzer, a former Utah schoolteacher who chucked it all in the early 1980s to pursue a career representing athletes. Tanzer stands 5'5" max, and many people note his resemblance to singer Paul Simon. But in bearing and demeanor, he's more a portable version of the stand-up comic David Brenner. This is only fitting, because when Tanzer ceases representing ballplayers for a living, he aspires to be a "sports gossip comedian."

Throw in a Joe Bick here, a Seth and Sam Levinson there, and the gang is all here in New Orleans. But in any gathering of agents, the attention invariably focuses on two above the rest. Scott Boras and Jeff Moorad share the same area code in Newport Beach, California, and a seemingly permanent place among the *Sporting News*'s list of the top 100 power brokers in sports. They're the new Lords of the Realm.

Whenever Jeff Moorad pops into the lobby to give the press an update on Manny Ramirez, he attracts a crowd. Moorad has a close-cropped beard and sleepy eyes; dresses in a blue blazer, loafers, and jeans, and speaks with a low nasal monotone that radiates self-assurance. He's the kind of guy who can feed three reporters the same "scoop," yet convey an air of confidentiality that makes them all feel special. Moorad is a serial user of the media—never inclined to return a phone call unless it's in his best interest, always helping the big paper in town at the expense of the little suburban guy who's busting his tail. But there's a roguish quality about him that makes him likeable, even when he's selling swampland.

Moorad's survival skills served him well during one of the ugliest episodes in the history of his profession. During a highly publicized trial in 2002, sports agent Leigh Steinberg had his reputation sullied as an alleged alcoholic, sexual harasser, and philanderer. And David Dunn, who took about 50 football clients from Steinberg to start a rival firm, was found guilty of breach of contract and ordered to pay $44.6 million in damages.

Moorad, the middle link in the Steinberg Moorad & Dunn triad, emerged from the nastiness unscathed. He remained the golden boy of Assante Corporation, the Canadian company that owned the agency, and then its spin-off, Loring Ward International, by continuing to bring in clients and signing them to lucrative multiyear contracts.

"Everyone else was bloody, gutted, the whole nine yards," says a competing baseball agent. "Jeff was the only person who came out on the white horse. That wasn't by mistake or happenstance. I give him his due for being the last guy standing. It takes an intelligent person to be able to do that."

Jeff Moorad is, by all accounts, a master at compiling and assimilating information. His most prominent early influence was his father, William, a buyer for the Gallo Wineries in California. The elder Moorad bought boxcars worth of raw materials that went into the manufacturing process, and he taught his son that everything was negotiable—that as long as you used logic and the proper tone, it was all right to question the sticker price.

Young Jeff Moorad, the aspiring deal-a-holic, attended UCLA and came in contact with Sam Gilbert, a wealthy booster who became infamous for giving improper gifts to coach John Wooden's basketball players while the NCAA was looking the other way. Jeff Moorad's father helped shape his worldview, but it was Gilbert who acquainted him with the magnetic pull of power and celebrity.

Some things just came naturally. As a Villanova law student, Moorad cold-called Indiana State basketball star Larry Bird to see whether Bird might be interested in hiring him as an agent. He ran up huge cell phone bills before it became fashionable, married the sister-in-law of a client, former Baltimore Orioles closer Gregg Olson, and became a prominent player in the world of baseball representation.

In 1997 Moorad nearly died from necrotizing fasciitis, commonly known as the flesh-eating disease, and had a spiritual awakening. "It affected me dramatically," he says. "I came out of the experience much more in touch with life priorities and a desire to do the right thing in a lot of ways." It wasn't lost on Moorad that Darin Erstad, Shawn Green, and Eric Karros, three of his most prominent clients, were among the first visitors to his hospital room. Their friendly faces substantiated the importance of relationships.

Now, Moorad gives speeches to church groups and talks about his faith. But his religious declarations are routinely mocked by his fellow agents, who accuse him of raiding their clienteles in the majors and the minors. "That's been his modus operandi," says one. When the Players Association sent a memo to agents outlawing All-Star Game parties because of complaints that they were an outlet for solicitation, Moorad was perceived as the main target because he threw the biggest All-Star bash.

Moorad is resigned to the concept of the agent business as snakepit, yet he venerates the skills required. He believes strongly that the best agents are "stars" at both the negotiating table and on the living room couch—where they recruit players and their families in the area he euphemistically calls "client procurement."

"It's not a profession for nice guys," Moorad says. "There's a toughness required that is both necessary and unfortunate."

A healthy ego, by all accounts, is also part of the equation, and when Moorad and his chief antagonist, Scott Boras, inhabit the same hotel space, a certain tension is inevitable. "There's a visceral hate there, no question," says another agent.

According to one popular tale, the rivalry played out several years ago in the Newport Beach Little League, where the two agent kingpins both had sons playing. Boras donated $25,000 for improvements to a local field and, in exchange for his largesse, had the field named in his honor and threw out the ceremonial first pitch.

As the story goes, the Steinberg Moorad & Dunn agency tried to undercut Boras by buying every sign on the outfield wall. But Moorad claims that's an urban myth. He merely bought the *biggest* sign in the park, for $500, in keeping with an annual agency tradition.

Boras and Moorad have taken turns representing some of the same prominent players through the years, and while their mutual Newport Beach ties have fueled a game of one-upmanship, Moorad is quick to point out that he moved to the town in 1981, well before Boras's arrival.

"There is no love lost between us," Moorad concedes. "But at the same time, it's fair to say we didn't spend enough time with each other one-on-one to conclude that we disliked each other for any reason other than competitive rivalry."

Sometimes, innocent bystanders can't help but get sucked into the Scott-and-Jeff tiff. When college pitching star Mark Prior was looking for an adviser before the 2001 draft, Moorad called his father to make a pitch.

"You have an outstanding son," Moorad told Jerry Prior. "Not only would I dearly like to have him as a client, I would also like to shove it up my Newport Beach neighbor's butt."

Jerry Prior, who only wanted the best for his son, was so shocked by the admission that he took the phone from his ear and stared at it for confirmation.

"It was incredible," Prior says. "You just don't say that to a kid's dad."

At the 2003 winter meetings, Scott Boras doesn't give briefings as much as educational primers that sound like sermons. While Moorad uses the press strictly on a need basis, Boras genuinely cares how he's perceived. He habitually returns phone calls, and he might spend an hour picking a beat writer's brain for insights. He enjoys the give-and-take of ball talk, and if the reporter can pass along a nugget that might help in contract negotiations, so much the better.

The writers that Boras courts often go to great lengths to describe him. In March of 2004, *Boston Herald* columnist Gerry Callahan laments the fact that Red Sox catcher Jason Varitek and pitcher Derek Lowe, both of whom will be free agents after the season, are Boras clients likely to scrape for every buck. "All agents are beneath head lice on the food chain," Callahan writes, "but Boras is the worst." Ken Rosenthal of the *Sporting News* refers to Boras as "Lex Luthor," in reference to Superman's evil genius arch-enemy, and Philadelphia columnist Bill Conlin once wrote that if Mother Teresa had been a Boras client, her image would have been transformed "from fragile saint to pushy shrew with a bad wardrobe."

Boras generally laughs off the monikers, at least publicly, except when inaccuracies are involved. In the mid-'90s, when a columnist observed that most baseball front-office people regard him as Darth Vader in an

Armani suit, Boras took offense. "I don't own an Armani suit," he huffed.

The less Boras shows his face in the Marriott lobby, the more the press speculates about the calls he must be fielding in his hotel suite. Unlike his agent peers, Boras refuses to be cowed by pronouncements that the sky is falling. Just a month earlier, during a gathering of general managers in Phoenix, Boras gave a defiant "State of the Game" address to the press. He said that big-league teams are cutting payrolls to increase profits rather than to reduce losses, and he cited Atlanta as a club that understates its TV revenue—because it owns the station that broadcasts its games—and pockets far more in media income than it reports.

"We're in the most successful economic place that Major League Baseball has ever been in," said Boras, spitting out a mind-numbing litany of facts and figures to support his thesis.

Let other agents cry and whine about collusion: Boras is pathologically opposed to the conventional wisdom. If Alex Rodriguez went on the market today, Boras tells reporters, he could fetch the same contract that Texas gave him in December 2000.

The underlying message is clear: A-Rod could get $252 million, Scott Boras seems to be saying, because he's a premium player. He also has *me* negotiating for him.

Paul Cobbe, the unassuming half of Sosnick-Cobbe, tries to overlook the fact that Scott Boras has taken three of his agency's best clients. He judges Boras in the context of his business model. Paul respects the manner in which Boras plows his profits back into his company, the way any good businessman should. The guy is the IBM of baseball agents, Paul concedes, and competitors who deny this are delusional or simply jealous.

"I think Scott sees himself as somewhat of a prophet," Paul says. "He has a responsibility to baseball and the players, and he has to fulfill his responsibility. Is he the root of all evil? Maybe, maybe not. The guy got 25 million bucks a year times 10 for A-Rod. He could sleep with his sister—he still got that deal done."

While the winter meetings are largely a showcase for agent egos on parade—*hey, look at me talking on my cell phone on behalf of my star free agent!*—Paul sits in the Marriott lobby nursing a soft drink and a low profile, which is the way he prefers it.

His partner, Matt Sosnick, never travels to the winter meetings because he's more comfortable in what Paul calls his "cocoon" back home in the Bay Area. Matt loves the social element of hanging out with friends, or the singular bond that comes with schmoozing a baseball front-office official over the phone. But the showiness of the big cattle-drive events—from high-school talent showcases to the winter meetings—makes him squirm, and he goes to great lengths to avoid them.

So Paul overcomes his initial reticence and buys a ticket to New Orleans. It's good practice for the day when they'll have some prominent free agents and work their way up the executive food chain. Maybe, one day, Paul will call big-time general managers such as Billy Beane and Brian Cashman and have business to conduct with them rather than calling the assistant GM or farm director. Then, he'll know he's arrived.

Paul is in New Orleans with a modest agenda. He'd like to meet Peter Gammons, the ESPN personality who's so influential that people refer to him as "the commissioner." And he'll spend time talking with Gus Quattlebaum, a bright young Baltimore Orioles scout that he's befriended. Gus and Paul have a bond because they're both prep-school types in a game that might have viewed them with a wary eye until the recent trend toward Harvard and Yale graduates in front offices. Gus was a star right fielder at Davidson, and Paul was a fine athlete in his own right, among the best in the whole water polo fraternity at Brown. But they don't chew tobacco or have tons of connections, so they're still making their way. Gus is raw when it comes to networking at the upper reaches, but Paul is convinced he'll be a general manager someday.

Paul's main order of business in New Orleans isn't schmoozing. About a 10-minute walk from the Marriott, baseball's trade show is taking place. Fans and club officials with money to spend will roam a giant warehouse for 3 days and check out everything from bobblehead dolls to pitching machines to ballpark cuisine and entertainment (including a dwarf dressed up to look like Elvis Presley). Paul is going to the trade show to see a Franklin sporting goods company rep about a deal that might be worth $20,000 in equipment for the Sosnick-Cobbe agency.

Say what you will about batting gloves in the cosmic scheme of things, but they go for $30 to $40 a pair retail, and every little bit counts. In conjunction with their business plan, Sosnick and Cobbe give each other a nominal annual salary of $36,000. The money they earn on draft commissions and baseball card deals certainly helps, but after more than 5 years, they're just now edging into the black.

Factor in recruiting costs, travel expenses, meals on the road, gloves and spikes for players who don't have deals with the equipment companies, tickets to fly players to San Francisco for visits, concert seats for entertainment purposes, and money for baby gifts, birthday gifts, funeral flowers and other "client service" costs, and you might be talking $500,000 a year. That's a heap of outflow.

"People say to me all the time that we must be making money in this business," Paul says. "If that's the case, we must be retarded. Because we aren't."

When union lawyer Gene Orza talks about young agents who like to brag at cocktail parties, he's certainly not referring to Paul Cobbe. If Paul is on a flight and a fellow passenger asks about his line of work, he invariably replies, "I'm a computer programmer." It's a sound strategy for two reasons: More often than not, the other passenger nods in bored assent and goes back to his magazine. And if by some miracle the person wants to discuss computer programming, Paul won't be caught off guard. His father, George, has a degree in electronic engineering from Stanford and once ran Samsung Hewlett Packard in Korea, and Paul is well-versed in computer lingo from his days as a consultant with Deloitte.

The agent business . . . well . . . it's not a topic he enjoys discussing with strangers. Paul saw *Jerry Maguire* 10 years ago, and he enjoyed the movie for its entertainment value. But now he chuckles at the incongruities. Jerry's only client was making $225,000, and Jerry got a 4 percent cut. That's not even $10,000, Paul calculates, and Jerry was still flying all over the country to games, loitering in the press box, and glad-handing with newspaper columnists. Jerry stood on the sidelines and badgered the general manager during practice, then showed up in the locker room—in the *showers*, even—to hang with his client. For a guy who was perceived as an underdog, Jerry pretty much had it made.

And don't get Paul started on the HBO series *Arli$$*. He never watched *Arli$$* once, under the assumption that it would only piss him off and make him dwell on the cutthroat, seamy side of his world. "Life is hard enough as it is," Paul says.

Mutual friends of Paul and Matt consider them diametric opposites. Matt makes his business decisions within seconds, on gut instinct, and is right-on maybe 95 percent of the time. Paul is the long-range thinker in the Sosnick-Cobbe agency, the careful one, the problem solver. He's perfectly comfortable hunkering down in an office examining spreadsheets and making forecasts, or troubleshooting a computer glitch. Paul's the one who's read the Basic Agreement several times over, and he's the agency's resident authority on issues ranging from termination pay to the grievance process. It's not glamorous work, but in any successful business, someone has to do it.

Paul's most impressive trait, other than his versatility, is his knack for concealing it. He was always the smartest kid in the class, the student body president, and most likely to succeed. Now he's approaching his mid-30s and has a wife who looks like she just stepped out of *Vogue* magazine, an adorable baby girl and a second daughter on the way, and a beautiful home in the San Ramon hills. But he's so unassuming, you can't possibly resent him for it. "Paul to me seems a lot more comfortable in his own skin than Matt," says a baseball acquaintance of both men.

Only the people closest to Paul, or those who dig, know that he scored 1440 on his SATs, or that he's licensed to fly single-engine prop planes, or that he dabbled in race car driving when he was bored and needed a diversion. Paul took classes at the Bondurant School in 1996 and competed briefly in the Formula Dodge Series before concluding that it was too expensive and he had better things to do with his life.

Paul practically revels in his low profile. On the first night of the New Orleans meetings, he strolled around Bourbon Street and saw Craig Landis, of the firm Reich, Katz and Landis, hanging out with several young associates at a restaurant. Paul knows them all by face or name, but most of them couldn't pick him out of a police lineup.

Paul and Craig Landis first met several years ago in Long Beach at the Area Code games, a summer showcase of high school talent where scouts take notes from the stands and agents troll the parking lots, dugouts, concession stands, and even the restrooms for the opportunity to hand out business cards and meet future clients.

Landis, a former professional ballplayer, introduced himself to Paul and complimented him on the stable of talent that Sosnick and Cobbe had amassed through the draft.

"You and Sosnick have some good guys," Landis said.

Then he paused.

"That's the easy part. Good luck keeping them."

The words resonated with Paul during the flight back to San Francisco: *What does this guy know that I don't know?*

The Sosnick-Cobbe Sports company brochure is modest as corporate promotional materials go. It consists of three glossy pages tucked inside a gray cardboard binder, with lots of information on baseball card deals, glove endorsements, and amateur draft bonuses negotiated by Matt and Paul.

The brochure features player testimonials ("Matt and Paul are like family to me," says Florida pitcher Dontrelle Willis) and praise from team officials ("Their clients are their first priority," say Jim Fleming, the Marlins' vice president of player development and scouting). Competing agents who criticize Sosnick and Cobbe for being too cushy with the clubs wonder if it's actually a good thing to crow about teams *liking* you.

But the words on the brochure pale in comparison with the photos. One picture features two *GQ*-looking dudes in sport coats with bats flung over their shoulders. That's Matt and Paul in their early 30s. The other photo shows them 28 years earlier, as little boys about to become lifelong friends.

Matt was 3 years old and Paul was 2 when they first met as neighbors on Via Ranchero, in an upscale development in the San Jose suburb of Saratoga, California. The Cobbes lived in a rambling, ranch-style tract house in Silicon Valley—a slice of upwardly mobile Americana—and Paul could almost always be found in the front yard kicking a soccer ball or riding a bike with Matt. Their sisters became best friends, too. "It was very clear even when they were little boys that they both were unusual," says Matt's mother, Victoria. "They were very bright and they tapped into each other. They'd give each other the giggles."

Matt was the idea machine, the intrepid one, his mind always racing in search of the next crazy scheme. Paul would stand off to the side and roll his eyes, then chuck his apprehensions and be Matt's partner in crime. "Paul was a little more reserved then, and easygoing, and that allowed space for Matt," says George Cobbe, Paul's father. "Some kids, if they are too much alike, they fuss and fight."

When Matt was in first grade, he brought several boxes of candy home from the company warehouse and set up shop with a plan to undercut the corner store. His garage became a battlefield, with Tootsie Rolls and licorice sticks as his weapons of choice. The plan worked, too, until one of the older kids grabbed a fistful of candy and refused to pay for it. "Matt and I just didn't have the muscle to back it up," Paul says.

Both boys were bored in school and felt hemmed in by the classroom walls, and they constantly tested authority or talked excessively in class. The other kids laughed when Paul propped a cup of water on the door and it came tumbling down just as the teacher entered the room. Lots of days, Paul would just skip school altogether. His parents finally packed him off to a boarding school, Harker Academy, and Matt's parents sent him to Harker's rival, Hillbrook. But their friendship endured. As high school freshmen, they had lots of money but no drivers' licenses, so they rented a limousine and offered to take two senior girls to dinner. The girls said yes, and the two couples enjoyed an evening of fine dining over Coca-Colas at the Velvet Turtle.

When Matt was 16 years old, he made a $24,000 score from the sale of 49ers season ticket rights, and he drove to a local bank with Paul to cash the check. The bank officer refused because of their age, and Matt threatened to call the police. The teens waited 2½ hours before the establishment backed down and gave them their money in wads of 20-dollar bills. Matt's Fiero didn't have a glove compartment and was so small that the money wouldn't fit beneath the seats, so the boys stacked the bills on the dashboard and just cruised around town.

Between sixth grade and high school, Paul attended five schools in a span of 5 years. He was a freshman at Robert Louis Stevenson School in Carmel in 1984 when his father accepted a transfer to Korea with Hewlett Packard. "We told Paul he could stay or go with us," George Cobbe says. "He wanted to go." And when George Cobbe's job eventually took him to Toronto, Paul went there, too.

As a freshman at Brown, Paul learned that the sons of big computer executives derived no special currency from their connections. His roster of classmates included the Prince of Greece, a Saudi Arabian prince, Ringo Starr's daughter, Michael Dukakis's daughter, and Rory Kennedy, whose wedding was scheduled to take place in Hyannisport the weekend that John F. Kennedy Jr. died in a plane crash.

Paul tried out for soccer, and on the first day of practice, the coach quizzed the team. How many were captain of your high school squad? And they all stepped forward. How many were all-state? They all stepped forward. Paul finally concluded that he didn't want to spend 6 days a week practicing and sweating to sit on the bench, so he quit soccer and signed up for rugby. Naturally, he was good at that as well.

Paul majored in international relations at Brown, and he traveled to France for a pilot program in conjunction with the University of Nice. Three days a week, he and his friend Jeff Lubow would rise early, ride their motorcycles to class, then head for the beach. They took a class called Science for Poets with Jean-Marc Levy-Leblond, a professor of theoretical physics. He'd sit with the two American boys and explain to them, in French, precisely why the grass is green or the sky is blue. They learned biochemistry from a marine biologist with a lab on the Mediterranean, and they immersed themselves in French culture at the office of the deputy mayor. During a break in their studies, they hopped a train and traveled to 30 cities in 3 weeks—Venice to Vienna and Salzburg and Prague. Paul handled all the logistics, and he was an easy travel companion. "At Brown, there was always a protest group of the day," Jeff Lubow says. "People were always spouting their passions or their political convictions. But Paul wasn't full of shit like a lot of people are. He didn't have any pretensions."

His friends knew he would amount to something because of his intelligence and sense of diplomacy. As a college senior Paul shared an apartment with three roommates, and one day his girlfriend came over and ate 90 percent of the groceries the boys had bought for the week. "I was a little pissed because she ate everything, and Paul was sort of a half-gentleman to this girl," recalls Brad Galinson, one of the roommates. "He did it so gingerly and masterfully that he continued dating her, yet she stopped eating our food. That's the kind of guy he is."

Paul made a smooth transition from college to corporate society. He began as a computer programmer, then found a niche with Andersen Consulting and, 2 years later, Deloitte. Big corporations need help setting up computer systems and new business models, and Paul had a gift for thinking analytically. He was also a people person, a rarity in the techno-geeky world of consultants.

In 1998 Paul married Ellen Encarnacion, a Cal-Berkeley grad, and they transferred to Japan to take his-and-hers consultant jobs. By age 27, Paul was earning $220,000 a year plus an annual bonus, and supervising 75 employees on a $25 million project. Ellen's job brought their combined family income to $500,000, enough for even the stratospheric cost of living in Tokyo.

They lived in a posh apartment in a swanky section of the city, in a building owned by Sony, and were neighbors of a singer who was hailed as the Japanese version of Madonna. They spent many a weekend night going to dinner with friends at 11:00 P.M., then hitting a dance club and rolling home at 6:00 A.M.

Paul enjoyed the fast-paced lifestyle and was on the track to partner at Deloitte. But when he stepped back and took stock, the future seemed strangely barren. "I had a pretty good affinity for technology, but it wasn't my passion at all," he says. "I did it because I was reasonable at it, but there are thousands of consultants out there." He fast-forwarded his life 30 years and saw a wealthy, comfortable executive who felt unfulfilled because he was a slave to his clients and never had the guts to take a chance.

When Plan B presented itself, Paul didn't wait to grab it. Matt Sosnick, his boyhood friend, needed help with his burgeoning sports agency and wanted Paul to come on board. On the face of it, the idea seemed ludicrous. But in the back of their minds, the two friends had always thought about working together. The sheer outlandishness of the adventure appealed to Paul, and it was evident for all to see.

"He was sort of a cog in a giant wheel-machine, and he hated it," says Brad Galinson. "When he broke away to do this with Matt, it freed him from the corporate constraints that everybody is pushed to by parents and family. You know: 'Be a doctor. Be a lawyer. Be a consultant.' That sort of thing."

Matt Sosnick, who hoarded trading cards as a kid and deftly worked a crowd selling tickets at concerts, derived energy from the *juice* of being a sports agent. Paul, in contrast, relished the prospect of diving into a business with no contacts or angles. There was something romantic about knowing that success or failure was based strictly on *you* and your own resourcefulness. "I thought it was new, and crazy, and interesting, and had potential all at the same time," he says.

Paul made the change in baby steps. He flew back to California to watch Matt's 1998 amateur draft for a first-hand glimpse of the insanity. He mailed the requisite application forms to the Players Association just in case. And in the fall of '98, he moved from Japan back to San Francisco with the intention of weaning himself off consulting.

Greg Staszko, the West Coast managing partner for Deloitte and Paul's mentor at the company, was accustomed to employees knocking on his door armed with competing offers from Price Waterhouse or Andersen. But he'd never sat across the table from an underling with a *Jerry Maguire* fantasy. He digested the news with a blank stare, and finally raised a question of his own.

"What does Paul Cobbe have to offer the baseball industry?" Paul's boss said.

Even Paul's father, while supportive of his son's ambition, failed to grasp the logic. "Let me understand," said George Cobbe. "You're going to give up what you've been doing for the last 10 years. You're going to represent players and work for them—a bunch of very young people—for potentially years at a time and you may never get paid? That doesn't sound like a very good business plan. Are you crazy?"

Paul worked his final day at Deloitte on December 31, 1998, then took the plunge. The mechanics of becoming an agent aren't especially complex. In the National Football League, aspiring agents must pay a $1,600 application fee, have a 4-year degree from an accredited college or university, pass a background check, attend a 2-day seminar, and successfully complete a written, proctored exam.

The aspiring baseball agent, in contrast, can't have a felony conviction on his record and needs to have a client on a 40-man major-league roster. Charles Manson and Jeffrey Dahmer fail to qualify under those rules, but they're more the exception than the norm.

The other requirement, obviously, is money. Money to travel and recruit clients. Money to buy equipment for players in the minors, because teams supply only the very basics. And money to buy groceries while those players are working their way through the minors.

Money isn't a problem for Sosnick and Cobbe. While Matt won't reveal the specifics of his finances, he entered the agent business with a stake sufficient to last years. He does, however, insist that it's not family money. "It's all money I made myself," Matt says. "It's enough. Enough that if this business failed and I wasn't doing anything, I could survive for a long time without a problem."

Paul, the product of an affluent family and well-staked from his days at Deloitte, was also in a strong financial position to take a risk. The friends agreed on a 50-50 partnership split, and Paul immediately kicked in $40,000 to $50,000 to cover his first-year expenses. Then he began thinking: What exactly did I get myself into?

The baseball agent business, Paul reasoned, wasn't unlike starting your own insurance company. An enterprising insurance agent needs patience to build up his "book" of clients. At the outset, you might sell automobile insurance to lots of single males in their twenties. Not much upside in that. But then the single male turns 30. He finds a wife, buys a house, and has kids. The family needs life insurance and long-term disability, and money for Johnny and Ashley's college tuition. Maybe they dabble in a little whole life or a universal policy, something to build equity for retirement. The most important factors in the insurance business are time and loyalty. Treat a client right and he'll stick with you for life. So, didn't it naturally follow that if you treat a baseball player right when he's riding buses in the minors, he'll be a faithful member of your stable 10 years later when he's hitting cleanup in the All-Star Game?

Paul and Matt looked at small shops that might serve as models—such as Tommy Tanzer's agency, or Eric Goldschmidt's, or Seth and Sam Levinson of the firm ACES, Inc., in New York. Paul dug up a March 17, 1996 issue of *Baseball America*, with brief bios of 12 "Agents of Influence" in the game. Most spouted clichés about providing excellent client service, or similar garbage. For Paul, the most insightful comments came from Seth Levinson. "Wow, is this business unregulated," Seth told *Baseball America*. "There are no ethics, no regulations. People are just running around doing whatever they want. It's very unscrupulous at times."

Agents with "inside" scouting information theoretically had an edge, but there were plenty of trails leading to amateur talent. You could subscribe to *Baseball America*'s premium service or the Area Code book and find names of highly regarded high school players. Then all you needed was a plane ticket and some chutzpah. In Paul's first 18 months, he flew all over the Midwest and Pacific Northwest in a feverish quest to "get guys." The first player he visited was Skyler Fulton, a multisport athlete who went on to play wide receiver for the Arizona State football team.

There were dozens more after that. Paul couldn't sell experience or contacts, so he spoke to kids in the gentle, reassuring tones of a big brother. The biggest challenge was getting a handle on his product.

"You're trying to sell things that are absolutely intangible," Paul says. "I'm a door-to-door salesman who goes in and tries to sell thin air, as opposed to a vacuum or cookies or something you can touch." But deep down, he sincerely believed in his mission. *There might be guys out there who are smarter than Sosnick or me*, he told himself, *but no two guys can possibly be smarter than the two of us combined.*

The hustle and frequent flyer miles paid off quickly. In 1998, a journeyman pitcher named Joe Davenport was placed on the Chicago White Sox's 40-man roster, a designation that meant Sosnick and Cobbe, as his agents, were eligible to be certified by the Players Association to conduct business and negotiate contracts. In 1999, Paul attended his first union briefing in Los Angeles. He introduced himself to the Players Association lawyers, took a seat at a picnic table, and found himself surrounded by men with stature and big-name clients. Over here, Scott Boras. Over there, Jeff Moorad. And on the other side, Don Nomura, the agent for Japanese pitcher Hideo Nomo. It later struck Paul as odd that agents were so civil to each other in person, then walked out the door and began stabbing each other in the back and pilfering each other's inventory. He came to regard the meetings as "big smile fucks."

Paul found his comfort zone by applying his business instincts to recruiting, and success gradually followed. In 2000, he landed his initial first-round pick, Phil Dumatrait, a lefty pitcher from Bakersfield College in California. He visited Dumatrait's house, and the kid came in the door fresh from a workout and removed a soaking wet T-shirt. He was so painfully thin, his ribs showed. But the velocity on his fastball had increased from 82 to 94 mph in the span of a year, and the Red Sox were sufficiently impressed to sign him to a $1.275 million bonus. Paul's 5 percent commission came to $63,750.

Paul's first big negotiation was with Wayne Britton, the beefy Boston scouting director and a man unlike anyone he'd encountered in the real world. Britton would begin every conversation by lamenting the state of the industry. "Fucking salaries are going up too fast," he'd say. "Kids are getting too much money. I ain't paying more than this." Wayne Britton, Paul decided, was a "punch in the face" style negotiator. His M.O. was to say something so volatile, it hit you like a punch in the face. By tuning out the first couple of sentences and waiting until the third or fourth, you could actually accomplish something.

There were adjustments all around. When Paul told his wife that a client was coming to the house for a visit, she laid out the best sheets and fancy linens. Then the doorbell rang and Ellen Cobbe opened it to find Phil Dumatrait, looking like a high school kid selling raffle tickets. "Hello, Ma'am," Phil said.

The next time a "client" visited the Cobbe household, Ellen made sure to bake chocolate chip cookies.

You have to embrace the humor in agenting, that's for sure, and God forbid you take yourself too seriously. Paul had one player who quit baseball to star in a porn movie. Another client left behind a trail of unpaid hotel and rental car bills and frayed relationships. Paul spent so much time cleaning up messes, he felt like a human pooper-scooper.

Several years ago, Paul got close enough to a young pitcher named Brian Bruney that he received an invitation to the kid's wedding. Then one day, Brian called and said he was leaving the Sosnick-Cobbe agency, in part because a competing agent was offering him a free cellular phone.

"So let me get this straight," Paul said. "All the work I've done for you means nothing. You'll switch for a $40 cell phone?"

It's just business, Brian Bruney told him, and Paul couldn't help but chuckle. *This kid's idea of a business transaction is buying a stick of gum,* he thought.

The association ended badly. Matt and Paul canceled a card deal for Bruney, who told them they were being mean-spirited. Then Paul told Bruney the Sosnick-Cobbe agency was going to charge him $2,000 for work done on his behalf. "He crapped in his pants when I told him that," Paul says.

Paul negotiated a $530,000 bonus for Danny Haren, an All-American from Pepperdine University who was selected by St. Louis with the 72nd pick in the draft. But Haren was barely into his pro career when he told Paul he was leaving for SFX, one of the multipurpose conglomerates. Haren liked Paul and was happy with the job he'd done, but he was looking for a big firm and didn't mind being 1 out of 100. What could Paul say in response?

Some clients, like Freddy Sanchez, flirted with leaving only to reconsider. Sanchez, a native of Burbank, California, took as unassuming a route to the majors as is humanly possible. He played at Glendale Community College, transferred to Dallas Baptist University, then signed with Boston for a $1,000 bonus out of Oklahoma City in the 11th round of the June 2000 draft. Freddy was quiet on the outside, but he burned with a competitiveness so deep he'd be pissed for days if you beat him in a game of HORSE on the playground. When Freddy showed he could hit and began moving through the Boston chain, he received literature from bigger agencies offering him free cell phones, clothing allowances, all kinds of perks.

Paul got on a conference call with the family, and Freddy's father, Fred Sr., started ticking off a list of areas where his son could have been better served by Sosnick and Cobbe. An emotional exchange ensued, and Paul lost his patience and dropped an F-bomb into the conversation.

The Sanchez family got off the line to confer, and 10 minutes later Paul's phone rang with the news: Freddy Sanchez was sticking with him.

But Travis Hafner didn't, and of all the emotional assaults over 5 years, nothing killed Paul like the Hafner ordeal. That one nearly drove him from the business.

Travis Hafner, now a star first-baseman with the Cleveland Indians, has come a long way from his roots in Sykeston, North Dakota, a glorified wheat field just up Route 52 from Jamestown. Jamestown proudly bills itself as the home of the National Buffalo Museum.

Sykeston, in contrast, has a restaurant, two bars, a gas station, and 150 residents who view a trip to the Wal-Mart as a potentially life-altering experience.

Sykeston High School had a student enrollment of 23 when Travis Hafner went there. Since there were only 4 boys and 4 girls in Travis' graduating class, he likes to joke that he was assured of graduating in the top 10 and getting a date to the prom.

The Hafner family leased several thousand acres of farmland to grow wheat, sunflowers, and beans, and Travis played basketball, ran track, and harbored dreams of two mutually exclusive athletic careers. He wanted to play baseball professionally, and if that failed to pan out, he told his high school guidance counselor he would be perfectly content as a WWF wrestler.

In high school, Travis attended a baseball tryout camp and attracted the attention of a bird-dog scout who steered him toward Cowley County Community College in Arkansas City, Kansas. The Texas Rangers saw potential and selected him in the 31st round of the 1996 draft.

Travis was just a raw Class A first-baseman with a single big-league tool—power—when Paul began recruiting him in 1999. But in spite of their differences, they quickly hit it off. Paul, the jet-setting son of a corporate executive, played varsity soccer in Korea even though he stood just 5'3" tall. Travis, the sheltered North Dakota kid, couldn't dunk a basketball in high school, but he strengthened his calf muscles until he could soar in the air and execute a smooth 360 jam. At different levels, they both knew what it meant to succeed when everyone around you said you were destined to fail.

As Travis rose through the minors, hitting 20-plus homers a year in Savannah, Charlotte, Tulsa, and Oklahoma City, Paul became his mentor and big brother. In 2000, Travis was invited to attend Major League Baseball's rookie development program in Lansdowne, Virginia, but he didn't own a sportcoat. Paul called every big man's shop in Bismarck in search of a size 54 blazer and size 14 dress shoes. Before the rookies visited the Capitol, Paul stood in front of a mirror for 45 minutes with a phone pressed to his ear and a necktie in his hands, teaching Travis how to tie a tie.

When Travis showed up at big-league spring training, a teammate began referring to him as "The Project," and others sized up his 6'3", 240-pound frame and began calling him "The Big Donkey." And just like that, a classic nickname was born: Travis Hafner would heretofore be known as "Pronk." But Ellen Cobbe looked beyond the big-lunk exterior and saw a sweet vulnerability. She kidded Travis about his resemblance to Vin Diesel, the action movie star, and Travis would blush with embarrassment.

In August 2002, at age 25, Travis made his major-league debut with the Rangers on a trip to Detroit. Before a game at the Oakland Coliseum in September, he stood on the field and posed for a picture holding Paul's daughter, Alexandra, in his burly arms. It immediately became the biggest, most celebrated photograph on the wall of the Sosnick-Cobbe firm's East Bay office. "It was one of those things where I just loved the guy," Paul says. "This is not an emotional, get-in-touch-with-your-feminine-side type of guy. Travis is a tough, strong person. But I think he felt the same way."

Business, unfortunately, is business. When Jim Thome left Cleveland for Philadelphia through free agency in December 2002, the Indians filled the void by acquiring Hafner in a four-player trade. And the Project-Donkey, already a hot commodity, was on the verge of a full-time gig in the majors. Darin Erstad, a fellow North Dakotan, told Hafner he might want to consider a more seasoned agent, and he put in a plug for his guy, Jeff Moorad. Phone calls started pouring in with increasing urgency from Pat Rooney of SFX and several other groups.

Cleveland general manager Mark Shapiro told Paul how happy the Indians were to have Travis in the fold. Then, Paul paid a visit to his parents' home in Grass Valley, California, during Christmas week and called Travis to say hi.

"I have something I need to talk to you about," Travis told him. "I've been interviewing other firms."

The revelation hit Paul like a punch to the midsection. He walked around his parents' house in a haze for 2 days, barely taking part in conversation and choking down his food. It wasn't at all unlike the feeling you get when a girlfriend suddenly dumps you.

George Cobbe urged his son to seize the advantage. "I don't know much about your business," he told Paul. "But you have a client who isn't loyal to you and obviously doesn't respect the service you provide. Why don't you fire his ass first?"

There was no time for pride. In January 2003, a month before spring training, Hafner called Matt Sosnick with the news that he was leaving for Jeff Moorad's agency. Rumors swirled through the agent grapevine that Moorad's group had given Travis a cash advance, a common practice, in anticipation of "marketing opportunities" down the line. To this day, Travis Hafner refuses to discuss his parting with Paul, but he insists he wasn't compensated for changing representation. "If anybody's given me any money, I haven't seen it," Hafner says in the spring of 2004.

Shortly after the switch, Matt drove to the East Bay office and removed the picture of Travis Hafner holding Alexandra Cobbe so that her father would no longer have to look at it. But Paul still felt humiliated for investing so much time and emotion in a friendship that could be severed so casually.

He had nightmares about the whole episode, bolting upright in bed with his eyes wide open and droplets of sweat dotting his forehead, like some character in a cheap TV melodrama. In 5 years in the business, no setback hit him harder or forced him to spend more time reassessing or self-flagellating.

Paul had trouble letting go for a while. He called Travis twice to maintain the lines of communication, but when the Indians visited Oakland on trips, Travis never reciprocated. Ellen even sent Pronk a Christmas card. But the Cobbes have since resigned themselves to watching Travis develop into a star from afar.

In hindsight, Paul took some consolation in the knowledge that Travis was destined to leave—if not for Moorad, then for someone else—and there wasn't a damn thing he could do. *I couldn't care less about the lost commissions*, Paul thought. He was more unnerved by the realization that his outlook on life was now defined by a callow North Dakota farmboy who had cast him aside. He was supposed to be the sophisticated one, and he had been duped.

"No decision to switch agents is based upon rational forethought," Paul says. "It's based on fear. Someone comes in and interjects some emotion and the kid says, 'Oh shit. If I don't do this, I'm really screwing myself.' That's exactly what Travis Hafner felt."

Some friends and even fellow agents urged Paul to pick up the phone, call the Players Association in New York, and raise a stink. But he refrained on general principle. He chose this cutthroat business, so why be a Mama's boy about it? *Accept the consequences and don't whine*, he told himself. *You're swimming with the sharks now, and you have only yourself to blame if you're not a good enough shark.* Matt, his partner, felt exactly the same way.

Sensitivity comes with a price. When Paul was 5 or 6 years old, the Cobbe family took a trip to Disneyland. While waiting in line for a ride, Paul saw a maintenance worker on his hands and knees with a razor blade, scraping bubble gum off the sidewalk. He felt sorry for the janitor, subjected to such indignity, and told his father so.

"You should never feel sorry for anybody that has a job," George Cobbe told his boy, "because they always have a choice to leave."

The sentiment still applies. Paul Cobbe made his choice, and now he's living with it.

Chapter

FIVE

Dontrelle Willis has a grand smile, a husky voice that heralds his arrival into every room, and all the traits of a young man born under the same astrological sign as Richard Nixon and Muhammad Ali. Capricorns enjoy prestige and fame but find that the accoutrements of success are only meaningful at the end of a long, hard road. They're strivers by nature, willing to put in the time and effort necessary to achieve. Therein lies the heart of the bond between Dontrelle and his agent, Matt Sosnick, the neurotic Taurus.

"I met Matt the summer between my junior and senior year," Dontrelle says, pausing every few minutes to sign another autograph in the lobby of his Philadelphia hotel. "He called me at my job one day at the Alameda Boys & Girls Club. At the time, I didn't know what an agent was supposed to be like, so I had nothing to compare him to. I just wanted to know how he knew I worked at the Alameda Boys & Girls Club.

"I was working as assistant gym manager and playing for a club base-ball team. High level AAU. I played on a North Cal team that was very good. Chris Carter and Jonny Ash played in the College World Series with Stanford, and Shane Costa played with Cal State Fullerton. I didn't think of myself as a hot prospect. I was just blessed to be on a good team.

"Matt called me again in December and went to my basketball games. I told him, 'Come check me out.' We were playing St. Elizabeth, a Catholic high school in Oakland, and I went off that game. I got a fast break, and before I went up for a dunk I looked over to see if he was paying attention. It was funny. He was so amazed that I was that type of athlete. That pretty much tied him down as far as wanting to pick me up.

"We stayed in touch. We'd go out to lunch and talk about what he does. It was never like, one day, he overwhelmed me. I liked Matt as a person because he was so energetic about what he did. He was so sincere and he cared about his players. He would fly them out and take them to games and share his resources. He seemed real happy to have people around him. He seemed real happy to have me around him. He puts on his shoes the way I put on my shoes. Real people are good people, regardless of where you're from.

"It wasn't until three-quarters of the season was over and I was doing really well that all the agents started coming around, but it was too late. I was like, 'Where have you been?' I don't want to come off as arrogant, but all of a sudden, now I'm getting national exposure because of how well I'm playing. I ended up getting All-American for the year. Then everybody started coming around. Matt was there from the start.

"He told me a lot of times players would say they'd go with him, then the draft would come and they wouldn't. We went to dinner and I told him, 'I'll go with you regardless of what you do.' He thought it was funny. He couldn't really mess up now. He told me what I needed to do. He said, 'Work hard and play well, and I'll be able to get what you need.'

"If I didn't get drafted, I was going to go to Sacramento City College, where a couple of my buddies played. My uncle Frank was key with scouts coming over, being firm with them. He'd tell them, 'You guys can do all you want; we're just looking for $200,000.' That's it. Point blank. We're not trying to get rich.

"I remember draft day like it was yesterday. A lot of people cut school that day. I live about a block from my high school, and there were 50 to 60 people at my house. Everybody was real nervous. They were watching TV and I was sitting by the phone. It was just hectic and everybody was like, 'I just hope 'Trelle gets drafted.' Everyone back home calls me 'Trelle, or D-trelle, or D-train. They were just rooting for me.

"I went to first period and walked home, and it was a long walk contemplating all the things that could happen. Next thing I know, five guys come in, then a couple of our girlfriends. All of a sudden I look outside and everybody's there with backpacks, walking in my house. Then I get a phone call from Jim Hendry of the Cubs, telling me they picked me in the eighth round.

"Everybody looked at me and I kind of pumped my fist, thinking, 'This is a blessing. Now we're in the door.' The area I come from is so tightly wound, everybody had seen what I went through—all the windows I broke throwing the ball around. People started screaming and going crazy, giving me hugs. My mom was so proud of me. She bought all this food, and it turned into an all-day, all-night party.

"After taxes and stuff, it didn't come out to a lot of money. But I knew what I wanted to do. I gave my grandpa and uncles a lot of money, and I bought my mom an Isuzu Rodeo. It was awesome. She put Raiders seat covers on it, black and silver. It was nice, man, just because I could do something for her to give her a lift.

"The Cubs were in the middle of all that fussiness about trading Sammy Sosa, so it took about 9 days for me to get signed. But Matt had good credibility with the Cubs' front-office people. He said, 'Look, this kid has a good attitude. He's a hard worker. You'll like him.' When you do good business with people, it goes a long way. Fortunately, Matt had in the past, and they took his word for it.

"I went over there and busted my butt. With so many people pulling for me, I can't give up or get lazy. A lot of guys I played with from 12 to

15 years old were the same caliber players. But something happened and they stopped playing, and baseball isn't a game you can just leave and pick up.

"Now, when I talk to those people they're like, 'Man, I wish I could still be playing.' They tell me, 'You did it with hard work.' Even when I was struggling, I dealt with adversity and kept getting after it. And now I'm here."

Today's version of "here" is Houston, on a Sunday afternoon in January 2004, when thousands of brides-to-be and their moms descend upon the George R. Brown Convention Center for the mother of all bridal extravaganzas. They carry shopping bags and peruse the latest in gowns, veils, caterers, and invitations, in hopes of finding just the right touch for that special day.

In an adjoining hall—smaller, but nevertheless huge—a marriage of sports and 21st-century capitalism is taking place. The annual Tri-Star Productions memorabilia show is in town, and Whitey Ford, Orlando Cepeda, Don Sutton, Juan Marichal, Gaylord Perry, Jim Palmer, and Monte Irvin take on all comers beneath a sign that reads, "We gladly accept MasterCard, Amex, TeleCheck, and personal checks."

This is the new reality for former sports stars who hit their peak in the 1970s and '80s, after the advent of free agency but a few years before middle infielders with .280 batting averages began to enjoy lifestyles more befitting the Sultan of Brunei than the Sultan of Swat. Gaylord Perry, who won 314 games and subsequently earned a degree of infamy by admitting to doctoring the baseball with Vaseline, looks like a cross between Santa Claus and Grizzly Adams, but that won't deter fans from lining up and paying him $30 to $50 per signature. The only thing standing between Perry and a lucrative payday is hand cramps.

While a Hall of Fame imprimatur is a guarantee of long-term appeal at memorabilia shows, warts are eventually exposed, and the shelf life for mortals is fleeting. In the summer of 1989, a young Chicago Cubs outfielder named Jerome Walton hit .293 in 475 at-bats. He won the Rookie of the Year award and was a popular attraction on the memorabilia circuit. Then he went home to Georgia and loaded up on soul food courtesy of his mother, whom he referred to as the "best cook south of the Mason-Dixon line." Walton arrived at training camp the following spring 20 pounds heavier, and teams were by now well-schooled on his problems hitting a curveball. The gold chains around his neck gave him the appearance of a star, but fans weren't so interested in waiting in line for a part-time player who hit .263. Demand failed to keep pace with supply, and the next thing you know, Jeff Rosenberg had a stack of Jerome Walton autographed photos collecting dust in his basement.

Rosenberg, a young entrepreneur in the Matt Sosnick mold, grew up in Houston with an affinity for Pete Rose and the desire to become a sports agent. He was working toward his degree from South Texas College of Law when he had a "harebrained" idea to get into the memorabilia business. In 1987, Rosenberg and two friends formed a company called Tri-Star and organized their first show at a Ramada Inn in Houston.

Mark McGwire, then a slugging young first baseman with Oakland, was the featured attraction. Rosenberg sensed he was onto something when he brought McGwire to the hotel and saw kids lined up for the next day's show as if they were waiting for a rock star. The event was a success, but on the way to the airport, McGwire revealed that his signature would no longer be for sale. He knew he was destined for big things, and he had no desire to spend his spare hours at a card table hawking merchandise.

"We weren't smart enough to listen to him," says Rosenberg, who quickly sold almost all his McGwire memorabilia. It was a decision he regretted years later, when McGwire broke Roger Maris's home run record and his autographed baseballs routinely sold for $500 to $1,000 each.

Rosenberg's two partners eventually left the business, and he found a new associate in Bobby Mintz, a Dallas native who grew up with the same fascination for sports memorabilia. Mintz was such an autograph hound that he once spent hours waiting outside the Baltimore Orioles' team hotel in 100°F heat for a glimpse of a player—any player. His reward: a hello and a signature from John Stefero, a backup catcher who hit .235 in 79 big-league games.

In 17 years of organizing autograph shows, Jeff Rosenberg and Bobby Mintz have grown accustomed to 15-hour days, cold pizza on the fly, and the notion that what's hot today might be lukewarm tomorrow. As the Jerome Walton episode taught them, fans are fickle and tastes come and go. The Tri-Star partners make a significant investment in the players they represent, promotions, advertising, and time. So, when they find a special commodity—an athlete with the charisma to strike more than the usual mercenary nerve—their antennae go up quickly in response.

Jeff Rosenberg's world first collided with Matt Sosnick's in 2002, when Rosenberg's sister returned from a trip to Israel and said she'd met an engaging young sports agent who represented baseball players. "I think I've heard of this guy," Rosenberg said. He called his partner, Bobby, who confirmed that Sosnick did, indeed, have some talented young players in the minor leagues.

Rosenberg and Mintz, through experience, knew the odds of a young prospect graduating to marketable commodity—with legs—were slim at best. But from the moment Dontrelle Willis joined the Florida Marlins in May 2003, his appeal transcended victories, innings pitched, or the standard calculus that defines a productive sports-business link.

As Dontrelle began to win games and appear on ESPN every 5 days, Jeff Rosenberg did some reconnaissance work. He called hobby store owners and reporters acquainted with the sports mindset in south Florida. His sources told him that Willis was generating a runaway enthusiasm that was impossible to define. Rosenberg's mind flashed back to when he was 11 years old and a curly-haired Detroit Tigers rookie named Mark Fidrych captivated America by hand-smoothing the mound and conversing with the baseball before throwing it. Fidrych, a blue-collar New England kid known as the Bird, was suddenly reborn in the person of an uninhibited black lefty from the Bay Area.

"We've seen a lot of kids come up, especially pitchers, and perform well," Jeff Rosenberg says. "But the differentiating factor was this excitement, this youthful energy that he brought to the mound. And the fans in Florida, they were just magnetized to this kid. Florida was drawing 7, 8, 9, 10 thousand people to a game, and then all of a sudden he's pitching and there are 25 or 30 thousand people in the stands. I remember telling Bobby, 'You know, we ought to take a look at this kid.'"

So it was that Tri-Star, which represents superstars from Joe Montana to Roger Clemens, took the plunge to become the exclusive representative for Dontrelle Willis's autographed merchandising opportunities. Matt had already signed baseball card deals for Dontrelle with Upper Deck, Topps, Donruss, Fleer, and a company called Just Minors. Now, Tri-Star was about to make a major commitment. If a Dontrelle-autographed ball was going to sell on QVC or the Home Shopping Network, it would be done through Tri-Star. If Dontrelle merchandise appeared on a Web site, in a catalog, at a show, or in a storefront and was going to be advertised as "authentic," it would go through Tri-Star.

Still, the framework of a deal needed to be negotiated. Plan A for Matt was to negotiate as high a guarantee as possible and take less money per "piece," or signature. Plan B was to take a lower guarantee and bet that Dontrelle's popularity would hold to the extent that he could fetch a high premium for signatures even if they weren't carefully rationed out. Plan B was clearly riskier, a bet that Dontrelle's performance and inherent likability—what Matt calls the "Ferris Bueller factor"—would win out.

Dontrelle's Uncle Frank hired a marketing firm to help with promotions, and one of the consultants told Matt it was a mistake to cheapen the value of Dontrelle's signature by pushing too much product on the market. But Matt was undeterred. He followed his gut instincts and took the higher-risk, higher-reward strategy.

"I wanted to leave as much room on the upside as possible," Matt says. "I told Tri-Star, 'I want you to max out how much money you can pay him per signature.' We don't need any guarantee at all, any signing bonus. I'll take my chances. If Dontrelle has a big year this year, he can make a quarter-million dollars with them in signatures."

The weekend of the Tri-Star show gets off to an inauspicious start. Matt absentmindedly leaves his jacket in a taxi cab, with his cellular phone in the pocket, and paces his room like a smoker in the throes of a nicotine fit. He'll misplace his cell phone—his lifeline to the world—twice in the span of a week.

"The tragedies are coming in groups," Matt says. "For some reason, I'm just retarded these days."

Short of finding a Verizon store that's open at 6:00 P.M. on Saturday, his only recourse is to hunt down the cab driver and see if an arrangement can be brokered. He makes contact, but the cabby says he's on the way to church and can't stop by the hotel until Sunday. "I'll make it worth your while," Matt says. He's ready to hand over $60 as a reward, until the cabby arrives in a huff and says there's $32 on the meter. Matt hands him $40 and tells him to keep the change. Cell phone in hand, Matt breathes a grateful sigh and determines that all is right with the world. "I feel like a parent who's just lost sight of his kid in a Toys "R" Us," he says.

Dontrelle has flown in from Miami, where he's spent much of the off-season working out with Marlins teammate Juan Pierre in an effort to prove that his rookie year was no fluke. He was lifting weights in November when Steve Copses, the Marlins' media relations director, called to tell him he'd just won the Rookie of the Year award. Dontrelle grabbed a towel to wipe off the sweat, spoke with baseball writers on a national conference call, then returned to the gym to resume his workout.

The Hall of Famers in Houston love Dontrelle because he reminds them so much of baseball the way it used to be. Don Sutton, now an Atlanta Braves broadcaster, was so bowled over by Willis's effervescent style of play that he sought out Marlins manager Jack McKeon during the season for an introduction. Dontrelle, making a sandwich in a room behind the clubhouse, nodded casually at Sutton. Then he realized who it was, nearly choked on his sandwich, and apologized profusely.

Whitey Ford, the old Yankee known as the Chairman of the Board, lives in Florida but watched Willis pitch numerous times on television in the summer of 2003. "I don't know about that windup, how long a career he's going to have," Ford says. "It's a little rough on his arm, the way he throws the ball. But no, he's the real thing."

Dontrelle, dressed in baggy jeans and an Akdmks Big Paper Maker throwback jersey, arrives at 8:30 A.M. to sign personal treasures that individual collectors have entrusted to Rosenberg and Mintz through the mail. For almost 2 hours, he autographs items ranging from a pitching rubber to a National League Rookie of the Year jersey that already includes the signatures of previous winners such as Jon Matlack and Steve Sax. And there are baseballs—baseballs upon baseballs—which will eventually make their way to memorabilia stores. Dontrelle churns one out every 10 to 12 seconds, eyeballing each ball for the sweet spot, then marking a big "DW" with a flourish. When he tires of sitting, he stands, and when his back feels the strain, he sits again. A few feet away, a Major League Baseball representative stands ready to affix a hologram to attest to the authenticity of each item. Tri-Star pays a licensing fee to MLB for the privilege.

When the private items are dispensed with, Dontrelle moves to a card table in the main hall, Sharpie in hand, and the line begins to form. Jeff Rosenberg estimates that 80 percent of the collectors here come from a 150-mile radius. If they're not from Houston, they're probably from Austin, Dallas, San Antonio, or somewhere in Arkansas or Louisiana.

Michael Douglas, a process operator at a Houston chemical refinery, pays $40 for a Dontrelle autograph and gets a freebie from Taylor Buchholz, a promising young Astros pitcher who's just come over from Philadelphia in the Billy Wagner trade. Douglas and his friend decide not to wait in line for a signature from Kansas City Royals shortstop Angel Berroa, the latest American League Rookie of the Year.

"When we got here, I told my buddy we need to get in Dontrelle Willis's line first, because it'll be the longest," Douglas says. "Dontrelle or Taylor Buchholz, they could be the Cal Ripken or the Roger

Clemens of tomorrow. How many Royals' Rookies of the Year have done anything? Bob Hamelin? Give me a break."

Dontrelle Wayne Willis was born January 12, 1982, in a rough section of Oakland. His name was the brainchild of his father, Harold, who liked "Dante" but preferred something more offbeat and original.

Harold split when Dontrelle was 2, leaving his wife, Joyce, with the promise of long hours fretting over her precocious baby. One of the first things Joyce noticed was that her son had huge hands and feet, like a Saint Bernard puppy. "If he grows into them feet . . . " the neighbors would say, and the rest never needed to be said.

The boy also had a mind of his own and a flair for adventure. One time, Joyce was driving down the highway and just like that, 18-month-old Dontrelle chucked his bottle out the window. Another time, he hurled the bottle against a glass case, sending shards flying in every direction.

He found hiding places so imaginative, Joyce would be on the phone with the police when his little face would appear and her heart would stop racing. On one harrowing occasion, Joyce roused the customers at the bar around the corner and raced up and down the block screaming. The search party returned to the house, where a neighbor asked Joyce what Dontrelle was wearing. "Hiking boots and some jeans," she said, with a tremble in her voice. "Would the hiking boots be brown?" the neighbor asked. "Would that be him?" And the heavy closet door was pushed back to reveal a 2-year-old boy, asleep in the back corner.

A single mom of limited means needed to use her head to keep a little boy entertained. Some days, Joyce would pack a bag of gummi bears and take Dontrelle to the movie theater on Jack London Square. They'd watch one movie, and when it ended, they'd slip into an adjacent theater to watch another.

Frank Guy Sr., Joyce's father and Dontrelle's granddad, was a ballplayer himself back in the day. He loved to fish, tell stories, and take

Joyce and her siblings to the Oakland Coliseum to watch Campy Campaneris, Reggie Jackson, and John "Blue Moon" Odom play for the Athletics. He'd sit on the front porch with his cane and roll a multi-colored ball to Dontrelle, who would dutifully retrieve it.

When Dontrelle was 9, the family left Oakland and moved to the apartment on Taylor Avenue, not far from the "Tube," the tunnel that separates Oakland from Alameda. He was an instant hit at Longfellow Elementary School.

"In the third grade, kickball was our life," says Mazonie Franklin, Dontrelle's best friend. "He shows up and we're like, 'Oh great, we've got a new kid—what team are we going to put him on?' Then we saw him play, and everybody was fighting to get him on their team."

Dontrelle and his friends graduated to four-square, then noon-league basketball, then Babe Ruth baseball. The house on Taylor has vertical siding above a 3-foot-high brick foundation. Dontrelle, Mazonie, Ross and Reid Muskar, and the other neighborhood boys spray-painted a red rectangular strike zone and pitched to each other for hours on end. Dontrelle adopted Dave Stewart and Rickey Henderson as his personal favorites, and he liked to pull his cap low and glare like Stew or good-naturedly style when he hit a home run, just like Rickey.

Mazonie lived five blocks away in the Buena Vista Apartments—the "BVs"—and came over for frequent sleepovers at Dontrelle's house. On one such visit, Dontrelle and another friend accidentally broke a vase in a "last man standing" pillow fight. The boys frantically used tape, glue, fingernail polish, and lipstick to repair the cracks before Joyce came home. Mazonie was so petrified that she would spot the damage, he slept in his clothes and shoes that night.

Joyce was one of two imposing parental presences in the neighborhood. The other, James Rollins, worked in the shipping and receiving department for Clorox and was once a competitive bodybuilder. Big Jim's son, Jimmy, was an undersize shortstop who graduated from Encinal High in 1996, signed with Philadelphia out of the draft, and made the All-Star team 5 years later. When Big Jim Rollins walked down the street, his biceps and forearms popping beneath his shirt-sleeves, the drug dealers and hustlers would cease their business and give him time to pass. They called him *Mr. Rollins*. And they learned that it was in their best interests to steer clear of Dontrelle Willis's mom, too.

"Joyce made it known that she was the law, and what she said goes," Mazonie says. "In Dontrelle's life, she was his mother and father figure. It was basically, 'If I have to discipline you, I'm going to make it stick to where you learn your lesson the first time.'"

As a teenager, Dontrelle worked for a company called Alameda Awards assembling trophies, and Joyce would let him keep $20 of the $80 he earned each week and apply the rest toward household bills. She was strict in any number of ways. Before sending Dontrelle to a neighbor's house, she'd call and say, "If you see Dontrelle doing something you don't like, chastise him and send him home to me." If he acted up at school, the teacher would call with an alert, and Joyce would storm through the front door while Dontrelle was looking for a place to hide. He even quit the football team because Joyce didn't want him to play and he grew tired of watching her stand there at practice, giving him the angry eye each time he took the snap from center as a quarterback.

Joyce's iron will and survival instinct were born of necessity. She served 3 years in the Army in Fort Knox, Kentucky, and dreamed of becoming a chef. But she never achieved her goal, and after a divorce in her early 20s, she took a construction job to pay the bills. She eventually graduated to welding and became a member of Iron Workers local No. 378. If the job required climbing the towers of the Bay Bridge or working high above ground on "Mount Davis," the monstrous addition to the Oakland Coliseum, she choked back the lump in her throat and commenced climbing. If it meant standing 20 stories above the street drilling in bolts at a building site with nothing beneath her but air, she obliged.

The life of a single mother is something only another single mother can fathom, with its constant bustle, sleep deprivation, and hail of worry. When Joyce was at work, she fretted over getting Dontrelle to his next game. When she was home, she worried about paying the bills. An emotional tug-of-war defined their relationship for many years. Joyce knew that Dontrelle could be embarrassed by this big, loud woman who was so natural at attracting attention. But he also saw her dragging her tool belt and lunch pail to his games after catching the bus from work, and he knew it wasn't easy. If anyone said a derogatory word about Joyce, the boy could get protective in a hurry.

Somehow she managed, finding time to squeeze in some baseball instruction along the way. Joyce was a catcher for 27 years, from her hitch in the army into her 40s, and she knew a thing or two about the right way to play. She played competitive softball when she was 6 months pregnant with Dontrelle. And when he'd wake her at 7:30 A.M. pounding that baseball against the wall of the house on Taylor, she was grateful he wasn't in trouble and had found a wholesome pursuit that he truly loved.

Joyce, like Dontrelle, remembers draft day like it was yesterday. Folks in the neighborhood are familiar with a gray-and-white cat that sits in the middle of Taylor Avenue like a feline sentry. On draft day, the cat could barely find a comfortable spot with all the traffic passing through. Joyce turned the corner and was shocked at the number of cars parked on the curb and well-wishers streaming into her yard. She barely entered the house to say hello before hustling to the supermarket to buy hamburger patties and hot links for the visitors.

Even though $200,000 seemed like a pile of money, Joyce initially resisted Dontrelle's overtures to buy her a car. She had "Old Faithful," after all, a 1983 Honda with more than 100,000 miles on it. Five dollars' worth of gas and enough time, and she could cover half the state. It even had those familiar, comforting coffee stains from the days when Joyce was running late to work and rounded a corner with too much speed, spilling her morning cup of java on the floor.

But the boy kept insisting on the SUV. "No mama of mine is gonna drive around in a jalopy like this," he said. Dontrelle would later buy his mom a 62-inch big-screen television to watch his games, but it was the Isuzu Rodeo, with the deluxe stereo and the Raiders silver-and-black motif, that served as the ultimate draft day keepsake.

"Dontrelle asked to borrow it, of course," Joyce says. "One day I come home and I get in it, and the ignition turns on and there's this *blare*. And I'm fumbling around because I can't figure it out. And I'm trying to yell at the top of my lungs, *Dontrelle!!!!*, and he's in the house. He can't hear me through all the noise.

"He says, 'Mom, that's the kind of system I need in case I drive around.'"

Encinal High, an unassuming blend of industrial off-white-and-blue trim, sits at the less fortunate end of Alameda. There's an outdoor pool and tennis courts with weeds pushing through the asphalt cracks—a metaphor for the aspirations of the kids who dream of something this town may or may not be able to provide.

Encinal's teams are called the Jets, a symbol of the Alameda Naval Air Station, which closed in 1997 and is now known as Alameda Point. In 2003, after considerable debate, the school mounted an A-4 Skyhawk fighter plane on a platform outside the front door. The Skyhawk flew in Vietnam, and some local residents thought its presence might be insensitive to Asian students at the school.

Jim Saunders, a physical education teacher at Encinal, is in his 15th season as the school's head baseball coach. Saunders lasted a couple of extended spring trainings as a catcher with San Francisco. But he lacked the talent to make it and the temperament to accept the punishment that former Giants coach Tom Haller doled out. "Tom Haller and I didn't see eye to eye," Saunders says. "I think it was when he turned the JUGS machine on about 95 miles an hour and we had to block balls. That was brutal."

Saunders, a stocky man with a friendly yet direct manner, is adept at taking kids from busted homes and underprivileged backgrounds and molding winners. Scouts who might fear bodily harm or a slashed tire if they set foot in nearby Oakland aren't as hesitant to sample the merchandise in west Alameda. While the kids here lack the material comforts of the upper-middle-class, predominantly white end of town, they've discovered that sports can be a great equalizer.

Drive 3 miles to the east side, and the houses are bigger and Alameda High School appears like a Roman coliseum. But Jim Saunders enjoys working with the kids on the west end because they're hungry and have no sense of entitlement. "I think there's a lot more character on this side of town," he says.

Alameda, an island city which was once home to the Skippy Peanut Butter factory, has a tradition of great baseball talent. It began with George "Duffy" Lewis in 1910 and eventually included more than a dozen big leaguers. The most renowned, Willie "Pops" Stargell, hit 475 career homers with the Pirates and made the Hall of Fame. The Encinal High ball field now bears his name, and his old jersey number—along with the numbers of former big leaguers and Alameda stars Tommy Harper and Curt Motton—will soon adorn the outfield fence in tribute.

Jim Saunders points to two retired numbers that have already been posted on the fence. Number 6 belongs to Jimmy Rollins, whose crowning moment at Encinal came in the 1996 playoffs when he hit a two-run homer to give the Jets the North Coast section title. Saunders anointed Rollins as an assistant coach of sorts, giving the kid the freedom to organize practices and ride herd on the other players, and "J-Roll" never disappointed him. Jim Saunders talks of Jimmy Rollins in tones normally reserved for a favorite son, and J-Roll affectionately refers to his heavyset coach as "Slim."

The number 15 on the fence is a tribute to Dontrelle Willis, who was about 10 years old when he first began hanging out on the fringe of the Encinal High field. "Just a little snot-nosed dude," Jimmy Rollins recalls with a laugh.

As a grade schooler, Dontrelle would shoot hoops for an hour, then migrate over to the ball field with his basketball beneath his arm. J. R. Rider, who later attended the University of Nevada, Las Vegas, and earned a degree of fame and infamy as NBA problem child "Isaiah" Rider, was a fixture on the local playgrounds. J. R. entertained onlookers with his skills, then punctuated the proceedings with several rim-rattling dunks.

Dontrelle was competitive playing hoops with the older kids because of his talent. He was versatile enough to play guard and forward, and he shot with his left hand, which caused numerous problems for a defender. "He did that 'And1' streetball stuff on the court," Jimmy Rollins says. "He was doing the legal version, but he was pretty slick."

Still, Dontrelle's demeanor earned him more respect than his jumper or his vertical leap. Little D knew it was a privilege to share the court with the older kids, so when they'd hack him on the way to the basket, he'd never whine or call foul. The older boys took advantage of his easygoing nature, chopping him on the arm and sending him to the asphalt rather than conceding an easy 2. But Dontrelle knew that crying was the quickest way to earn a seat on the sidelines, so he never made a peep.

Saunders heard that the kid was an athlete—so good that he wasn't allowed to play with the other fourth graders—and he made him a batboy for the squad. Dontrelle never stopped coming. Each spring, he'd chase down stray balls, keep the equipment in order, and enjoy the privilege of playing catch with the varsity players. When Dontrelle showed up as a freshman and made the squad, he stood 5'11" and 125 pounds. But his heart was undeniable.

Encinal went 26–3 that year, and Dontrelle was the number-four pitcher on the staff. But when Saunders needed an emergency reliever in the title game, he knew where to find him.

"I had a guy who struggled in the second inning, so I went right down the bench," Saunders says. "My reliever, a big, stocky guy who's had a great year, he didn't want it. One guy was too damn scared. So I'm like, 'Who the hell wants the ball?' And Donny's arm went up."

Dontrelle pitched 5⅔ innings and struck out seven batters, even though Encinal lost the game. Saunders has a picture of Dontrelle sitting in the outfield grass, a portrait in dejection. But the events leading up to the portrait said more. "Just the courage factor," the coach says. "You could see it happening there, and that was neat."

At the end of the 2003 season, Dontrelle Willis returned to the Bay Area and was honored with a "this is your life" tribute before 300 friends and well-wishers at the Alameda Little League complex on Grand Street. His old coaches got up and spoke and shared memories of his youth. Shelly Osborne, his fourth-grade teacher, recalled how polite Dontrelle was at Longfellow School, and how considerate he was to take something off his fastball when throwing to the girls in school-yard games.

A future in baseball almost never came to be. As a sophomore at Encinal, Dontrelle said he'd had enough of the sport and was going to concentrate on basketball. There were rumors that he was upset over a breakup with a girlfriend, but his real issues were with his coach, Saunders. "That guy was a knucklehead and he would always get on me," Dontrelle says. "He'd make me do pushups and embarrass me in front of my peers all the time. Finally I just said, 'Forget it.'"

It took a collaborative effort for Dontrelle to return. Slim Saunders wore down the kid's resistance by following him around campus for 5 weeks. "I went to his English class, his math class, and his history class, and he already had PE with me," Saunders says. "I told him, 'You can't not play baseball. You're throwing away too much potential.'"

Joyce made her feelings known, and Dontrelle's teammates appealed to him to play. After he failed to show for the first practice, Saunders made a pact with him: Give me one practice, the coach said, and if you don't have fun I'll disappear and you can play basketball to your heart's content. I'll never bother you again.

The next day, Dontrelle showed up at baseball practice, jumped in the cage, and fell victim to the same spell that had afflicted him since he painted his first strike zone on the side of the house on Taylor. The lure of baseball had nothing to do with the promise of a major-league contract. Once Dontrelle smelled the grass and the dirt, he was power-less to resist.

Chapter
SIX

Arn Tellem, a devout fantasy baseball player who
runs the basketball and baseball groups for SFX, was once described
by Oakland general manager Billy Beane as having the intelligence of
Alan Dershowitz coupled with the neurotic behavior of Woody Allen.
He's a profound man as well. It was Tellem, after all, who observed
that the average Jewish boy realizes by age 13—the time of his bar
mitzvah—that he stands a better chance of owning an NBA team than
of playing for one.

Arn Tellem also believes that *The Godfather* is a wonderful how-to
video for aspiring agents, an observation that resonates with Matt, even
though he's too conflicted to do more than fantasize about ambushing
one of his rivals at a causeway tollbooth.

"I can't decide whether I want to kill myself or my competitors first,"
Matt says. As life decisions go, it's a lot tougher than choosing between
the traditional burr walnut and the gray-stained maple veneer for the
interior of his Jaguar.

Sometimes it's hard to know where you stand, given the shifting nature of alliances in the agent game. Several years ago, Matt became aware that Scott Boras's group was hawking Jerome Williams and Tony Torcato, two San Francisco minor leaguers represented by the Levinson brothers' agency in New York. So he called the brothers with a heads-up, and Sam Levinson thanked him for the courtesy. Not long after that, the Levinsons took Mets outfielder Jeff Duncan from Sosnick-Cobbe, while claiming, naturally, that it was strictly Duncan's initiative.

Other veteran agents have taken turns providing counsel to a kid with ambition. Tommy Tanzer, who represents Steve Finley, John Burkett, and others, encouraged Matt in the early going, and Joe Bick, a former Cleveland Indians front-office man who now runs a successful agency in Cincinnati, listened patiently when Sosnick was frustrated by several client defections and needed somewhere to turn.

"He had some issues that were bothering him, and he asked me for opinions on how he should handle it," Bick says. "He seemed like a nice enough guy, so I tried to give him my thoughts."

The fraternity usually isn't this collegial. Talk to almost any agent, and he'll quickly point out that he works longer hours and has higher standards and a more devoted client base than the competition. The agent will recoil with horror at the slightest negative commentary about his own business practices, while gladly pointing out that Agent B has the emotional and moral depth of your average protozoan.

Professional wrestlers are more inclined to say nice things about each other. Tony Attanasio, who's represented big leaguers since the early 1970s, appeared on a talk radio show several years ago when the host stumped him with a question: If you had a son about to enter pro ball, which agent would you choose to represent him?

"Once I got past Ron Shapiro and Barry Axelrod, I couldn't think of anybody," Attanasio says.

Furthermore, if you had a dollar for every agent who said, "You know, I was the *real* basis for the movie *Jerry Maguire*," you wouldn't have to invest in a 529 plan to fund your kids' college tuition.

Given the tendency for agents to undercut each other and players to change allegiances so cavalierly, it's no wonder that insecurity abounds in the profession. At the All-Star Game, where baseball's best and highest-paid players congregate, agents walk around with their heads on a swivel to make sure rivals aren't sampling the merchandise. A Major League Baseball official recalls an All-Star tour of Japan several years ago, when agent Adam Katz was so hyper about competitors stalking Sammy Sosa, "You wanted to shoot him with an animal tranquilizer."

When Paul Cobbe was doing his early research, he came across a profile of David Falk, the king-making agent who represented NBA pillar Michael Jordan. Falk seemingly couldn't ask for more, but when the interviewer asked him to identify his biggest regret, Falk didn't hesitate. He said it was difficult for him to get over losing out on Grant Hill.

It struck Paul as odd that an agent could represent the greatest player in basketball history, yet feel such remorse over not representing one who was merely very good. The anecdote showed Paul that for the big boys, maybe it wasn't just about money after all.

Sosnick and Cobbe invite skepticism in the agent ranks because of their ambitious business model. If they were content to represent 10 players, they could grow their firm quietly and inconspicuously. But they've taken the approach that veteran agent John Boggs calls "panning for gold," signing up dozens of players through the draft on the theory that many of them will fall by the wayside through lack of talent, injuries, or attrition. They represent more than 80 clients, and other agents claim they're overextended.

David Rawnsley, a former Houston Astros assistant scouting director who spent 20 months as a draft recruiter for Sosnick and Cobbe, heard the same two knocks all the time: (1) They represent too many guys; and (2) they're too cozy with the teams. "A lot of agents would tell kids, 'They do sweetheart deals with the clubs. They're on too good of terms with the general managers and scouting directors,'" Rawnsley says. "But we thought that was a positive. We tried to build on that reputation."

Matt's big financial stake, which allows him to weather the tough times, isn't about to make him popular with small agents who can barely pay the electric bill, or with young agents who are cogs for corporate entities. And his reclusive tendencies create an air of mystery. He never attends the union's agent briefings or travels to the Arizona Fall League or the Cape Cod League, because they're beyond his comfort zone. So, an image of him has formed in a vacuum.

He's a kid with a rich father who got into this business because he thought it would be fun, the other agents say, *and he doesn't know anything about baseball.*

Andrew Lowenthal, a New York agent who twice approached Sosnick and Cobbe about a job, only to be turned down, has since blown hot and cold in his relationship with the twosome.

"Matt's buddies with these players, where he's not really selling the business part of it. He's selling the friendship part of it," Lowenthal says "He tells them, 'I'm going to be your best friend, I'm going to be your buddy.' And then other agents come in and say, 'Well, it's great that you have a buddy in Matt and he takes you on trips, but is he going to be able to arbitrate for you? Can he negotiate a contract with Brian Cashman? What in his background makes you think he'd be successful at that? Why do you want to be the guinea pig?'

"That's the pitch. That's what Boras is saying. That's what Moorad's saying. That's what any one of these guys who are stealing his players are saying. And once the player gets to the point of a Jesse Foppert or a Travis Hafner, where they're knocking on the door, they realize, 'Wow, you're right. I don't need a buddy right now. Maybe when I was 20 or 18, I needed a buddy. Now, I need a business partner.'"

While Matt believes he's proven his mettle by consummating dozens of big nonsports transactions, he makes little effort to debunk the notion that he's a baseball dilettante. He's more inclined to sit down at his desktop computer and punch up the Drudge Report than ESPN.com, and on a given day he's probably better versed in the West

Bank than in the American League West. If being a well-rounded person precludes him from knowing Albert Pujols's slugging percentage by heart, so be it.

When Dontrelle Willis made the All-Star Game in 2003, Matt and Paul were riding a party bus and struck up a conversation with Lance Carter, a marginal reliever who made the American League squad for the simple reason that Tampa Bay had to send *somebody*. Sosnick had no idea who Lance Carter was, by face or by name. When he asked Paul, "Wasn't Lance Carter in *NSync?," they both had a good laugh over it.

That hip-outsider irreverence helps define the Sosnick-Cobbe niche. Lenny Strelitz, a former minor-league ballplayer and Texas Rangers scouting director who's now an agent, has made inroads through the draft by selling young players on his industry contacts and ability to break down their baseball skills. Matt Sosnick is a guy in his 30s who remembers what it's like to be in his mid-20s, or younger. He shares the kids' tastes in movies, music, consumer electronics, and finding eligible women to date, so he can relate on their terms. "If they view me as an adult, I'm in trouble," he says.

But Matt has also learned some very grown-up lessons in the world he now inhabits. For starters, the most dangerous enemy is often the one that you don't see.

In 2001, Sosnick and Cobbe were pursuing a highly regarded Iowa high school player named Matt Macri when the family received a call with an anonymous "tip" that the agency was under investigation by the NCAA for rules violations. The tip was apparently a plant by a competitor—and purely fictional—but it basically killed any chances Matt and Paul might have had with Macri.

In 2002, Matt was in line to represent Humberto Sanchez, a 6'6", 230-pound Dominican pitcher out of Connors State College in Oklahoma. Detroit had selected Sanchez in the 31st round of the draft the previous year, and Matt was ready to help him negotiate a $1 million bonus with the Tigers before he went back into the next draft. But Sanchez changed his mind and switched advisers late in the game, and

Matt allegedly went into a panic. According to a story that made the rounds among agents, Matt called Connors State coach Perry Keith and offered to deposit $10,000 in the coach's bank account to help him win back Humberto Sanchez.

Perry Keith, the story goes, pitched a fit and warned Matt never to show his face around the Connors State campus again. But this, too, is fiction.

Sosnick, Keith confirms, was upset about losing Sanchez and the $50,000 commission he would bring. But there was no bribe attempt—or even a hint of it—and Matt is still welcome on the Connors State campus provided he can find his way to Warner, Oklahoma.

"Matt was upset, I guess," Keith says. "That's a big payday for him that went out the window. But there was none of that other stuff going on. I'm not bitter toward him at all. If anything, I felt bad for him."

The other prominent rumor about Sosnick and Cobbe is that they slip some cash to scouts now and then for leads on players. Scouts can be a fertile source of information on young talent, and since an area scout for a big-league team earns $35,000 to $50,000 annually as a rule, it's not exactly a lucrative line of work. Other agents are perplexed that Matt and Paul, two Silicon Valley guys, could build such an extensive network so quickly with no previous ties to the business.

Jim Lindell, an agent who competes with Sosnick and Cobbe in the Pacific Northwest, wonders how they're so adept at finding players who sneak up on people as second- and third-round draft picks. "I'm not the super-brightest guy in the world, but it's taken me a long time to build a network where I can get good information," Lindell says. "Those guys are right there, right now, with no baseball background. They don't know anybody, so how are they figuring all this out?"

Sosnick replies that the available information—through Baseball America, Perfect Game, and other media/scouting sources that identify budding stars as high school freshmen—negates the need to pay scouts. If scouts are inclined to help Sosnick and Cobbe, it's because they have a reputation for working harmoniously with teams.

Matt admits he was viewed skeptically by the fraternity when he broke into the business, in part because of his designation as an outsider. He hadn't played, coached, or scouted, and came across as a little too *GQ* for some scouts' tastes. But he had a respect for the job because it was so thankless and demanding by nature.

Scouts ran the gamut, Matt found, from duplicitous to scrupulously honest, from hound-dog lazy to obsessively hard-working. A scout was like an independent contractor—constantly on the road, lonely and underpaid, with only one mission: to get players. The definition of disaster for a scout was to recommend a prospect, then have his team fail to sign the player based on misleading information from an agent or "adviser."

"Some scouts looked past the fact that I hadn't done it and realized I was trying to fulfill a dream," Matt says. "And they were willing to try to help me, particularly when I showed that I just wanted to get players signed and get them out playing, because I thought that was the right thing."

If Sosnick has a classic agent foil, it's Steve Canter, whose principal claim to fame was representing Jim Morris, the former high school science teacher who tried out for the Tampa Bay Devil Rays on a dare from his students and made 21 appearances in the majors in 1999–2000. Canter's high-water mark in the industry was helping Jim Morris navigate Hollywood in the making of *The Rookie*, a Disney film starring Dennis Quaid.

Steve Canter is balding, awkward-looking, and not particularly dashing when he shows up at the park in sandals, baggy pants, and a ball cap. He is, in many ways, the antithesis of what people perceive an agent to be. One general manager calls him a charter member of the "Seinfeld Whining Club."

Paul Cobbe concurs that Canter is a repository for nerdy stereotypes but gives him points for persistence.

"He's like the Energizer rabbit," Paul says. "He gets pummeled and pounded and pilfered. He's so awkward and risk-averse, it's uncomfortable for anyone to deal with him. But he loses his guys and somehow stays in it."

Among agents, the story is told of Kevin Christman, a former Milwaukee Brewers scout who once worked for Canter as a recruiter. Christman, a walking unmade bed whose wardrobe consists almost entirely of T-shirts, was on the road constantly, chasing prospects like a madman. Then he'd turn in his expenses and Canter would punch up a map on the Internet and check to see if Christman could have taken a different route and avoided paying a toll. If so, he might chastise Christman for the oversight.

In a parallel universe, Matt Sosnick and Steve Canter might find a way to peacefully coexist. Before Matt had his heart broken by Jeff Duncan and Jesse Foppert, Canter was losing major leaguers Robert Person and Joe Mays to the bigger agencies. When Person was a promising young pitcher with Philadelphia, Canter collected his meager commissions a year at a time. Then Person cashed in with a $6.25 million deal, but only after he'd departed for Jeff Moorad.

Matt's dislike of Canter stems from the 2001 amateur draft, when Sosnick and Cobbe were advising junior college pitcher Jake Woods and trying to get him signed quickly with Anaheim as the 89th overall pick. Through the years, Matt and Paul have found that by acting decisively, you can squeeze some extra money out of a club before teams start falling in line and paying draft picks strictly on where they go in the overall pecking order.

But there was a problem. Angels scouting director Donny Rowland couldn't act on Woods until he signed Steven Shell, an Oklahoma high school pitcher who'd gone with the 81st pick. And Shell's negotiations were proceeding glacially because his representative, Steve Canter, wouldn't return anybody's phone calls.

"Steve Canter's M.O. is, he doesn't negotiate anything," Paul says. "He just waits to see where the numbers come and slots himself in there. He's Mr. Safety. Our job is to do the absolute best we can for our client, so if we're being hamstrung by someone and we're both in the same spot, why not find out how the negotiations are going and share information? The teams do it all the time."

Matt and Paul initially hoped to get Jake Woods a bonus in the $470,000 range, but as signings trickled in, it became apparent that he would be locked in closer to $440,000. After several futile attempts to reach Canter, Sosnick left a message on his answering machine.

"I'm trying to get something facilitated for both of our clients so they can make money, and you're holding the whole thing up," Matt said. "So I no longer will avoid going after your guys. If you don't call me back, I'll steal all your fucking players."

Canter, "Mr. Safety," apparently wasn't as wimpy or risk-averse as Sosnick and Cobbe believed. He sent a copy of the answering machine tape to the Players Association, prompting union lawyer Bob Lenaghan to call Matt and Paul on a combination fact-finding mission and etiquette lecture.

"You really can't be threatening people like this," Lenaghan told Matt.

"It really wasn't a threat," Matt replied. "It was a posturing remark in the heat of the moment. I was just trying to rattle the guy's cage because he wouldn't have any sort of conversation with us. The money was falling more and more with every hour. I was just trying to goad him into responding."

Lenaghan, who deals with juvenile behavior of this sort routinely, seemed to understand—to a point. "It was a poor choice of words," he said, "and you shouldn't do it again. I'll speak to Steve and we'll convince him to drop this thing. But in the future, you can't threaten other agents."

And, by the way, unless you feel the need, please try to avoid leaving an answering machine tape as evidence.

The matter went no further, and after a fitting lapse of time, Matt contacted Canter again. On Yom Kippur, the Jewish Day of Atonement, he called and offered to make a truce. But after several minutes of olive-branch rhetoric by Sosnick, Canter was noncommittal. "I'll get back to you," he said.

Steve Canter never did call back, and, in Matt's eyes, was forever branded as spineless and deserving of whatever he got. If Canter had told him to take a flying leap off the Coit Tower, Matt might have respected him for it. But nothing elicits ire in a man with a can-do mentality like a half-hearted "I'll get back to you." Matt determined that if the opportunity ever arose to put a dent in Canter's talent base, he would jump at it.

In January 2004, opportunity finally knocks in the person of Kevin Jepsen, an Angels prospect represented by Steve Canter. Just before the New Year, Matt accompanied Dontrelle Willis to Reno for a card show and struck up a conversation with Jepsen, who flew to San Francisco for a visit. They hit it off, and Jepsen, whose fastball touches 100 mph on good days, decides to leave Canter for the Sosnick-Cobbe agency.

Now Jepsen is working his way through the Anaheim chain, and Matt feels little remorse about taking him from another agent who's just trying to get by.

"I'm not such a wonderful person that I'm not going to take guys who are poorly represented, by an agent I don't like—an agent who would take a player from me in a minute," Matt says. "I can be a good guy and I can be polite and respectful, but there's no way in the world I'm going to let people pick off my guys and be afraid to go after their players."

Matt has permanently sworn off going after any players who are represented by Tommy Tanzer and Joe Bick. After that, just about anyone is fair game.

Gene Orza, second in command at the players union, has a formidable IQ and a knack for inserting enough clauses and parenthetical phrases in conversation to make it clear he's the smartest man in the room. The son of Italian immigrants, Orza was trained in Latin and Greek at Fordham University and has law degrees from Georgetown and St. John's. Around the Players Association offices, he's known as one of the last true Renaissance men.

Orza plays poker with Pulitzer Prize–winning author Robert Caro, and he's one of the rare New Yorkers fortunate to have a table at Rao's, a restaurant so exclusive that someone has to die for a seat to become available. He's a connoisseur of theater, opera, show tunes, and fine wine, and he's well-versed in Shakespeare by the standards of anyone but a Shakespearean scholar. When Orza casually drops a reference to Virgil or Dante, there's a 95 percent probability that it's not Ozzie Virgil or Dante Bichette.

Gene Orza is overqualified for the role of Daddy Daycare, but these agents sure need supervision. The baseball union certifies more than 300 agents to negotiate contracts and represent players, and they come from all educational backgrounds, walks of life, and ethical orientations on what is or isn't kosher. What's standard practice for one might make another physically ill.

Barring another round of expansion, the number of players remains finite. There are 750 players in the majors at any one time, and another 450 minor leaguers who are part of 40-man big-league rosters. While the revenue pie might increase—as evidenced by the rise in the average salary from $438,729 in 1988 to $2.37 million in 2003—there are only so many beating hearts and ambulatory bodies to go around.

The player's only commitment is an "agent authorization" form, which must be filled out once a year and is as disposable as yesterday's lineup card. If the player designates Adam Katz as his representative on Tuesday, Scott Boras on Wednesday, and Jeff Moorad on Thursday, his status can be tougher to sort through than an Olympic figure-skating judging fiasco.

No matter how bad things seem, Orza has probably seen worse in his two decades with the union. During the 2003 World Series, Florida second baseman Luis Castillo was being courted by three groups, and there was speculation that his unsettled agent situation was a factor in his poor October performance.

Gene Orza can top that. He once encountered a star player, a former league MVP, who signed five agent designation forms in 5 days. The guy made Luis Castillo look like a monument to loyalty and decisiveness.

"Why are you doing this?" Orza asked the MVP.

"Because these guys are like leeches," the player replied. "They come to me and I just say to them, 'Yeah, sure, fine.'"

The union generally regards poaching with a laissez-faire attitude. That's French for "Go ahead and slit each others' throats." Agents with concerns about client stealing are free to drop a note in the suggestion box, yet they're resigned to the likelihood that little will change. When veteran agent David Sloane sent Orza an e-mail listing ways to change the system for the better, he received a response reading, "Thank you for your input."

"If anything comes of it," Sloane says, "the shock would kill me."

Orza and Michael Weiner, the Harvard-trained lawyer who hears many of the agent complaints, are typically so preoccupied with the fate of the Montreal Expos or the ramifications of the BALCO steroid scandal that they have to prioritize. And the truth is, the union believes that players who leave small mom-and-pop shops for industry behemoths are usually well served. So a certain elitist mentality prevails.

"The laws of competition are what they are," Orza says. "I can give you a hundred illustrations. The Dallas Symphony Orchestra comes across what happens to be the next Yasha Heifetz. They nurture this guy or this gal. And they train this person and give him or her solos in the Dallas Symphony Orchestra, until one day, along comes the New York Philharmonic, and they say, 'Do you want to play in the big time?'"

The result is easy to predict. Salmon swim upstream. Lemmings march into the sea. Every spring, the cliff swallows of the San Juan Capistrano Mission in California make the 6,000-mile journey home from Argentina. And a big-league ballplayer with nine-figure aspirations has only so many places to turn to maximize his bargaining power.

"New York is bigger than Dallas," Orza says. "New York will always have a better symphony orchestra than Dallas. And Scott Boras, based on his reputation and all the great contracts he's negotiated, has a natural advantage over you, which he'd be crazy not to try and exploit."

In the old days, there was such a thing as a code of civility. If a player called Randy Hendricks with an interest in his services, Hendricks would immediately inquire into his current representation. If the player mentioned Tom Reich, Jim Bronner, Ron Shapiro, or some other respected agent, Hendricks would most likely reply, "What are you calling me for?"

Now Reich hates Jeff Moorad, and Moorad detests Scott Boras, and Boras privately disparages Beverly Hills as a "partying group," and they're always standing in judgment of each other's tactics and results. If an agent goes to salary arbitration too often, or too infrequently, it will be duly noted and exploited by the competition. Some agents are hesitant to even exchange arbitration figures with clubs, because if you settle on a salary below the midpoint, competitors are going to savage you for it.

The 30 big-league clubs have skillfully exploited this division in the ranks. Former Boston general manager Dan Duquette might have been the most disliked man in baseball. But if Duquette were preparing an arbitration case for, say, Jason Varitek, and Jorge Posada were a fitting comparison, he could phone the Yankees' Brian Cashman in search of information and get his call returned. Those are the rules under which the clubs operate. Agents, in contrast, view "cooperation" as a four-letter word.

"I think competition among agents has had a profound impact on the way contracts have been negotiated over the last 5 to 8 years," Michael Weiner says. "It's had a negative impact, and it's not simply the case of the young, inexperienced agent who's afraid some big guy is going to pick him off."

Lord knows, there are plenty of examples of that. In 2004, Arizona Diamondbacks pitcher Brandon Webb signs a 3-year, guaranteed $3.3 million contract that many agents privately knock as substandard. In theory, Webb should be free to sign for whatever he wants, but the truth is that no transaction takes place in a vacuum. If a competitor undersells his client today and your player has similar statistics or service time, you might feel the squeeze tomorrow.

Client stealing is so rampant that agents now try to leave a paper trail—or an e-mail trail—to show that they've laid some groundwork in case a player bolts for a competitor. That way, if your rival negotiates a multiyear deal, you, too, can stake a claim on the commission.

During a meeting of the union's executive board in December 2002, client stealing was a prime topic of conversation among players, who groused about the Wild West feel of the agent wars. A month later, the union sent an e-mail to agents telling them that it planned to strictly monitor fees. If agents are playing games with commissions and doing favors for selected players, they might have more than altruism on their minds.

"This whole topic comes up every year," says New York Mets pitcher Tom Glavine. "It's something everybody is concerned about. You want players picking their representation based on these guys doing a good job for them—not what they promise them."

The stars are usually the ones who hear the biggest promises. The organizational soldiers—less promising players who fill out rosters to aid in the development of the stars—aren't as fortunate. They get their one pair of spikes each year and their standard-issue bats, and they stand idly by as the stars revel in the "concierge mentality."

Minor-league pitcher Chris Rojas, one of Matt and Paul's favorite organizational soldiers, grew up in a New York ghetto best known for producing junkies, crackheads, and weapon-toting gang members. Bedford-Stuyvesant, the Brooklyn neighborhood that served as the backdrop for the Spike Lee movie *Do the Right Thing*, offers little hope and lots of temptation, either to sell drugs or to consume them. Violence and tension are constants in Bedford-Stuyvesant, where the motto is "Bed-Stuy—Do or Die." The locals say it with a sense of pride, and they view survival as a badge of honor.

Chris Rojas was born on March 30, 1977, and never knew his father. His mother, Supilda, moved to New York from Puerto Rico at an early age, and she wanted the best for her only child. But life was pretty much a day-to-day proposition. Supilda, known as "Soupy" to her friends, did odd jobs and worked as a messenger in the city, but she existed primarily from welfare check to welfare check. She lived with Chris in an apartment on Kosciuszko Street, and it was nothing to flick on the lights—when the lights were operational—and see mice or cockroaches scurrying in all directions.

Chris Rojas can summon a slew of childhood memories that revolve around being menaced or threatened. When he was 6 years old, two knife-wielding thugs cornered him and his mother at a bus stop. Soupy fended off the attackers, but not before suffering a stab wound that landed her in the hospital. On Chris's first day of high school, he saw a kid burst through a set of double doors and sprint down the corridor with an Uzi in one hand, a trail of bullets falling out of his backpack, and security guards in hot pursuit.

The apartment building at 279 Kosciuszko was headquarters for a neighborhood drug ring, and half the cops, it seemed, were on the take. Neighborhood residents would congregate on the front stoops, and one summer night when Chris was 12, he was hanging out with his mom and some friends when a car pulled up and started blasting away. Soupy grabbed her boy, shielded him with her body, and stumbled toward the front door in search of sanctuary—but not before a bullet struck her in the arm. She survived the shot, but it was a bleak reminder of the randomness of life in a drug haven.

Supilda had her share of personal problems, but she tried to teach her son the proper values and her heart was in the right place. She was conscious of Chris's long-term interests, and the need for him to be tough, when she pitted him against neighborhood boys in sparring matches. When Chris developed an interest in football, Soupy invested what little money she had in a helmet and shoulder pads. Then she schooled the boy on the realities of the game, ramming a shoulder into him with sufficient force to make his ears ring.

Baseball was Chris Rojas's passion, and he was content to play without a fancy Little League uniform. Fields of dreams were nonexistent in Bedford-Stuyvesant, so Chris and his friends painted a square box on a brick wall and threw fastballs to each other until their elbows throbbed. If there weren't enough kids for a traditional game, they'd use half a field and designate landmarks as hits. This patch of asphalt was a double, and that fire hydrant was a triple. Ebbets Field, it wasn't.

Chris's relationship with Soupy grew strained as he reached high school, and he moved in with an aunt in Queens and transferred to Great Neck High School. He attended the New York Institute of Technology, where he obtained a degree in criminal justice and played baseball beyond the realm of scouts and pre-draft "buzz." After a summer in the independent Frontier League with the Canton Crocodiles, he took a shot at professional ball through that last refuge for dreamers—the tryout camp.

In September 1998, about 40 kids, mostly stiffs, showed up and spent several hours displaying skills and trying their best to impress Bill Bryk, field coordinator for the Pittsburgh Pirates. Chris, an infielder by trade, decided to take a turn on the mound to show that he had some arm strength. He was the last pitcher to throw, and the Pittsburgh people were intrigued. They told him to go home and wait for a phone call, and a day later it came. "Consider yourself a Pirate," Bill Bryk told him, and in the fall of 1998, Chris Rojas left New York for the Instructional League in Florida.

He quickly came to understand the double standard and handy euphemisms inherent in pro ball. A first-round draft pick prone to emotional highs and lows might be classified as "competitive" or "high-strung." Chris, mindful that qualifiers don't apply to tryout camp refugees, kept his emotions in check because he feared being labeled a "hot-headed Latino." In hindsight, he felt like a fraud. But he held his own, posting a 5–7 record with Williamsport in the New York–Penn League.

The Pirates released several prospects during a front-office overhaul that winter, and Chris, out of a job, called Bill Bryk, now with San Diego, and begged for a chance. "I can't promise you anything," Bill told him, "but if you can get to Fort Wayne, I'll see what I can do."

Chris rode a Greyhound Bus for 18 hours to Indiana and threw for some Padres minor-league people. San Diego signed him to a contract, and he went 6–4 for Idaho Falls and Fort Wayne.

He saw that other kids in the minors had agents to represent their interests, so he hired a local guy to negotiate with the Padres. The dude made all sorts of promises, until Chris discovered that the money in the low minors is etched in stone. You take what they give you. *This guy is a knucklehead,* he concluded, before firing the agent over the phone.

In spring training of 2001, Chris asked one of his Lake Elsinore teammates, Dennis Tankersley, for a recommendation on a new agent. Tankersley had two California guys named Sosnick and Cobbe working for him, and he spoke highly of them. Matt and Paul supplied him with equipment and card deals, and were always accessible by phone. Sosnick had even attended Tankersley's wedding in St. Louis, and he had helped counsel Tankersley and his wife over the phone when they'd had some marital problems.

Dennis Tankersley, known as "Tank" around the clubhouse, was a climber. The Red Sox selected him in the 38th round of the 1999 draft, and he was stagnating in their system when they sent him to San Diego in a trade for fading third baseman Ed Sprague.

The Padres tinkered with Tankersley's pitching mechanics and he immediately blossomed, going 5–2 with a 2.85 ERA for Fort Wayne in the Midwest League and striking out 87 hitters in 66 innings. He was rewarded with an appearance on *Baseball America*'s list of top Padres prospects. "Tankersley is yet another example of the Red Sox underestimating the worth of their prospects before including them in trades," wrote *Baseball America*, which compared his delivery to big leaguer Kevin Appier's.

The 2001 Lake Elsinore team was stacked—with Jake Peavy, Xavier Nady, and other highly regarded prospects—but Tankersley had a certain golden-boy luster. His fastball registered in the mid-90s, and he dominated opposing lineups by throwing the ball past them. "He was the 'man' in the Padres system that year," says John Scheschuk, a first baseman on the Lake Elsinore team.

Tankersley attracted the attention of the San Diego front office, which began debating when to promote him to Double-A Mobile. Unbeknownst to Matt Sosnick and Paul Cobbe, he also attracted the attention of Jim McNamara, who was covering the California League on behalf of the Scott Boras Corporation.

McNamara, a former North Carolina State University player, spent 6 years as a catcher in the minor leagues before a cameo with San Francisco in 1992 and '93. When the regular players went on strike and the call went out to journeymen, plumbers, and pizza deliverymen to fill in as "replacement players," Jim McNamara's conscience got the better of him. He didn't want to be a "scab," so he fulfilled a promise to his mother and went to Arizona State to obtain his college degree. During a trip east, McNamara had a chance meeting with Bob Brower, a former big-league outfielder working for the Scott Boras Corporation, and he landed a job with Boras's group.

McNamara, one of 46 big leaguers born in New Hampshire, once told baseball writer Peter Gammons that he couldn't understand why his family moved so often when he was a youth. Then, his father retired and told the family that he'd worked many years for the CIA. Jim McNamara, who stood 6'4" and weighed 210 pounds during his stint in the majors, apparently inherited his dad's talent for sleuthing.

According to one team's scout, McNamara is a gregarious, engaging, eminently likeable guy. He's also the kind of guy "whose eyes are in six different places" when you're having a conversation with him.

When McNamara began showing up around Lake Elsinore's home park with regularity in the spring of 2001, it didn't seem particularly odd. Boras represented Padres prospects Jake Peavy and Xavier Nady, and it stood to reason that McNamara, as a Boras surrogate, would be around to keep tabs on them and make sure they were content.

But within a short period of time, it struck some Lake Elsinore players that they were seeing a little too much of Jim McNamara.

"He followed us a lot," says Troy Schader, a former Lake Elsinore infielder and Sosnick-Cobbe client who missed much of the 2001 season with a back injury. "If we'd go on a road trip, he might follow the bus.

He was always at the games, sitting right there, trying to get in good with the coaches or something. I thought it was weird."

If the team bus pulled up at a Burger King or a McDonald's, the players would look out the window and see Jim McNamara's car. When they entered a rest stop, McNamara did everything but follow them into the john.

McNamara's fervent hawking of Dennis Tankersley became a running joke among the Lake Elsinore players. When he was around the clubhouse someone might pipe up, "Here comes corporate America!" Or Tankersley's teammates would exhort him to stand his ground and not to succumb to the pressure. "Don't go corporate, Tank!" they'd yell at him.

Paul Cobbe eventually caught wind of the situation through the grapevine. Players on the Lake Elsinore team invented nicknames for Jim McNamara. They referred to him as "Dennis's balls," or "Dennis's nuts," because everywhere Dennis went, Jim McNamara was sure to follow.

The entire scene made Chris Rojas uneasy. In spring training, he had been looking for an agent, and Tankersley had introduced him to Matt Sosnick and Paul Cobbe. For Chris's entire life, he'd been conditioned not to trust anybody, but he quickly found himself on the phone with Paul routinely, confiding in him about baseball and life as if they were best friends. He was a full-fledged member of the Sosnick-Cobbe stable now. And ironically, Dennis Tankersley, his entrée to Matt and Paul, was headed out the door.

Chris raised the issue with Tankersley early in the season, and Tank swore up and down that he wasn't changing his representation. But gradually, inexorably, Jim McNamara seemed to be wearing down Tank's resistance.

"They'd send him gear and stuff," Rojas says. "Every other day was something new. New sneakers, new cleats, stuff like that. I was like, 'Dang, this is Christmas time for you, Tank.' He was getting so much stuff. It's not like we weren't getting taken care of by Matt and Paul. They took care of us perfectly fine."

Chris Rojas remembers passing through Visalia and seeing Jake

Peavy hand off his tax return to Jim McNamara, and asking Tank if he needed his taxes done too. "The guy was literally everywhere he went," Chris says.

Dennis Tankersley pitched 52⅓ innings in the California League that spring before earning a promotion to Double-A Mobile, Alabama. He made only eight starts in Lake Elsinore, but it was plenty of time for him to be swayed. In May, the Storm made the trip north to San Jose, and Matt drove down from San Francisco to see the game. The ubiquitous Jim McNamara, naturally, was in attendance.

Chris Rojas watched the entire thing unfold, and it was like seeing a car wreck in advance. "I told Tank, 'Hey, Matt is here,' and he just blew it off," Chris recalled. "And I thought, 'Oh, man, there's some fishy shit going on.' Matt was waiting for Tank to come by, and he never even said hello."

The odor got ranker the next day when Paul invited Chris Rojas, Troy Schader, and Dennis Tankersley out for breakfast, and Tank begged off because he said he was sick. Within a few days, Matt finally tracked down Tankersley by phone, and Tank assured him he was happy and there was nothing to the rumors.

That pledge was still fresh in Matt's mind a few days later when he received a letter signed by Dennis Tankersley. It thanked him for all he had done, and informed him that Dennis had decided to go in a different direction. The letter never mentioned a word about the Scott Boras Corporation.

Chris never discussed the break with Tankersley, but he overheard Tank explaining his decision to other players in the clubhouse. *Boras has been around and he knows how to handle the system*, Chris Rojas recalls Dennis Tankersley telling the other Lake Elsinore players. *I'm going to go through arbitration in a few years, and my agents have never done that. They don't even have any players in the big leagues yet. I don't want to be the first guy they have to represent in arbitration and get screwed.*

This was Dennis Tankersley's prerogative, of course, Chris realized. He couldn't be begrudged the opportunity to protect his long-term interests or look out for number one.

But after seeing Jim McNamara's face more than chalk lines and roadside Denny's in the spring of 2001, Chris Rojas wondered how much forethought and free will weighed into Tank's decision. Chris wondered when the line between loyalty and self-interest began to blur, and when exactly salesmanship turned into strong-arming. He wondered whether a player was wrong for lacking the spine to say no, or if Boras's guy in the California League was so persistent he simply refused to take no for an answer. There had to be a line somewhere— didn't there?

"He was sent out to do one thing and one thing only," Chris Rojas says of Jim McNamara. "It was, 'Don't come back until you get it done.' That's what it seemed like."

This agent business, Chris determined, was do or die—just like Bedford-Stuyvesant without the bullet holes. But there sure were plenty of cockroaches.

Chapter

SEVEN

One day, Matt Sosnick is hanging out at an autograph show with his star client, Dontrelle Willis. A month or two later, who knows? Fate and the chase might take him to Tomball, Texas, home of Dr. Tony's Pet Cottage and Joe's Barber Shop & Salon, where every mile on the odometer brings him closer to the next phenom for his stable.

In late February 2004, Matt and Toby Trotter met in Houston for a day of recruiting, in an effort to nail down three new advisees for the year and a potential star attraction for 2005. The June draft, more than 3 months away, always assumes a prominent place on the agent's calendar. And the more competitive the pursuit of young talent, the earlier you have to get up in the morning, and the more hustle and anticipation are required.

"I'd go see a kid if he was 7 years old, as long as he was left-handed and he threw hard," Matt says. He laughs—*really, it's a joke*—but cradle-robbing humor is inevitable in a business where it pays to be ahead of the curve.

Amid the draft planning, Matt checks in regularly with his players in spring training camps in Florida and Arizona, and in many cases, they convey positive news. Florida Marlins catcher Josh Willingham, a slugger from Alabama, tells Matt that he caught Brad Penny and Chad Fox in a spring training game yesterday, a sure sign that he's moving up in the world. And pitcher Chad Qualls, invited to his first big-league camp with Houston, enters the clubhouse in Kissimmee, Florida, and sees the two newest Astros, Roger Clemens and Andy Pettitte, hanging out in a mind-blowing Yankees reunion.

When Clemens comes over and introduces himself, with his firm handshake and Texas drawl, Qualls feels like an intruder in someone else's dream. Clemens's 310 career victories are a testament to his ability to intimidate hitters. But he also has a rare capacity, with his Hall-of-Fame aura and six career Cy Young Awards, for turning otherwise confident young athletes into awestruck fantasy campers.

"He's such a down-to-earth guy," Chad Qualls tells Matt. "He's awesome. But I'm scared to even talk to him."

Dontrelle Willis is chatty and upbeat about the Marlins' prospects for this season, and he's ready to go after a winter filled with perks and obligations. His excellent post–World Series adventure included a tour of the Negro League Museum in Kansas City with old-timer Buck O'Neil as his guide, and a December visit to New York, where he rang the opening bell at the NASDAQ and mingled at Jay-Z's exclusive nightspot. He made television appearances on Carson Daly's late-night show and *The Best Damn Sports Show Period*, and he would have met with President Bush if not for a prior engagement. While his Florida teammates were visiting the White House, Dontrelle traveled to New York to accept the National League Rookie of the Year Award at a writers' dinner.

"It was unfortunate," Dontrelle says. "But I apologize to Mr. President. Hopefully we'll win again so I can go next year."

The next trip to the White House just better not take place in January: Dontrelle and his girlfriend, Kim, are engaged to be married, and they've set a tentative wedding date before the start of 2005 spring training.

Houston isn't one of Matt's favorite stops, and his distaste for the city is exacerbated by the Sunday morning traffic and the maze of power lines and orange highway barrels. Matt and Toby kill time in the car ranking their top 10 favorite movies and discussing *The Passion of the Christ*, the new Mel Gibson film. Toby, as a devout Christian, says it had a profound impact on him both spiritually and emotionally. Matt hasn't seen it yet, but he plans to catch it as soon as possible.

They discuss world events and trivia. Toby just saw a newspaper item listing the top U.S. states in terms of per capita cigarette consumption. What's number one? After several futile guesses by Matt, Toby reveals that the correct answer is Kentucky.

"Right," Matt nods in assent. "After you have sex with your first cousin, you've got to have a cigarette. It takes the edge off."

Their first appointment is at a local cantina, for a Mexican-style breakfast with two area high school kids and their dads. Mark McGonigle is a skinny outfielder from Bellaire, and Brian Juhl is a catcher from Katy, home of Roger Clemens. Mark's stepfather, Rommie Maxey, is an associate scout for the Colorado Rockies and shakes your hand with a grip that's both firm and sincere. Brian's dad, Charlie Juhl, bears a resemblance to former Mets third baseman Howard Johnson.

The kids wear pullover shirts and jeans, and their dads dress just as casually, but Matt goes to great lengths to project an air of professionalism and class. He wears a dark pinstriped suit from Maxwell's, the Hong Kong tailors, and he brings a spare in a garment bag in case it gets wrinkled during the trip. He has also packed two extra dress shirts for the trip to Texas, just in case one doesn't suffice.

Both boys have all but officially committed to Sosnick-Cobbe, and over breakfast, Matt walks them and their dads through the upcoming draft process. He talks about the intricacies of the draft and tells the families to consider every question and formulate a response for interested clubs. *How badly do you want to play pro ball versus attending college? What kind of money do you expect as a bonus?* And he advises the boys that they're now being watched by scouts, and that every action on the field sends out a message. *If you lose your cool in the heat of a game, the scouts will naturally wonder how you'll handle the scrutiny of pro ball.* Even parents aren't immune. It's great to be a concerned, involved father. But if you come on as overly demanding, you risk being branded as a "nightmare" dad by the clubs. That's never good.

Matt tells Brian and Mark that it's important to be truthful with major-league teams. But that doesn't mean you have to share every single thought whirling through your head. If a club is really hot to draft you, it doesn't hurt to leave a shred of doubt about college as an alternative just for the sake of leverage.

The next stop is the upscale, master-planned community of The Woodlands, about 40 minutes from downtown, where Matt and Toby pass through a wrought-iron gate and enter the Dodson family's 6,500-square-foot English country-style home. Jordan Dodson is a star two-sport athlete at The Woodlands High, and his father, Richard, is a former Marine and managing director for an oil services company. The Dodsons and their visitors eat filet mignons from the grill and discuss baseball and their tastes in music. When Richard Dodson reveals that he's a John Denver fan, Matt nods in assent. "If I can ever find a victim, I might play 'Annie's Song' at my wedding," he says.

After dinner, Matt, Toby, and the family retire upstairs to watch Jordan's high school baseball and football exploits on a big-screen TV, directly beneath a deer head on the wall. They're ecstatic when Jordan Dodson, like the two high schoolers before him, confirms that he will use Sosnick-Cobbe to advise him in the draft.

The hoped-for prize catch of the day comes on the final visit. Kyle Russell, a 6'4", 180-pound junior outfielder from Tomball High School, is lanky and athletic in the mold of the Tampa Bay Devil Rays' Rocco Baldelli. He has long sideburns and an easy smile, and he's sitting in a T-shirt and a pair of shorts, eating pizza, when Matt and Toby arrive for their meeting. It doesn't take much to envision Kyle chasing down a line drive in the gap, or uncoiling his swing and sending a fastball to the nether regions of some fenceless high school field, and having it roll all the way to next week.

The dynamic in the Russell household is easy to discern. Kyle seems alternately flattered and embarrassed by the attention from agents, and he's hesitant to embrace it because he's such a nice, sincere kid. He knows he'll have to say no to someone eventually, and he finds that prospect unappealing.

Gerald Russell, the dad, is assistant controller for a $400 million-a-year steel company in Houston. A bookish-looking man, he's proud of his son's accomplishments but not pushy or overbearing. When Gerald lets it drop that Kyle hit a home run recently that traveled 460 feet, it's more out of pride than braggadocio. He's under no illusions that stardom and a huge payoff are inevitable for his boy; Gerald Russell has heard plenty of sad stories about ballplayers who sign pro contracts out of high school, never make the majors, and have no college degree as a safety net. He's concerned that Kyle might get starstruck, take the money, and hit a dead end in baseball at age 22.

Kyle's mom, Joyce, is the resident hard sell in the family. While she offers the visitors soft drinks and makes an effort to be congenial, her body language suggests that she's wary of the hucksters parading through her living room under the guise of "representing" her son. She listens to Matt's talk with her arms folded, and it's readily apparent that gaining her trust will be a challenge.

While Sally, the Russell family dachshund, scurries in and out of the living room in pursuit of a green tennis ball, Matt begins his presentation. The higher the stakes, the more he believes in speaking slowly and quietly to project an air of authority. And the salesman in him knows that every word matters.

As Paul Cobbe points out, if you're talking to a player from the South, it never hurts to slip a "y'all" into the conversation for bonding purposes. Or if the player is black, maybe you squeeze in a "bro." As in, "Nice game last night, bro." Cynical? Perhaps. But the tactic is subliminally effective.

All kinds of crazy things can happen on a recruiting visit. Two years earlier, Sosnick and Cobbe spent a lot of time pursuing a highly regarded high school pitcher named Chris Gruler, out of northern

California. At 6'3" and 200 pounds, Chris had the repertoire of a young Curt Schilling and strong legs in the Tom Seaver mold. After being besieged by would-be advisers, the Gruler family invited a handful into the house to get acquainted.

Chris Gruler was a formidable catch. When he worked out for Cincinnati officials at Cinergy Field before the 2002 draft, Hall of Famer and Reds consultant Johnny Bench said he had a better breaking ball and changeup than Seaver—who merely won 311 games and made it to Cooperstown with 98.84 percent of the vote.

Chris was more intelligent and mature than the average jock, and he had a strong family foundation. His dad, Steve, is in charge of quality control for Gerber, and he has the businesslike air of a man accustomed to making decisions and seeing people jump in response. He's not going to be overwhelmed by two agents, that's for sure.

The Grulers sat across the table from Matt Sosnick and Paul Cobbe, and Steve Gruler made it clear that picking an adviser was no minor consideration for his son. Chris had a special talent, there was a lot of money at stake, and it was vital that no detail be overlooked.

A sense of trust was also important. The Grulers wanted to feel comfortable that the agency they selected was sincere.

"I don't want anyone fucking with my kid," Steve Gruler said.

The declaration resonated with Matt because of the value he places on loyalty, and the Grulers sensed a light going on in his eyes. Matt doesn't like people messing with the people he holds dear, either. He began speaking passionately to the Grulers about the emotional investment he's made in his company, and his lifelong friendship with Paul, and about how the two entities—the business and the friendship—are now inextricably linked. The more he talked, the stronger he felt, and the more his emotions gained momentum, like a boulder rolling down a hill.

Words were cheap, Matt knew. He wanted the Grulers to see that he and Paul were a team in every sense of the word and different from the other agents who might pass through their living room under the guise of caring, when all they really cared about was the commission. Had any of those agents known their partners since they were 3 years old? No way.

"This man is my fucking buddy right here," Matt said, pointing to Paul. "This is my partner, and I'd fucking die for him."

Accounts vary as to whether Matt tossed in another stray F-bomb or two, or as many as a dozen. But to the Gruler family, he might as well have been Andrew Dice Clay strutting his stuff on stage. Rather than create a bond, his earthy language made Chris Gruler and his parents squirm in their chairs. The meeting ran its natural course, but the family had already checked out mentally. By the time Matt and Paul hit the driveway, it was a lost cause.

Irene Gruler, Chris's mom, was the last to say goodbye.

"Well, Steve," she told her husband as the door swung shut. "I guess you shouldn't have said 'fuck.'"

The atmosphere was considerably less tense 3 years ago when Matt sealed the deal with Mike Hinckley. The courtship was dicey for the first few hours, but that's the risk you take when you're forthright and assertive with a family: It can go either way.

Sosnick, true to form, didn't waste any time when he heard about the formerly scrawny Oklahoma left-hander who was gradually climbing the draft rankings. At the start of his high school career, Mike Hinckley had his thoughts trained on a scholarship to the University of Oklahoma. But as he grew bigger and his fastball got faster, Mike began generating a buzz among scouts early in his senior year.

"The Cubs told me they'd take me in the second round if I was there," Mike says, "and I was thinking, 'This can't be happening. If they're saying I might go second round, I might go in the first round.' It was nuts. To start the year I was a 15th rounder, maybe. It was crazy."

He was evolving into the kind of stealth pick that Sosnick and Cobbe consider a specialty. So Matt operated at Autobahn speed. He called the Hinckley house and spoke to Lyn, Mike's mom, and told her that he would be flying from California to Oklahoma in a few days for a visit.

"Wait a minute," Lyn said, before the conversation got too far along. "We're from Oklahoma. We don't talk that fast." Matt's schedule was a little too ambitious for her husband's tastes. But in spite of their reservations, the Hinckleys decided to be hospitable and welcome him into their home. When Matt arrived at 6:00 P.M. on a Tuesday, the prospect and his dad were still at a game, so he peeled off his sweater and sneakers and challenged the family's 9-year-old twins, Jeff and Chris, to a game of Nerf basketball. Lyn Hinckley, puttering around the kitchen, heard good-natured trash talking coming from the back room. Then Matt leafed through some photographs of Mike before settling in with Lyn to watch *Who Wants to Be a Millionaire* on television.

The twins immediately took a liking to the visitor from California, and Lyn was impressed because he seemed, for want of a better word, so *normal*. "He wasn't at all what you'd expect," she says.

But when David Hinckley rolled home around 7:30, tired from a long day of teaching history and coaching baseball at Moore High, he was naturally suspicious of the interloper in his midst. While he and Mike were out, Matt Sosnick had scaled the moat, climbed the drawbridge, and planted his corporate flag atop the Hinckley castle. The California agent had made a few too many assumptions, in David's opinion, and it brought out the Papa Bear in him.

"Matt was very brash and very, 'I'm here, and I'm the best, and this is what we need to get done and we need to do it now,'" David Hinckley says. "And I'm like, 'Hold on a minute, bud. Don't come into my house and tell me what I'm going to do.' I had to yank his chain a bit. I didn't want to run him off, but I wasn't necessarily very happy with his attitude in the beginning."

Still, the Hinckleys bore with Matt, in part because he'd flown halfway across the country and merited a fair shot. And he never sugarcoated anything. When they looked him in the eye, he looked squarely back. When they began pumping him with questions, he answered patiently and methodically.

"What happens," Dave Hinckley asked Matt, "if my son reports to pro ball and his roommate is a carouser or a troublemaker or a pot smoker? How can you protect him? And what about the money aspect? Are you going to view him as a person or just a commission?"

Lyn Hinckley asked questions, too, about baseball groupies and life on the road, and the hazards of a diet filled with midnight stops at Burger King.

Matt's responses were measured, thoughtful, and, most important, sincere. *The guy sure seems to know what he's talking about,* Dave Hinckley thought. And the refreshing part was, he never tried to absolve Michael of personal responsibility. "I can't shelter your son from the world," Matt told the Hinckleys. "He's going to have to make proper decisions or this isn't going to work. But if I didn't think he could, I wouldn't be here."

When Matt walked out the door at 11:00 P.M., the Hinckleys had given him their seal of approval. He fulfilled his promises in the coming months, relaying word from the scouts on when Mike might go in the draft, if not necessarily where. Mike Hinckley's third-round bonus with Montreal, $425,000 plus a college scholarship, was equivalent to 17 years' worth of David Hinckley's salary as a high school teacher. And Matt made sure that the money was invested wisely, hooking Mike up with CSI Capital Management, a financial services company in California. Even when September 11 hit and the stock market took a dive, Mike's investments came through all right.

As time passed, Matt became more an extension of the family. He was constantly sending the twins presents, be it boxed sets of baseball cards or an autographed Shaquille O'Neal–Kobe Bryant basketball. When Matt traveled to Atlanta on business and turned on CNN and saw footage of an F-5 level tornado tearing through Oklahoma, he called Lyn Hinckley in a frenzy to see if the family was all right.

Lyn has a hard time explaining why her son Mike, a humble Christian boy from Oklahoma, and Matt Sosnick, a fast-talking Jew from San Francisco, bonded so readily. She suspects it's because they're both passionate about life and have strong convictions. They're also similarly consumed by how they're perceived. "They both want to be loved by other people, and they're curious what other people think about them," Lyn Hinckley says. "Mike might not want to admit it, but it's true."

In November 2002, Mike's older sister, Cari, married Toby Trotter, an assistant football coach at Southern Nazarene University in Oklahoma, and Matt flew in for the wedding. As part of a ceremonial tradition, male guests lined up to dance with the bride. "I don't dance," Matt told Cari, "but here's something for you." And he quietly handed her a $100 bill.

Matt and Toby Trotter struck up a conversation over cake and punch, and they found that they had some common ground. Toby, a boyish-looking 24, was no baseball guy, but he could appreciate the art of salesmanship as a college football recruiter. Toby loved his job and took pride in molding character in young men, but the rewards were meager on the 1st and 15th of every month. Toby worked 50 to 80 hours a week, depending on the season, and made about $15,000 a year.

So, when Matt called several months later with a proposition—*come work for my agency as a recruiter*—Toby saw the potential. He went home, talked it over with Cari, and they prayed in search of guidance.

Toby had believed in the power of prayer since age 9, when he bolted up in bed with a sheen of sweat across his forehead, and his mother burst into the room in response to his cries of rapture for the Lord Jesus Christ. Debating whether to take a job as a sports agent wasn't as momentous, obviously, but it fit with the overall plan. "I believe that God puts you in different areas for different reasons," Toby says. "This was out of the blue. It kind of came chasing after me. That showed me it was a step of faith that God wanted me to take."

As the ambitious sort, Toby became a disciple for Matt and Paul Cobbe. He moved from Oklahoma to Dallas in July 2003 and quickly ran up $7,000 in expenses each month. He traveled to Georgia, Missouri, Illinois, Tennessee, Kansas, and Oklahoma in search of talent, and made enough forays to Houston to be considered an honorary resident of the city.

On a trip to Cape Cod that summer, Toby and Paul watched four games in a day with just a roadside hot dog or two for sustenance. Their reward came when they wangled a few minutes with Rice University pitcher Jeff Niemann, a sure first-round pick and a veritable Sasquatch at 6'9" and 260 pounds.

When 5 minutes to sell yourself is like an eternity, every gesture matters. Subtle things matter. Toby made some nice, comfortable chitchat with Niemann. But he also forgot to remove his fake Oakleys— or "Foakleys"—thereby limiting eye contact with the kid. He'd violated a cardinal rule of the agent business, and Paul gently alerted him to the gaffe as they headed to the car.

"You never want to burn a bridge, and you always want to do something so they'll remember your face," Paul said.

As a high school receiver in Oklahoma, Toby was undersize for football. But he had vise grips for hands, ran precise routes, and made himself a player through focus and hard work. *If I apply the same work ethic and attention to detail in this job, I'll succeed*, he told himself.

At his first high school showcase, in Joplin, Missouri, Toby met two scouting directors, five national cross-checkers, and a bunch of area guys. Scouts are a chatty bunch, Toby discovered, and they might tip you off to prospects if you treat them with dignity and respect. At one game Toby sat beside a scout, and it wasn't long before the guy started pouring out his heart about marital difficulties and other problems at home. "Pray for me, if you can," the scout told him.

Toby quickly grew suspicious of other agents, with their slicked-back hair and unctuous demeanors. He found it unsettling, the way they queued up for the privilege of sucking up to kids. You might be talking with a young ballplayer, handing him your card, and it was nothing to see rival agents standing there waiting like customers at a supermarket deli.

Toby came to believe strongly in Matt and Paul's venture. He respected them for running their business honestly and ethically, and he viewed himself as a frontline soldier for the cause. Still, he knew that competitors were pulling into the same driveways an hour before or after him, and he wondered what kind of promises they were making to families.

"I saw some of these guys, and it didn't seem like there's a lot of integrity in the business," Toby says.

As a new agent, he regards each commitment as a form of personal validation. Tyler Beranek, a power-hitting high schooler from Wisconsin, commits to the Sosnick-Cobbe agency several months before the 2004 draft, as does Grant Hansen, a rangy pitcher from NAIA powerhouse Oklahoma City. Garth Iorg, the former Toronto Blue Jays infielder and the de facto "godfather" of the Tennessee baseball scene, invites Toby to the house and agrees to let him represent the three Iorg boys, Isaac, Eli, and Cale. The Iorges, devout Mormons, even haul out some family videos and show them to Toby. "As long as I take care of Garth's sons, I have a great reference who believes in me and my company," Toby says.

But for every victory, it seems, there is a disappointment or degradation to endure. Toby spends a lot of time this spring hot on the trail of Troy Patton, a top pitcher from the Houston area. He goes to dinner with the family and is taken aback when Troy's father, Dave, pulls out a questionnaire and begins screening him on his approach to the agent business.

Toby is fine with that until Troy, the free-spirited type, stands up mid-survey and excuses himself. "I'm going to a friend's house, because there are some girls swimming there," Troy says. Here's a dad seemingly obsessed with his kid's future, and a kid who apparently can't be bothered. Toby is dying to leave the restaurant too, but he bites his lip and shakes Troy's hand and keeps it civil, even though he knows his chances of landing the kid are nil.

Deep down, Toby also knows his first draft will be a sign of whether he can make a living as a sports agent. With 3 months and counting until June, he spends a lot of time taking stock and praying.

"It's kind of a crapshoot," Toby says. "I could have six guys go in the first five rounds. Or I could have zero."

Matt now keeps the R-rated language to a minimum on home visits, but he's still prone to laying his emotions bare. He lets families know that it's a tough business, and that he's had his heart broken several times by players with weak constitutions and no sense of loyalty. He's become more active recruiting in Texas and Oklahoma, he tells Kyle Russell and his parents, because he prefers religious kids with strong family backgrounds. They're more reliable and values-oriented, and less inclined to switch agents as casually as batting gloves.

Less than a minute into his presentation, Matt tells the Russells that he's a bit of a "weird guy," then drops the Big One: His most prominent player, Dontrelle Willis, is such a loyal Sosnick-Cobbe client, he has the company logo tattooed onto his arm.

"I won't ask you to do that," he tells Kyle, and everyone laughs. He's off to a good start.

Matt's 90-minute talk with the Russells is part educational seminar and part personal catharsis. The "agent" designation, he explains, is a misnomer. The Russells are picking an adviser who will help guide them through the process, and must be referred to as such. It's a gentleman's agreement that's considered binding, Matt says, and if you sign anything with us, your college eligibility is shot. Under the rules, you can't accept anything of value from us—even a meal.

Why does a high school junior need an adviser? Matt tells Kyle and his parents that it's in their best interests to pick a college early, even if Kyle plans to play pro ball, or choose an adviser, even if he plans to attend college, because then he's covered either way. And he can concentrate on the most important things—playing ball and having a great senior year—without being overwhelmed by strangers with an agenda.

Matt also shares his personal story with the Russells. How he wanted to be a professional athlete himself but chose the agent business because he was naturally suited for it. He's intent on proving that an entrepreneur with morals and ethics can succeed, even if it's as a lone crusader.

"We're not agent-y agents," Matt tells the Russells. "We really run this like a family. Everyone we represent in the draft actually comes out for a few days to the Bay Area. We are not a group like a Scott Boras or an IMG, where you're just a number. We're very close to our players."

The Russells seem to like what they hear, and the meeting rolls along congenially until an hour into the conversation, when Gerald Russell fills in a few blanks on the competition. What other groups have shown interest in Kyle? Gerald says the family has positive vibes on J. D. Smart of Octagon, for starters.

J. D. Smart pitched briefly in the big leagues with Montreal and Texas, and Octagon is a mega-conglomerate that runs the gamut from athlete representation to event management to TV rights sales. The company represents athletes in 35 sports, from football to tennis to snowboarding, and has offices in 51 cities worldwide, including Amsterdam, Rotterdam, and Shanghai. Advising high school and college players on their draft bonuses is only a small part of Octagon's business. Managing athletes' finances and handling their marketing and endorsements once they've made it big is a far more lucrative proposition.

Matt Sosnick, who has one office in a 1,700-square-foot duplex 5 minutes from the San Francisco Airport, has bought a plane ticket via Priceline and flown 1,650 miles for the privilege of sitting in the Russell family living room for 90 minutes, or however long they'll have him. And he wants the family to know he's not some corporate cog. Which leads to the following exchange:

> *Matt:* I have nothing bad to say about Octagon. The issue with them is, they go after 40 to 50 guys a year in the draft. They do seven or eight different sports, so they have hundreds of athletes and dozens of agents. It doesn't mean we're right and they're wrong, but you have to decide: Do you want the relationship to be more business, or do you want it to be a combination of business and personal?

> *Gerald:* But my understanding of J. D.'s situation is, he has two guys a year that he follows.

> *Matt:* That's absolute B.S. That is so not true at all.

> *Gerald (laughing nervously):* We don't know.

> *Matt:* That's a lie. Let me ask you this: From a realistic standpoint, do you really believe that a company would hire a guy and ask him to

only go after two players a year, and they're going to pay that guy a salary where he's going to be able to support his family?

Gerald: I've tried to figure that out myself.

Matt: That guy was in no less than 15 to 20 houses this year.

Joyce (trying to lighten the mood): Maybe he meant only two baseball players.

Matt: You're talking about a corporation, and that's the problem. These people are going to say anything. His job is to get a bunch of guys, and he's paid a commission based on the amount of guys he gets. He's paid a commission based on signing bonuses.'

Toby (changing the subject in an attempt to lighten the mood): Say it's 15 months from now, we're past the point of you getting your signing bonus and having a contract, and you're in minor-league ball. The relationship you develop with us is going to be totally different than whomever. Maybe it's something outside of baseball. . . .

Kyle (perking up): Like girls, maybe.

Toby: Say it's a Friday night. It's 2 A.M., you're on a bus trip back from somewhere to somewhere else, and you just went 3-for-4 against a really good pitcher and you want to talk to somebody. You better give me a call, because my wife understands what I do. She's excited about the relationships I have with my players.

Matt (unable to get his mind off J. D. Smart): It's my company. You're going to come out and stay at my house after you're drafted. It infuriates me, because this is exactly what we were talking about. You say he goes after two guys a year . . . he tells you that. Say he goes after two guys a year and he gets both of them. Do you really think the company is going to pay that guy $40,000 or $50,000 or $60,000 or $80,000 a year as an agent? If he goes after two guys a year, you're talking about him taking 5 to 10 minutes a day to recruit a guy, plus maybe visit with him twice or go see him play. What does he do with the other 39 hours in a week? That's the thing: People will say anything to make you feel like you're important or you're their biggest priority, and it's a bunch of crap. This is what infuriates me about this business.

The meeting winds down amicably enough. Everyone agrees that Toby will keep occasional tabs on Kyle—enough to stay on top of the situation without becoming a pain or an intrusion. Matt and Toby cordially say their goodbyes and head out the door into a humid Houston afternoon.

During the car ride back to the hotel, they stop for soft-serve ice cream and agree that the meeting went relatively well—although Matt took notice of the nine crosses on the Russell family wall. During a bathroom break, he found three more crosses hanging in the john.

"I had a hard time even taking it out," Matt says.

Kyle Russell, unfortunately, is not in Matt's future. In May, Gerald makes it known that the family has passed on Sosnick-Cobbe and will choose from three other agencies—Octagon, the International Management Group, and Michael Moye, an Atlanta-based agent who represents Colorado's Todd Helton, Houston's Lance Berkman, and Florida's Josh Beckett, among others. Moye, a devout Christian, runs his business with former big-league pitcher Scott Sanderson. He charges a 3 percent commission compared with the 4 percent that Octagon and IMG charge.

Sosnick decides that if he's on the outs, he'd like to see the sole proprietor win out over the corporate concerns. So he calls Moye and gives him a 15-minute tutorial on the Russells and the factors that he considers important in their decision-making process.

Gerald later reveals that the family had two reasons not to pick Sosnick-Cobbe. The biggest factor was Toby's lack of baseball experience. Scott Sanderson, Michael Moye's partner, pitched 19 years in the big leagues. J. D. Smart, the Octagon recruiter, pitched for the University of Texas and spent parts of two seasons in the majors with the Expos and Rangers. The Russells find it comforting that both know first-hand what Kyle is about to encounter.

"I told Scott Sanderson, 'Kyle is going to be your little brother. If he calls at 1 A.M. and he needs a roll of toilet paper, I expect you to help him,'" Gerald Russell says. "I told all of them that. When Kyle starts going through the season, he's going to have down and up times, and he needs someone who can relate to him.

"I like Toby, and Kyle did too. He seemed like a real nice fella. But he wasn't a baseball player. He hadn't been there and done that. That was the major thing that drove us away from Sosnick."

Gerald also points out that it wasn't very sporting of Matt to be so critical of the Octagon recruiter. As for the issue of how many players J. D. Smart recruits in a year, it will never be completely resolved. But Matt was right about this: It's more than two.

Smart, who just began working for Octagon in the past year, will help the agency land University of Texas pitcher Huston Street and three other players in the 2004 draft. And if he has a 100 percent efficiency rate on the kids he targets . . . well . . . he must be God's gift to recruiting.

"Nobody gets every guy they go after," says another agent. "If you get four, you have to be going after a minimum of eight to ten."

Sosnick attains a degree of satisfaction in the end when the Russell family, after careful deliberation, chooses Michael Moye and Scott Sanderson over the big corporate concerns.

Moye, who's been in the business 18 years, can't recall whether a fellow agent has ever called to give him a heads-up on a potential client the way Matt Sosnick did.

"I appreciate very much that they recommended me when they didn't think they were going to get the player," Moye says. "That's not a very common occurrence in this business."

Score one for the sole proprietor.

Chapter

EIGHT

If Dontrelle Willis ever wants to trace his baseball lineage, he can log on to the Internet and look up Bob Gibson and Ferguson Jenkins, and before that, Satchel Paige and the other great Negro League pitchers—men named Bullet Rogan, Rube Foster, and Hilton Smith. It's not such an easy task for Matt Sosnick. There's no agents' wing in Cooperstown or "dead ball era" for free agency and salary arbitration. Baseball's agent pioneers were fast-talking, quick-thinking men, with a brand of knowledge you couldn't cram into a briefcase. But they were promoters more than businessmen.

In the first half of the 20th century, the definitive baseball agent was Christy Walsh, a former journalist who made money for Babe Ruth, Lou Gehrig, and others by putting their names on ghostwritten articles in newspapers and magazines. Walsh's ultimate judgment call was advising Gehrig to end his consecutive games played streak at 1,999, under the theory that 1,999 was a more memorable number than, say, 2,048. Gehrig weighed the advice, ignored it, and kept playing until

2,130—thereby forcing Cal Ripken Jr. to play almost an entire extra season to make history.

Frank Scott, a Pittsburgh native and World War II Navy veteran, brought the role of the agent to a new level. Scott worked in the Yankees' front office as traveling secretary in the late 1940s, only to be pushed out when general manager George Weiss determined he was too cozy with the players. His foray into athlete representation came by happenstance. Scott was visiting Yogi Berra's house when Yogi's wife, Carmen, noticed that he wasn't wearing a wristwatch. Carmen retired to another room and returned moments later with a tray of watches, maybe 20 in all, and told Scott to take one. The watches, she said, were Yogi's compensation for personal appearances.

Scott, using his Rolodex and his imagination, embarked on a mission to make the term "in lieu of cash" obsolete. He negotiated a lucrative deal for Berra to plug Yoo-Hoo, and when cameras caught Mickey Mantle blowing a bubble in the outfield, Scott parlayed it into a $1,500 endorsement. Soon, Joe DiMaggio, Willie Mays, Hank Aaron, and prominent athletes in basketball and football sought out Scott, who drummed up personal appearances and arranged for them to be audience plants at the *Ed Sullivan Show*, where they would acknowledge the host's wooden introduction with a wave from the crowd. Scott helped Don Larsen capitalize on his perfect game and Roger Maris make $200,000 in endorsements for breaking Babe Ruth's home run record. His only caveat to players was that the spigot would cease to flow if they stopped producing on the field. "I tell them, 'If you don't win, you get nothing, and I get 10 percent of nothing,'" Scott told the *New York Times Magazine* in 1961.

But even a go-getter like Frank Scott knew that a club's ability to dictate salary terms was sacrosanct. "Scott knew an agent's place," Shirley Povich wrote in the *Saturday Evening Post*. "He was too smart to meddle in the players' salary debates with the ballclub. He knew, too, that there had to be rigid respect for the rule that the players' first obligation was to the ballclub."

Bob Woolf wasn't so quick to adhere to tradition. Growing up in Portland, Maine, Woolf embodied the writings of Horatio Alger, whose dime novels in the late 1800s celebrated gritty little street urchins who became great successes through hard work and determination. As a pre-Kindergartener, Woolf would fill a pitcher to the brim and sell ice water to neighborhood construction workers for a penny a glass. He delivered newspapers at age 8, braving howling New England winds off the Portland peninsula with the knowledge that at the end of the day, there would be ample reward: an entire dollar for 100 papers delivered.

Woolf played basketball for Boston College, went to law school, and was running a legal practice above a fast-food restaurant when Earl Wilson, a Boston Red Sox pitcher who lived in the neighborhood, came to him in 1964 looking for assistance after an auto accident. Woolf helped Wilson with his taxes and personal appearances, then graduated to contract negotiations even though baseball didn't welcome him at the time.

When the Red Sox traded Wilson to Detroit 2 years later, Woolf secretly helped the pitcher work out a deal with the team. During a meeting with Detroit general manager Jim Campbell, Wilson excused himself several times and ducked out to a pay phone to call Bob Woolf. Wilson was pleased with Woolf's handiwork, recommended him to several Boston teammates, and a thriving sports agent practice was born.

Several years later, baseball owners had no choice but to field Bob Woolf's phone calls and grant him a seat in the room. For that, he had Marvin Miller to thank.

More than 2 decades after his retirement as executive director of the baseball Players Association, Marvin Miller remains spry into his late 80s. He still enjoys swatting a tennis ball over the net but gave up ice-skating a few years back after hip replacement surgery. Two generations of Major League Baseball owners might observe that it's the first concession he ever made.

When Miller left his job with the Steelworkers Union in 1966 to run the new baseball union, the sport was a bastion of old-line thinking. The average big-league salary was $19,000 a year, and baseball executives liked the fact that players were forced to take what they could get. Players griped plenty about substandard medical treatment, a horrendous schedule, and the lack of an adequate pension plan, but they had almost no recourse.

"I used to hear people say, 'Look, if this guy doesn't sign, we'll send him to Podunk,'" says Roland Hemond, who spent 23 years as a general manager with the Chicago White Sox and Baltimore Orioles. "I never figured out where Podunk was."

Miller, as an ardent unionist, identified with the little guy and was aghast at the way teams could simply dictate terms and laugh in your face. Sure, Joe DiMaggio held out for more money during his heyday, and Sandy Koufax and Don Drysdale joined forces in a 1966 spring training holdout with the Dodgers, but those were more symbolic gestures than a sign of a collective purpose. A player needed star power to even try and buck the system, and it was a misnomer to refer to contract talks as "negotiations."

"The owner said, 'This is what I think I'll pay,' and that's it," Miller says. "If you don't like it, well, you're always free to become a doctor. You want to become a psychologist? You want to become a truck driver? There's no slavery here. You're free to leave. But baseball you will not play, because we own you, kid."

The owners feared and despised this left-wing egghead who traveled from camp to camp spreading the gospel of economic progress through unity, and they weren't alone. Former American League President Joe Cronin went berserk when Miller suggested that players should have input in scheduling matters. And when Miller was banned from the Chicago Cubs' clubhouse and forced to have a meeting in the outfield, manager Leo Durocher grabbed a fungo bat and tried to pepper him with fly balls.

Tom McCraw, who played first base for the Chicago White Sox and three other big-league teams from 1963–75, was at a union solidarity meeting in the late '60s when Miller was blistered by Eddie Stanky,

Chicago's redneck manager. For the better part of 10 minutes, Stanky assaulted Miller with vulgarities and insults designed to make Miller lose his cool, and Miller responded as if Stanky were chatting him up about the weather. He just stood there, placidly nodding his head and saying "Yes, Eddie; yes, Eddie," until Stanky, all huffed out, slammed a blackboard with his fist and stormed out of the clubhouse.

Miller, the players determined, was a master at exerting force without strong-arming, making noise without raising his voice, and inducing the fruit to fall to Earth without shaking the tree too hard. "Marvin Miller was like King galvanizing the blacks, or Gandhi pulling a group together through adversity," Tom McCraw says. "I'm gonna eat the rest of my life because of him, and it burns me up that some of the guys playing now don't even know who he is."

McCraw and his contemporaries had grown up with the reserve clause, which contractually tied a player to an organization for life. But with Miller as their guide, players experienced a sea change of events over the next decade. In 1970, St. Louis outfielder Curt Flood went to court and challenged the reserve system rather than accept a trade to Philadelphia. Although Flood lost his case, he emboldened the players and laid the groundwork for future challenges.

In late 1974, arbitrator Peter Seitz issued a decision making pitcher Jim "Catfish" Hunter a free agent after Oakland owner Charlie Finley defaulted on Hunter's contract by reneging on a promise to pay a $50,000 annuity. Hunter took advantage of his newfound freedom and signed a 5-year, $3.75 million deal with the Yankees, thus alerting players to the riches that awaited them. Emancipation day came on December 23, 1975, when Seitz issued a ruling that made pitchers Dave McNally and Andy Messersmith free agents. Baseball would never be the same.

Marvin Miller's brilliance lay in his ability to anticipate change and to envision how one development would lead to another until they eventually meshed into a coherent whole. Before Curt Flood, Catfish Hunter, Andy Messersmith, and Dave McNally began making waves, he negotiated a paragraph into the labor agreement allowing players to use agents in contract talks.

When Miller saw how ballclubs hoarded information and unilaterally dictated terms, it bothered him that players didn't even have the benefit of seeking professional advice. The 1970 labor agreement was the first to make specific mention of agents. Under the category of "Representation during Individual Salary Negotiations," Article V included the passage, "A player may be accompanied, if he so desires, by a representative of his choice to assist him in negotiating his individual salary with his employing club."

Miller's plan called for the Players Association to negotiate the overall framework of a contract—minimum salary, pension benefits, and such—and for players to strike their own deals with clubs. The union lacked the resources to hire a staff capable of negotiating dozens upon dozens of contracts. But Miller believed that agents, if properly trained, could fill a valuable role, particularly after players won the right to take their contract disputes to salary arbitration in 1973.

The union held meetings and educational seminars for agents and schooled them on contract language. Agents now had access to comparable salaries, and they were able to assess the market from a more broad-minded view than players. Miller believed that even a high-priced Wall Street lawyer, who might charge a whopping $400 an hour, would be worth the investment to a player.

Still, Miller was worried that the lure of a quick buck might attract a parade of fly-by-nights to the profession. It wasn't long before he heard reports of agents gouging players, charging commissions of up to 10 percent. And lord knows what their qualifications were. Miller began seeing strange, unfamiliar characters hanging around fields at spring training. "Who's that guy?" he inquired on more than one occasion.

Eventually, Miller came to regard himself as a sort of agent clearinghouse and industry watch dog. He'd plumb his sources for opinions and compile dossiers on agent misbehavior. In many cases, he found the agents too accommodating, too willing to roll over on a deal rather than buck ownership.

Even the most skilled agents weren't above scrutiny. Tom Reich, a Pittsburgh lawyer whom Miller liked and respected, was representing

Pirates outfielder Willie Stargell in free-agent talks one year. Miller had long regarded Stargell, one of baseball's premier sluggers, as underpaid. So he winced when he saw a newspaper quote from Reich saying how much Stargell loved Pittsburgh and wanted to remain a Pirate. Miller immediately placed a call to Reich's office and lectured him on the importance of leverage.

"For Christ's sake, Tom, what the hell are you doing?" Miller said. "If Stargell has a long-term contract and you want to talk about his feeling of loyalty to the city and the team, that's fine. It's good PR. But in the middle of negotiating, you're undercutting the interests of your client."

In the early days, an agent with foresight and energy could make a splash through word of mouth and hard work. And nobody was more enterprising than Jerry Kapstein, a Rhode Island native who showed at a young age that he was never at a loss for energy—or ideas.

At 15, Kapstein talked his way into keeping the scorebook for the Providence College basketball team. He later attended Harvard, where he introduced himself to broadcaster Keith Jackson during a Crimson football game and parlayed the association into work as a statistician for ABC Sports. It was young Jerry Kapstein who introduced time-of-possession and other stats that later became standard fare for TV football viewers.

Stories abound of Kapstein popping up, in Zelig-like fashion, in places you couldn't imagine. He was a broadcaster for the Providence Steamrollers at the world's first professional indoor football championship game in 1962 in Atlantic City. Ten years later, he worked briefly as a television commentator for the Baltimore Bullets, of Earl "The Pearl" Monroe and Wesley Unseld fame.

Kapstein's introduction to the agent world came in football. He represented his brother Dan, an aspiring tight end with the New England Patriots, and enjoyed it enough to branch out to baseball. The brothers Kapstein became a team, traveling to Florida for spring training, hustling for business and stretching their meager funds to the limit. The Kapsteins only had enough money to sleep in a hotel four nights a week, so they'd sleep the other three in Jerry's 1974 Grand Prix.

Kapstein's career began to take off when an old Navy friend introduced him to three Baltimore Orioles—Don Baylor, Bobby Grich, and Johnny Oates—who were amenable to his sales pitch. But he caught his big break with the advent of salary arbitration, which allowed him to exploit his encyclopedic grasp of facts and figures. In 1974, Kapstein and Charlie Finley spent 10 hours over 2 days debating the merits of Athletics pitcher Kenny Holtzman, in a tête-à-tête that rivaled a Nixon-Brezhnev summit for sheer intensity. Major League Baseball, sensing that the arbitration process might spiral out of control, put a time limit on arguments.

Kapstein loved to schmooze, and he tried to create an atmosphere in which both sides could feel positive about the result. "Jerry was very good at selling his position—that his player wanted to come to you, but there was a huge amount of interest," says Pat Gillick, former Toronto general manager. "He had a nice style of selling his client and making the bidders think there was a deep market for this guy."

After Kapstein beat Finley out of $26,000 in arbitration cases for Holtzman, Rollie Fingers, and Darold Knowles, his clientele grew exponentially, and he emerged as a sort of unavoidable force on the horizon. Even general managers who liked him personally grumbled about the crimp he put in their schedules. "Dammit, I used to be able to come to spring training and see my team," one executive told Kapstein. "Now I have to spend all this fucking time under the stadium talking contracts with you."

Larry Lucchino, then general counsel for the Orioles, came to know Kapstein well when they negotiated long-term contracts for pitcher Mike Flanagan and outfielder Al Bumbry. "Jerry, as I see it now, you've made several million dollars over the last month, and all I did was get my salary," Lucchino said during a break in negotiations. "What's wrong with this picture?"

Kapstein had once served in the Navy's Judge Advocate General's Corps, presiding over court-martials and other disciplinary matters, and his dealings as an agent had a certain military efficiency. By force of habit, he checked the chandeliers to make sure they weren't bugged upon entering a hotel room to talk contract, and he was a stickler for having the chairs positioned just so. "He would have made a great CIA agent," Don Baylor says.

General managers grew accustomed to seeing Kapstein in the same corduroy sportcoat and receiving phone calls from him with explicit, yet shadowy instructions. *Call me at 3:15 P.M.*, he would say. *I'll be at this phone booth at the corner of Eighth and Vine.* "Jerry didn't need much in the way of overhead," says Lucchino.

In the winter of 1976–77, when the free-agent market started percolating, Kapstein rented a room in the Hospital Trust Bank Building in Providence and turned his hometown into the hub of the baseball universe. Of the roughly 60 players who became free agents that year, nearly one-third were Kapstein clients, and the agent negotiated seven-figure deals for the likes of Baylor, Gene Tenace, Joe Rudi, and Montreal second baseman Dave Cash—the most appropriately named client in his stable.

Many of Kapstein's clients swore by him. When Baylor signed a 4-year, $3.6 million contract with the Yankees in 1982, Kapstein told him to forget the commission and invest the money in his son's college fund.

"He was a guy who'd lay down his life for you," Baylor says.

Yet as Kapstein stockpiled players and expanded his client base, other agents began to regard *him* as a Providence Steamroller of sorts. After pitcher Ed Figueroa won 16 games for California in 1975, agent Tony Attanasio charged him a $150 commission to negotiate his contract. Then Attanasio lost Figueroa to Kapstein, who worked out a multiyear deal for the pitcher with the Yankees.

Attanasio later cornered Figueroa in Texas to ask why he'd switched. "Well, Jerry told me you were only charging $50 an hour," Figueroa said. "He asked me, 'Would you go to a doctor and have your appendix taken out for $50?'" If Kapstein was charging more money, Figueroa believed, he *must* be doing a better job.

When Kapstein negotiated a sweet deal for a young Boston catcher named Carlton Fisk, Marvin Miller was impressed. But it didn't take Miller long to sour on the young mega-agent. He began receiving calls from players telling him that Kapstein was difficult to reach by phone.

Then Dick Moss, Miller's union lieutenant, watched Kapstein in an arbitration hearing and reported that Kapstein was obsessed with charts and exhibits in a "show-off" sort of way.

The following spring, Miller traveled to camps and gave players the lowdown. Jerry Kapstein, he told them, was spread too thin to properly service his clientele, and had a "damn know-it-all attitude."

The level of resistance that Miller encountered was testament to the loyalty that Kapstein inspired. At Boston's camp in Winter Haven, Florida, Carlton Fisk confronted Miller, and they had a heated exchange over the merits of Jerry Kapstein. When Miller gave the same speech in Bradenton, Pirates outfielder Richie Zisk passionately defended his agent's honor.

There might have been a touch of jealousy in Miller's anti-Kapstein crusade. Players who had formerly viewed themselves as "union guys" now made up a different band of brothers as "Jerry Kapstein guys." And while Miller was earning a modest salary as head of the Players Association, Kapstein, other agents, and the players were getting rich off a system he helped create.

Jerry Kapstein eventually drifted from the agent business into baseball management through family ties. He married San Diego Padres owner Joan Kroc's daughter, Linda, and was decertified by the union in 1989 for his links to management. Players Association lawyer Gene Orza claims that Kapstein never informed the union that he was overseeing the sale of the Padres—a professional conflict if there ever was one.

Some players, like former San Diego pitcher Rich "Goose" Gossage, thought Kapstein abandoned them by switching to management. When Gossage heard rumors that Kapstein might leave the agent business to work for the Padres, he told friends that it was impossible, because Jerry had never mentioned the possibility to him. Then the news came down, and Gossage felt a sense of betrayal that lingers to this day.

"Jerry Kapstein is a phony," Gossage says. "He had a reputable business, and he sold out all his players so he could nose up to Joan Kroc. He's just a big, power-hungry guy who had the limelight and can't stand to be without it."

In the 1990s, Kapstein drifted into obscurity and had an awakening of sorts. He got divorced, sought comfort in the Bible, and spent 8 years on the streets of San Diego working with the homeless, a world removed from his formerly fast-paced existence.

Then suddenly, in a flash, he was back. Larry Lucchino, his old negotiating counterpart in Baltimore, took over as Boston Red Sox president and hired Kapstein as a senior adviser. Kapstein, who now prefers to be called "Jeremy," is a visible presence at Fenway Park, as tight with the ushers and parking attendants as the front-office bigwigs.

Once the games begin, Kapstein has a seat directly behind home plate at Fenway. Whenever Goose Gossage turns on his TV and the Red Sox are playing, he sees his old friend, Jerry Kapstein, staring right back at him.

The lure of the agent business was so powerful that even Players Association officials couldn't resist. Dick Moss, who had spent a decade as Miller's assistant, left to represent players in 1977, and he eventually counted Nolan Ryan, Andre Dawson, and Jack Morris among his clientele.

Miller received several overtures of his own, the most notable coming on a flight from Chicago to New York in 1981, when Reggie Jackson asked him for help in free-agent talks with the Yankees. "I don't think Marvin would have ever wrung out the rag and squeezed out every nickel," says Jackson, now a special adviser to Yankees owner George Steinbrenner. "Marvin was about fairness. He just wasn't in a position to be able to do it."

Even though Miller was close to stepping down as head of the union, he declined Jackson's request because of the hypocrisy involved: After criticizing union officials in other sports for representing individual players, how could he profit by favoring the interests of a few over the membership at large?

And even without Marvin Miller's involvement, players had plenty of options in their search for quality representation. In the 1970s and '80s, men who would become giants in the profession began flocking to it, from all walks of life, in a frenzy reminiscent of the California gold rush.

Some had baseball in their genes. In the mid-1960s, Tony Attanasio was a scrappy, mouthy second baseman for a Portland Beavers Triple-A team that included Luis Tiant and Tommy John. Attanasio returned home each winter to his hometown of Stamford, Connecticut, and handed out trophies to a hotshot youth league ballplayer named Bobby Valentine. Years later, when Valentine turned pro, he hired Attanasio as his agent.

Dennis "Go Go" Gilbert was a struggling minor-league outfielder in Jamestown, New York, when manager Jackie Moore was forced to release him. When Gilbert offered to play for free, Moore shook his head. "Sorry, Go Go," he said. "I need the uniform." Gilbert went into real estate and became a prominent agent. Several years later, he took his old manager to lunch and picked up Moore in front of the hotel in a Rolls Royce.

The Hendricks brothers, Randy and Alan, built a thriving agent practice in football before meeting Cleveland Indians pitcher Fritz Peterson at a real estate investment seminar in 1975. The Hendrickses wore cowboy boots and jeans, and they became known for their good-cop, bad-cop routine. "Alan would come in and schmooze and laugh and slap backs and lay things out," says Tony Siegle, a long-time front office executive. "Then Randy would come in and wallop you with a club."

Jim Bronner was a successful lawyer in Chicago and Bob Gilhooley was in the marketing business when they were riding a commuter train and saw a newspaper story in which Marvin Miller complained about the growing abuses among baseball player agents. *We could do this*, they agreed. They began by representing Cubs pitcher Steve Stone, a family relative of Gilhooley's, and he passed them along to teammates Rick Reuschel and Bruce Sutter. When the firm won a $700,000 salary arbitration award for Sutter in 1980, Bronner and Gilhooley no longer had to rely on relatives to find clients.

David Sloane, the son of a Russian immigrant and labor union activist, began representing athletes by negotiating a professional basketball contract for a friend at Arizona State University. Not long thereafter, he was dealing with sports franchise owners and discovering, to his amusement, that F. Scott Fitzgerald was right about the very rich: They are different from you and me.

Charlie Finley, the eccentric, colorful Oakland A's owner, certainly was different. Oakland players used to joke that they knew Finley was lying when he cleared his throat. But Sloane found him to be candid to a fault. In 1975, Sloane represented Stanford catcher Bruce Robinson, who asked for $50,000 and a Porsche as the team's number-one draft pick. "Tell him to Porsche it up his ass," Finley said. Another time, Finley, exasperated by the lack of progress in negotiations, told Sloane to "take a flying fuck at a galloping goose."

Ted Turner, Atlanta Braves owner, media baron, yachtsman, philanthropist, and future husband of Jane Fonda, was also a trip. In 1977, Turner invited Sloane to the Braves' suite at the Los Angeles Hilton to discuss John "The Count" Montefusco, a pitcher that Sloane was representing at the time. They were sitting down to breakfast, Sloane recalls, when Turner offered to flip a coin with the Mexican busboy over the bill. When Turner lost and tried to go double-or-nothing, the busboy, who barely spoke English, stood wide-eyed and on the verge of panic. But that wasn't even close to the weirdest part.

Midway through the meeting Turner remarked, "Oh, I didn't do my jogging today," and stood up in his suit and wing-tipped shoes and ran several laps around the table before stopping. "Screw it," he said. "I might as well sit down and eat."

Sloane figured any guy with a billion dollars was entitled to act however he wanted in the privacy of his hotel suite. But he still had to bite his lip. "It was insane," Sloane says. "I was just sitting there trying to eat my eggs and keep it together and not bust up and look like I'd seen a ghost or something."

While owners could be eccentric, front-office men often bordered on hostile. The hard-liners, like Detroit's Jim Campbell and Boston's Haywood Sullivan, thought agents were sticking their noses where they didn't belong, and commiserated over this unfortunate turn of events. Others were downright scared of the agents, with their briefcases and college degrees. Milwaukee general manager Jim Baumer referred to agents and their "blue oxford shirts," as if an entire class of people could be characterized by their wardrobe choices. And it was common knowledge that Frank Cashen, who ran the Orioles and later the Mets, loathed Dick Moss. According to one contemporary, Cashen swore off Moss's clients for eternity.

Players who retained agents in the early days found that it could be hazardous to their job security. Don Money, the former Phillies infielder, brought an agent into the room with him, and general manager John Quinn escorted the guy right out the door before resuming his discussion with Money. The converse also applied. When Kansas City signed role player John "Duke" Wathan to a particularly generous contract, some observers thought that Wathan had helped his cause by negotiating the deal *sans* agent.

The more enlightened executives could see the wave of the future and were more accommodating. Lou Gorman, a former Navy officer who ran teams in Kansas City, Seattle, and Boston, had such a teddy bear quality that agents ranked him as their favorite front-office executive in a poll taken by the *Sporting News*. Even when the Hendricks brothers made his life hell in the spring of 1987, convincing Roger Clemens to pack his bags and leave Boston's spring training camp in a contract dispute, Gorman realized that the brothers shared his desire to get a deal done.

Some others, he wasn't so sure about.

"A contract negotiation should be a give-and-take, a win-win," Gorman says. "But some agents don't negotiate. They demand. They're immutable. They're like talking to the wall. You can't deal with those kinds of people. When an agent comes in you want to say, 'Okay, here's our common ground. I think this. What do you think about that?' Then you try and work it out. Now *that's* a negotiation."

The agent-player relationship is also rooted in trust, and this, too, can be a source of problems because players place so much faith in men who seem to have their best interests at heart but are often on a power-tripping agenda.

The truly unscrupulous have the power to ruin lives. In the 1970s and '80s, a junior college professor named LaRue Harcourt attracted a large following of players with his upbeat persona and boundless energy. His clients swore by him until he began investing in airplane-leasing deals and other shaky investments under the guise of tax shelters. Rick Wise, Bill Campbell, Ken Reitz, Don Sutton, Bob Forsch, and Bert Blyleven were among the players who got burned, to one extent or another, by Harcourt's fraudulent schemes. After losing millions of dollars for more than a dozen players, Harcourt was working behind the counter at a Yorba Linda, California, liquor store in 1987.

Bob Woolf, who craved the limelight, represented celebrities ranging from TV personality Larry King to Boston Celtics star Larry Bird before dying of a heart attack in 1993. Only then did reports surface of problems in his kingdom. Clients came forward to file lawsuits and complain about excessive commissions, failed investments, and conflicts of interest—a series of bad news items that stained Woolf's legacy and reputation.

Joe Rudi, the former Oakland outfielder, considers his former agent, Jerry Kapstein, "one of the most honest people I've ever met." Kapstein always told Rudi that he didn't want to get involved with handling a player's money because it was such a conflict. But Rudi came to discover that several prominent agents recommended their players to specific financial advisers and received kickbacks for the referrals.

"I met several super-big agents, who are still big agents to this day, that I wouldn't trust with a dime," Rudi says.

Padres outfielder Tony Gwynn was in the prime of his career in 1987 when he declared bankruptcy because of bad investments and the misconduct of his agent, Lew Muller, who had bailed on some six-figure bank loans that were co-signed by Gwynn. After firing Muller, Gwynn turned to John Boggs, who had previously worked as a marketer for Steve Garvey. They drove home together from the ballpark the night Gwynn filed his Chapter 7 petition, and Boggs gave him a pep talk.

"We're going to get through this together," Boggs told Gwynn. "I guarantee you that you will never, ever put yourself in this position again." Nearly two decades later, Gwynn and Boggs are still together.

In recent years, several big leaguers have taken a more activist approach to all facets of their business dealings. Jamie Moyer, Curt Schilling, Matt Morris, and Gary Sheffield are among the prominent players who have negotiated their own contracts, with only the help of a lawyer to peruse the language. Morris, who valued his relationship with St. Louis general manager Walt Jocketty and manager Tony LaRussa, was hesitant to have an agent push too hard in contract talks and make him feel like a "schmuck" in the clubhouse. So he negotiated a 3-year, $27 million deal before the 2002 season, with relatively little sweat.

"We just FedExed a couple copies to each other, talked on the phone a little bit, and it was done," Morris says. "Not to make light of it, but it reminded me of trying to get a date in high school, you know?" When the union lawyers observed that Morris was selling himself short coming off a 22-win season and driving down the price for 15-game winners, he was unsympathetic. *Tell them to win more games*, he thought.

Matt Morris didn't need an agent to book his plane tickets, pay his bills, get him Metallica tickets, or bolster his confidence during losing streaks. But many of his peers weren't so independent-minded. The average ballplayer is wracked by the same self-doubt as everyone else but works in an environment that's not very tolerant of weakness. To concede that weakness to your wife might violate the code of "macho." To confide in teammates . . . well . . . it might not be something you want floating around the clubhouse. So you call your agent and unburden yourself to him.

And when difficult times arrive or tragedy strikes, you expect that he'll be there. When St. Louis pitcher Daryl Kile died suddenly of a heart ailment in a Chicago hotel room at age 33, his agent, Barry Axelrod, assisted with the funeral arrangements and helped Kile's widow, Flynn, carry on with three small children. When Dennis Eckersley entered the Hall of Fame in 2004, he credited his agent, the late Ed Keating, with helping him overcome alcoholism. Eckersley has described Keating as a "father, uncle, brother, and friend."

One of Keating's other clients was Curtis Leskanic, a free-spirited pitcher who's played for several big-league clubs. Leskanic was with the Colorado Rockies in 1996 when Keating died of cancer, and the void in his life was palpable. He interviewed nearly 10 companies before replacing Keating with Jim Turner, a veteran St. Louis agent who impressed him as both a smart businessman and a potential lifelong friend.

"You know what I wanted most in an agent?" Leskanic says. "I wanted somebody that I can put in a headlock and give a noogie to." Sure enough, one night, player and agent had pizza and a few beers after a game in Chicago, and Leskanic gave Turner a headlock-noogie combination on the way back to the hotel.

The best agents help players help themselves, and the big leaguers who find them consider themselves fortunate. Clint Hurdle, a former Kansas City prospect who never lived up to his early promise, hired Ron Shapiro in 1977 on the basis of a batting cage recommendation from Brooks Robinson. Over the next 25 years, Shapiro was with Hurdle through signings, releases, marriage, divorce, and children—including the arrival of a daughter with a birth defect.

"After my father, Ron Shapiro has been as influential as any man in my life," Hurdle says.

Hurdle looks at agents and some of them remind him of Mr. Haney, the old Pat Buttram *Green Acres* character who was bound and determined to sell you something you didn't need. But Shapiro wasn't a huckster or an enabler.

When Hurdle asked for help with his taxes, Shapiro handed him a worksheet and showed him how to figure it out himself. And when Hurdle began managing in Colorado and it came time for contract talks, he attended one of the negotiating seminars that Shapiro holds regularly for corporate executives.

Armed with the Shapiro mantra of "Prepare, Probe, Propose," Hurdle walked into Colorado general manager Dan O'Dowd's office and negotiated a 2-year contract with 2 option years. It was a win-win resolution, and he had his agent to thank for it.

"It goes back to the Biblical thing," Hurdle says. "If you want somebody to fish, are you going to give them a fish or teach them how to fish? Ron teaches you how to fish."

As the move toward corporatization gained momentum, it became harder to find old-school mom-and-pop agents like Tony Attanasio or Tommy Tanzer, who took the business so to heart that they'd negotiate your deal and become part of the family. Feisty by nature and inclined toward profane, stream-of-consciousness rants when angered, the 5'5" Tanzer embodied what one baseball man called a classic case of "little man's syndrome." But he provided great entertainment value, and when other agents saw him get in the face of guys like Boras and Moorad, some got a vicarious thrill. "Tommy Tanzer is the only guy in this business with any balls," says one.

The son of a middle-class Pittsburgh family, Tanzer was teaching school in Utah in the early 1980s when he decided to enter the sports agent business. As a diminutive bundle of energy and idealism, he was right at home in the classroom. "I could teach math to a rock," he says. Tanzer was also a union representative, and management quickly came to regard him as formidable in contract talks.

But the politics of teaching overwhelmed Tanzer, and he grew disillusioned and decided one day that he'd like to represent athletes for a living. Through the help of Les Zittrain, a family friend from Pittsburgh who represented Terry Bradshaw, Mean Joe Greene, and Pete Maravich in the 1970s, Tanzer had lunch with Utah Jazz coach Frank Layden. They hit it off, and Layden told him, "Sure, you can represent me."

It wasn't much of a gig. Layden, a regular guy known for his lovable-fat-man shtick, was content with doing endorsements for R. C. Willey furniture at $1,500 a pop. Tanzer clearly aspired to more, so Layden, as a favor, referred him to some basketball players at Brigham Young and the University of Utah. It was an instant wakeup call for the 33-year-old schoolteacher.

"Frank would introduce me to these 19-year-old Mormon boys who didn't shave yet, and they'd ask me for $10,000 and tell me I could represent them," Tanzer recalls. "I had kids say, 'The guy here this morning offered $25,000 but I like you better. If you give me 10, you're my guy.'

"I was like, 'Uhhh, I don't know what you're talking about.' And they'd pat me on the head and tell me, 'When you grow up and learn what the world is like, come back and talk to us.'"

Baseball ultimately provided a more realistic and bribe-free route. During the 1984 Olympics in Los Angeles, Tanzer saw agent Barry Axelrod speak at a seminar at UCLA. Tanzer introduced himself, and Axelrod recalled how he'd met pitcher Rick Sutcliffe in the minor leagues. Axelrod helped Sutcliffe with his equipment, taxes, and some personal business, and a few years later, Sutcliffe won a Cy Young Award with the Chicago Cubs. That sounded a lot more appealing than condescending pats on the head from 6'11" power forwards looking for payouts.

Tanzer decided to chuck his teaching career, but he needed a financial stake. His parents had sold the family clothing store back home in Pittsburgh, and there was some money in that. His brother Peter, a doctor, was kind enough to lend him $40,000, and in the summer of 1985, Tanzer bought a Chevy van and outfitted it like a small apartment—with a generator, microwave, toilet, shower, hot water heater, two beds, and a computer. It was just him, his wife, and their cat, Lady Samantha, who would return from periodic wanderings, jump on the roof, and start scratching when she wanted to be let in for the night.

Tanzer's brother kept lending him $40,000 in dribs and drabs, until the total due surpassed $400,000. Tanzer, in return, hustled like a maniac, visiting camp after camp and collecting clients like toll receipts. He signed up Charlie Hayes and John Burkett in the early years, then Steve Finley and Dave Hollins and Dante Bichette. It was easier in those days, before the competition became so outrageous.

When pitcher Les Lancaster made it to the majors with the Cubs in 1987, it was a proud moment for Tanzer. The low point came 3 years later, when it sunk in that no matter how diligently he tended to his players' needs, there was no guarantee that they'd stay with him. After first baseman Lee Stevens left him for the Beverly Hills Sports Council, Tanzer confronted Dennis Gilbert in a parking lot. He shoved his client list in Gilbert's face, essentially challenging him to steal the rest.

The more customary it became for agents to steal from each other, the harder they all had to work in the name of client service. For Dennis Gilbert, it meant going out on a fishing boat with Mike Piazza and Jose Canseco even though he didn't fish, or trekking into the mountains with Bret Saberhagen on a bear-hunting expedition even though he'd never shot a gun in his life. An agent had to do what an agent had to do.

For Tommy Tanzer, it meant glimpsing the miracle of childbirth almost by accident. In September 1995, Tanzer was at Jack Murphy Stadium to watch the San Diego Padres when his cell phone rang during batting practice. It was Steve Finley's wife, Amy, with news that she was going into labor.

Tanzer flagged down Finley, and they quickly drove two exits to the nearest hospital. Finley insisted that his agent accompany him into the delivery room, and before Tommy Tanzer knew it, he was a witness to the blessed event.

"There's music playing, then we're listening to the game, and Amy goes into the throes of these contractions and just goes berserk," Tanzer recalls. "Then she comes out of it in about 20 seconds and says, 'What did I miss? Are the bases still loaded? Did we score?' And I'm like, 'Does anybody want a pizza? Does anybody want something to drink?' I was trying my ass off to get out of there."

Here's the really amazing part: Little Reed Finley entered the world in barely 2 hours, so his dad had time to hustle back to Jack Murphy with his agent and play an inning in center field. For the record, Steve Finley went hitless in one at-bat in a 6–3 victory over the Phillies.

Nine years later, Finley remains a productive player at age 39, and his agent is taking a step away from the insanity. In 2004, Tommy Tanzer decides to sell his agency to Alan Nero of CSMG, one of the big all-purpose firms. Tanzer will continue representing the same clients under a new umbrella. But he's so tired of the backstabbing, the client-stealing, and the nasty downward turn the business has taken, he'd prefer to let someone else deal with the major headaches.

The world just isn't very kind to mom-and-pops these days, although a few years ago Tanzer received a call from a pleasant young guy in California who was just starting out as an agent and seemed sincere about making it work. It was heartening to know that the breed wasn't completely extinct.

Can Matt Sosnick make a go of it? Sure, says Tommy Tanzer. But in the immortal words of Jeff Moorad, it's not a profession for nice guys.

"It was hard enough when I started out, and you needed a combination of resources and hard work and luck to succeed," Tanzer says. "Now you need one more thing—the teeth to keep all these other guys away from you."

Chapter
NINE

Matt is amused that many of his friends, accomplished professionals with a passing interest in sports, think he's hit the mother lode with Dontrelle Willis. They assume that since Dontrelle can't cross the street or stroll through a mall without attracting a crowd, his agent must be capitalizing on his fame.

Here's the reality: After making chicken scratch in the minors, Dontrelle earned the prorated portion of the rookie minimum salary of $300,000 in his first season with the Marlins. The agent receives none of that because it's the minimum.

The second year won't be much better. Under the baseball labor agreement, a player needs between 2 and 3 years of big-league service time before he's eligible to have his salary determined by a three-member panel in arbitration. Dodgers reliever Eric Gagne, who earned $550,000 in 2003, goes to arbitration in February 2004 with Scott Boras in his corner. If Gagne wins his case, he'll get a raise to $8 million. But he loses and has to *settle* for the team's offer of $5 million, and concern is rampant that his feelings might have been hurt in the process.

The stakes are comparatively miniscule for Dontrelle Willis, who still resides in a service category where he has to take what he can get. But that doesn't prevent his agent from giving it his best shot. Sosnick plans to wow the Marlins with details of Dontrelle's impact on the team's championship season, and the 14–6 record and 3.30 earned run average are only part of the equation.

In Dontrelle's 15 appearances at home during his rookie year, the Marlins drew an average of 21,643 fans per game. When he wasn't pitching, attendance dipped to 14,826. Slice and dice the figures, and the Marlins drew an extra 102,255 fans with Dontrelle on the mound. Those people all have to pay to park and buy nachos and sodas and game programs. Every smile and high-five from Dontrelle Willis, in essence, put money in owner Jeffrey Loria's pocket.

The team designed a special ticket package for him, the Dontrelle Willis Flex Pack, and sold a raft of No. 35 jerseys in the team store. Matt figures that the Marlins earned an extra $2.5 million off of Dontrelle in ticket sales and pocketed an additional $500,000 in merchandising revenue generated by him. Sosnick also factors in the gobs of publicity from local TV news shows and the national headlines and "goodwill" that Dontrelle helped generate for a franchise that's generally considered a poor stepchild to the NFL Miami Dolphins.

So, Matt approaches the Marlins in early 2004 with reams of data and pleas for "fairness," in hopes that the team will see his side. General manager Larry Beinfest is tending to other business, so Sosnick spends most of his time dickering with Michael Hill, Florida's assistant general manager.

Hill, a Harvard graduate, is on the move. In 2003, he was named to *Black Enterprise* magazine's "Hot List" as one of the best and brightest African-Americans under age 40. Michael Hill is a smart guy, for sure, but he spends too much time spouting the company line for Matt and Paul's tastes. In several conversations, Hill explains that the system assures that Dontrelle will make his money down the road if he remains healthy, productive, and patient. Sosnick counters by trying to apply the minimal leverage at his disposal. There are consequences,

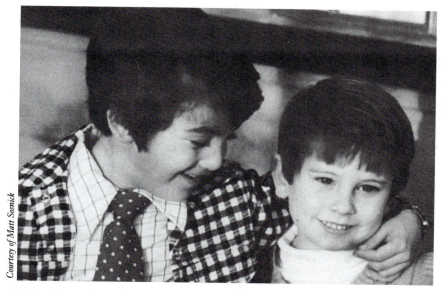

Matt Sosnick *(left)* and Paul Cobbe as childhood friends in Saratoga, California.

Sosnick and Cobbe nearly 30 years later, as 50-50 partners in a growing baseball agency.

Pitchers Dontrelle Willis and Jon Pridie pledged allegiance to Sosnick-Cobbe Sports by getting tattoos of the agency logo on their arms.

"It was like death," Joyce Guy-Harris said of Dontrelle's Fort Mustang when she saw it after his accident.

Dontrelle's deceptive pitching motion gave big-league hitters fits when they first saw him in the summer of 2003.

Dontrelle and Matt engaged in some good-natured role reversal at a Halloween party in 2002.

Sosnick client Mike Hinckley went 9-5 with a 3.64 ERA for the Class A Savannah Sand Gnats in 2003.

Just three years out of Moore High School in Oklahoma, Hinckley has emerged as the Washington Nationals' top prospect.

Paul Cobbe with his wife, Ellen, daughter Alexandra, and the baby, Rachel, in late 2004.

Mike Hinckley, Adam Donachie, Matt Sosnick, Paul Cobbe, Mike Wood, and Dontrelle Willis at the 2005 Orange Bowl in Miami.

Scott Boras, lawyer and former minor-league infielder, has built baseball's most prominent agency from scratch.

Scott Boras with a famous former client—San Francisco Giants slugger Barry Bonds.

New York Yankees scout Fay Thompson, pitcher Jeff Marquez, and Matt Sosnick after the 2004 June draft.

Cory Dunlap, drafted in the third round by Los Angeles, hit .351 in the Pioneer League in his first professional season.

he warns, to taking a hard-line approach with the spiritual heart of the team.

"Do you know how many times Dontrelle showed up somewhere or was on a commercial or signed stuff for the team?" Matt asks Hill. "If you're not willing in good faith to compensate him for that, you're never going to compensate him for anything.

"He'll sign for whatever you want. But we'll charge you $25,000 or $50,000 every time you want him to sign extra baseballs for a promotion, every time you want him to do anything. I guarantee you, Dontrelle will not make one appearance for you off the field. Not one."

The decision to reward or risk offending a player with minimal service time is up to the club, and there are precedents for teams to be either generous or dismissive when they're in a position of strength. Nomar Garciaparra, Kerry Wood, and Albert Pujols are among the players who received more than garden-variety salary bumps after big rookie years. Eric Gagne, in contrast, was 2 years into his career and establishing himself as baseball's most dominant closer in 2003 when the Dodgers unilaterally renewed his contract for $550,000—about $250,000 less than the figure Boras wanted.

So it can go either way. The key is understanding that business decisions should not be taken personally—yet another piece of wisdom from the *Godfather* agent handbook.

Encinal coach Jim Saunders sensed that Dontrelle Willis was on the cusp of big things in January 2003, when the precocious lefty dropped by practice and threw the ball so hard in the bullpen, he brought the rhythms of a winter workout to a standstill. Dontrelle was throwing at maybe 80 percent of capacity, and the ball was hissing and the catcher's mitt was popping with such authority that all activity ceased and the entire roster came over to watch.

The kid won't be in the minors for long, not with that kind of stuff, Saunders thought.

Dontrelle, grateful just to be on a ball field again after the auto accident, exceeded his quota of joie de vivre in spring training. The equipment manager handed him a No. 77 jersey—offensive lineman territory—but Dontrelle didn't stay anonymous for long. In a March game at Melbourne, he was standing on first base when teammate Juan Pierre laid down a bunt that was bobbled by the infielder, then thrown awry. The D-Train chugged around the bases only to be thrown out by 10 feet. He punctuated his journey with a headfirst slide, a coronary-inducing breach of etiquette for a pitcher.

"Nice slide, kid," the umpire said, raising a knotted fist, "but you're out."

Dontrelle got up, dusted himself off, and encountered a faceful of manager Jeff Torborg, who told him to tone it down immediately. Torborg read *Baseball America* like everybody else, and he knew that Willis was too valuable a commodity to be risking injury in a meaningless game in a cow pasture in Florida. "Kid, I'm a big fan of yours," Torborg admonished, "but if you do that again, I will fine you $1,000." The threat resonated, given that Dontrelle was accustomed to making $850 a month in the minors.

Although the other Marlins gave Dontrelle the obligatory mock–cold shoulder when he returned to the dugout, they could feel his energy like a refreshing gust of wind. They didn't begrudge Dontrelle his enthusiasm or consider him a hot dog because his love for the game was so palpably, undeniably real.

The day after his headfirst slide, Dontrelle walked into the clubhouse and his teammates jokingly referred to him as "Stunt Double." The nickname stuck for the rest of spring training. "He's a full-size bobble-head out there," Brad Arnsberg, Florida's pitching coach, told the *Miami Herald*.

While Torborg lobbied to keep the kid, the Marlins took the cautious approach and sent Dontrelle to Zebulon, North Carolina, home of the Double-A Mudcats, to begin the season. Dontrelle's first six starts proved that he was destined for bigger things than the Southern

League. He went 4–0 with a 1.49 ERA, and circumstances soon conspired to advance his timetable. Three Florida starters went down with injuries, and by the time assistant GM Jim Fleming called Zebulon to tell Double-A manager Tracy Woodson that Willis was an option, the Marlins were out of Plan Bs and Cs.

Carolina was playing a road game in Orlando, Florida, at Disney's Wide World of Sports Complex, when Woodson and Mudcats pitching coach Reid Cornelius gave Dontrelle the news that would change his life forever.

"Albuquerque is great in May," Woodson said. "It's beautiful out there."

Dontrelle's face lit up when it dawned on him that he was headed for Triple-A ball—just a step from The Show.

"But you're not going there," Woodson said. "You're starting Friday night in Miami."

The initial numbness soon morphed into a sense of shared jubilation. One by one, the Mudcats lined up to hug Dontrelle and wish him the best. One of the happiest Carolina players, Billy Hall, was a former Korean Leaguer still waiting for a big-league shot at 33. Billy Hall cut Dontrelle's hair in the clubhouse, and Dontrelle affectionately referred to him as "Pops."

On Dontrelle's big day, Hall pulled him aside and provided quiet words of encouragement. "Act like you belong," Hall told him, "and just be yourself."

When the shock wore off, Dontrelle began fretting about logistics. There were only 2 days until his debut, and he wondered how Joyce would make it across country in time. Should he put her on a bus or a train from San Francisco? Even with his new $300,000 salary, he was too accustomed to economizing to consider splurging.

"I have to hurry up and pay for it now, because she has to be able to get there,'" Dontrelle told his manager.

Tracy Woodson couldn't help but laugh. "Dude," he said, "you're going to *fly* your mom to Florida."

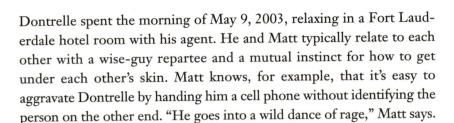

Dontrelle spent the morning of May 9, 2003, relaxing in a Fort Lauderdale hotel room with his agent. He and Matt typically relate to each other with a wise-guy repartee and a mutual instinct for how to get under each other's skin. Matt knows, for example, that it's easy to aggravate Dontrelle by handing him a cell phone without identifying the person on the other end. "He goes into a wild dance of rage," Matt says.

Sosnick's weak spot is his compulsive neatness. At his Burlingame duplex, he keeps several coffee table books stacked just so on a glass table in his living room. When Matt leaves the room, Dontrelle and his friends will shift a book an inch this way or that and wait to see how long it takes before he notices.

"Maybe we'll get a drink and we won't use a coaster," Mazonie Franklin says. "Every time we go over there, we test his patience."

On the morning of Dontrelle's major-league debut, Matt tried to maintain a sense of normalcy while deferring to the momentousness of the occasion. He tried to coax Dontrelle into taking a walk to work off the nerves, but Dontrelle would have none of it.

"I'm just going to stay here in the room," Dontrelle said, "and be Incog-negro."

Matt solved the bus-train dilemma by paying for Joyce Guy-Harris to fly to Florida, and she walked onto the field at Pro Player Stadium with her sister Sharon and her nephew. Her mind flashed back to Dontrelle's boyhood, when he pretended he was Dave Stewart, firing tennis balls off the wall of the Taylor Avenue apartment.

Dontrelle was so nervous warming up before his start against Colorado, he couldn't throw a strike in the bullpen. But once the National Anthem played and his left spike pushed off the rubber, muscle memory took over and everything clicked into place.

Ever since the car accident, Dontrelle had made a habit of dropping to one knee, saying a silent prayer, and pointing to the sky before throwing his first pitch. It was a moment to put things in perspective, catch a deep breath, and refocus. And it served him well.

Dontrelle retired his first major-league batter, Chris Stynes, on a grounder to shortstop, and ended the inning by inducing Todd Helton to bounce into a double play. He finished with 93 pitches in six innings, and the Marlins won 5–4. The most important thing was that he pitched well enough to assure there would be a next time.

Two days later, the Marlins were 16–22 and fourth in the National League East when Jeffrey Loria got serious. The Marlins fired their manager and pitching coach, Torborg and Arnsberg, and replaced them with 72-year-old Jack McKeon and minor-league pitching coordinator Wayne Rosenthal. McKeon, a cigar-smoking turnaround specialist, ultimately received much of the credit after the Marlins went 75–49 for the rest of the regular season and beat the Yankees in the World Series. He had a gruff demeanor and a take-no-guff approach that resonated with the players, and an obliviousness to detail that kept the team loose. But in September and early October, when the Marlins sensed they had a special team with a title shot, many of them cited Dontrelle Willis's arrival from Carolina as the turning point in the season. Given Dontrelle's lack of experience and tender age—21 years and 4 months—the Marlins hoped he could help them stay afloat until Josh Beckett and Mark Redman returned from the disabled list. In hindsight, they seriously underestimated him.

The motion that Dontrelle Willis concocted to deceive his neighborhood friends was equally confounding to big-league hitters the first time they saw it. Even the best hitters were at a disadvantage if they couldn't find the ball, and many were unable to start their swings until it was too late. The baseball, wrote Ross Newhan of the *Los Angeles Times*, came out of Dontrelle Willis's hand "as if launched from a camouflaged silo."

Dontrelle went 1–1 with a 7.07 earned run average in his first three starts in Florida, then kicked it into gear. He beat Cincinnati in consecutive starts and shut out Oakland at Pro Player Stadium. In June, he tossed a one-hitter to beat Tom Glavine and the New York Mets 1–0. Then he followed up with a complete-game shutout to beat Tampa Bay. As the All-Star Game approached, he was generating a momentum that seemed impossible to stop.

His teammates could sense something special was happening, and they embraced it. First baseman Derrek Lee bought Dontrelle some suits, and one day, outfielder Todd Hollandsworth came over to shag fly balls and shoot the breeze. Hollandsworth, a 9-year veteran, told Dontrelle he was proud of him for handling his sudden fame so well. "You don't even realize what kind of impact you're having on people," he said.

Reporters tracked down Vida Blue and Mark "The Bird" Fidrych for perspective. Blue, who'd had a similarly meteoric rise as a kid pitcher with Oakland in the '70s, also threw with a contorted motion that defied convention. Fidrych went 19–9 for the Detroit Tigers in 1976, started the All-Star Game, and quickly attained rock-star status for his animated mound antics. Female admirers lingered at the barber shop to scoop up souvenir locks of Fidrych's frizzy hair, and a Michigan state legislator submitted a resolution recommending that his $16,500 salary be increased. The Bird appeared in *Rolling Stone* magazine and made some money on the side doing commercials for Aqua Velva aftershave.

It all came tumbling down in a flash. In 1977, Fidrych hurt his shoulder, and by 1980, he was out of baseball. Twenty years later, he appeared at the occasional autograph show or baseball legends game just for old times' sake, but he paid the mortgage doing construction work with his 10-wheel dump truck.

Fidrych, a walking example of how fame can go south, was asked what advice he might give Dontrelle Willis in the summer of 2003. "What would I tell that kid?" Fidrych said. "Be polite, and don't be afraid to ask questions. He's got a good road ahead of him. Hopefully he keeps his head straight."

When the 2003 All-Star Game rosters were announced and Dontrelle wasn't chosen, there was a national backlash. Of more than 150,000 voters in an ESPN.com poll, 49 percent said Willis was the overlooked player they'd most like to see in the game. He received more votes than Pedro Martinez, Sammy Sosa, and Roger Clemens combined. In a media conference call, Fox broadcaster Tim McCarver said baseball was missing an opportunity to market itself to younger fans by leaving Dontrelle off the National League roster. "He's as charismatic as anybody in the game," McCarver said.

Baseball eventually reached the same conclusion and, through a series of injuries and machinations, found a way to send Dontrelle to Chicago. NL manager Dusty Baker warmed him up in the bullpen in the late innings, but Dontrelle never appeared in the game.

Still, the extent of his popularity and the obligations of fame were gradually becoming evident. More frequently, Dontrelle would step outside his hotel room, hear footsteps close behind, and turn to find a fan or three following him down the street. In St. Louis, he was standing outside the team hotel with his girlfriend when the valet pulled up and shouted, "Hey, you're Dontrelle Willis!"

At the All-Star media session, he filled more notebooks than any National Leaguer but Barry Bonds. And when he returned to the Westin hotel from the Players Association party on the eve of the game, the fans behind the barricade on Delaware Street were thrilled to see him.

An autograph seeker hailed him for a signature, and Dontrelle turned and explained that it had been a long day and he was heading upstairs to sleep.

"Yeah, that's right," the fan yelled. "You owe us!"

Even on the streets of Alameda, there's such a thing as etiquette. Dontrelle walked across the street, looked the offender in the eye and proclaimed, "I'm signing for every single person—except you." And as the crowd broke out in nervous laughter, he applied a distinctive "D. W." to every baseball card, ball, and game program but one.

Twenty minutes later, Dontrelle relinquished his pen and waved to his loud-mouthed antagonist. "Have a nice night," he said, as he walked into the Westin lobby.

While average Joes derived a thrill from meeting Dontrelle, the little boy in Dontrelle felt a tingle from meeting Joe Torre and Frank Robinson. The Marlins played the Expos in Montreal, and Robinson, a product of McClymonds High in Oakland, signed a baseball for him. Torre, four-time World Championship manager of the Yankees, shook hands with him at the All-Star Game and told him, "Don't stop smiling."

Dontrelle's new status also gave him access to celebrities from the non-AARP ranks. The tennis-playing Williams sisters, Venus and Serena, became regulars at Marlins games in the postseason. At the World Series, Spike Lee asked how he kicked his leg so high and Dontrelle responded, "Can I be in one of your movies?" On a trip to New York, Dontrelle met the rapper Jay-Z, who jokingly asked him, "Why you trying to beat my Yankees?"

While Dontrelle shrugged embarrassedly over the notion that he was somehow famous, it was inevitable that others came to regard him that way. Although he disdained the concept of an "entourage" of old school buddies and hangers-on, he began to understand why the truly famous might feel the need.

"People think that's part of the 'being famous kit.' You get a nice little chain and five or six guys," Dontrelle says. "But 9 times out of 10, it's just to be safe." One day, he rode the subway in New York City and later told his friend C. C. Sabathia, a young Cleveland pitcher with 2½ years of major-league experience, about his urban adventure. Sabathia up-braided him for his recklessness. "You can't be running around town like that," he told Dontrelle. "People know who you are, dude."

People close to Dontrelle, by extension, basked in the glow of his fame. Kim, his girlfriend, wore a T-shirt with Dontrelle's picture around campus at San Jose State University. And Joyce reveled in her newfound acclaim as the D-Train's mom. She'd go to the park and just like that, Dave Winfield or Benito Santiago would come up and want to chat about her boy.

One day, Joyce received a call from one of those "extreme makeover" shows, where people undergo plastic surgery for the sake of self-improvement and Nielsen ratings. She tactfully declined, in part because she didn't want to make a spectacle of herself. "I'm a 6-foot-tall, 250-pound black woman," Joyce says. "It's not like you're not going to see me or know who I am." She knew her penchant for dressing colorfully and behaving in a loud or overly gregarious manner in public would occasionally embarrass her son. "I don't want you to be poolside conversation," Dontrelle told her, but she knew the objections were rooted more in protectiveness and love than in self-consciousness.

Joyce Guy-Harris also knew that no matter how hard she tried to protect her son, there were times when he had to experience life for himself. Harold Willis's emergence from the distant past was one of those occasions.

Joyce, by her admission, hasn't had the best of luck with men. She was in her early twenties, just back from her Army stint, when she married Harold Willis. He was a product of Houston's Third Ward, a place where toughness was a prerequisite. Harold played football at Texas Southern University and served in the Navy before trying and failing to make it as a defensive back in the NFL. He was charming in his own way, but he and Joyce argued in the car all the way to and from their honeymoon in Reno, and it was all downhill after that.

Joyce quickly became fearful of Harold and his moods. The only saving grace was that he didn't hang around very long. He suggested the name "Dontrelle" as an option early in Joyce's pregnancy. But when their son was born in the winter of 1982, Harold had long since disappeared.

Joyce went on to marry two more times. She had a second son named Walter with Kelvin Blakely, a kindhearted yet free-spirited musician who stuck around for a few years, then took Walter and moved to South Carolina. Kelvin did, however, teach Dontrelle to ride a bike *sans* training wheels before he split.

In the mid-1990s, Joyce wed George Harris, a fellow iron worker who treated Dontrelle like his own son. Early in the courtship, Joyce warned George, "If Dontrelle doesn't like you, I won't date you." Then one day, George asked to take Dontrelle for a ride, just the two of them, and Dontrelle came home 2 hours later beaming and holding bags of shoes from the local Foot Locker. George had discovered that the way to Dontrelle's heart was through his size-13 feet.

Harold Willis, out of the picture for so long, made a final cameo in the summer of 2003. He was working 5 nights a week at an International House of Pancakes in Denver when his brother in Houston saw a kid named Dontrelle Willis pitching on television for the Florida Marlins. One thing led to another, and Doris Willis, Dontrelle's paternal grandmother, contacted the Marlins and left a message.

Dontrelle then approached Joyce, who had periodically received letters from Harold asking about the boy.

"Dontrelle hadn't seen the man for 20 years," Joyce says. "He left us, and that was pretty much a good thing. But I had to ask myself, is it very unfair if Dontrelle wants to know him? I asked Dontrelle, 'Do you want to see your dad?' And he said, 'Yeah Mom, I do. I just want to meet him.'"

Harold, it turns out, had almost 2 decades of baggage and a dark, ugly secret to bring to the reunion. Just 8 months earlier, he had been paroled from the Arrowhead Correctional Center in Canon City, Colorado, after serving 16 years of a 40-year sentence for the kidnapping of a Florida woman who was 7½ months pregnant.

Joyce was aware of Harold's story and thought long and hard before giving her approval. "People can be cruel," she says, "and I was concerned that with his father's background, it would strip from Dontrelle and his image. I just prayed about it. But Dontrelle is so mature. He's like, 'Mom, don't worry about it.'"

Mike Berardino of the Ft. Lauderdale *Sun-Sentinel* tracked down Harold Willis at his job busing tables at the Denver IHOP and wrote a poignant, largely sympathetic story of a man with good intentions whose life had gone horribly wrong. Harold was living in a seedy, $199.99-a-week motel, with cinder block walls and minimal creature comforts, and trying to piece his life together when he saw his son for the first time in nearly 20 years. The meeting, at an ESPN Zone in Denver, was by all accounts cordial yet short on sentiment. Harold's first reaction was to gush over the size of his son. "Man, you're a tall drink of water," he observed as Dontrelle walked through the door.

Although Harold had drifted out of Dontrelle's life, he wasn't completely oblivious to the boy's existence. When Dontrelle was 12 years old and named MVP of his Little League, Harold sent him a mirror with a picture of a lion walking through the jungle, and the inscription, "Dontrelle Willis, future major-league ballplayer." Harold also sent Dontrelle several letters in the early 1990s, but they were never answered.

Given Dontrelle's high profile, the meeting was destined to cause a stir. John "Boog" Sciambi, the Marlins' play-by-play man, mentioned on a radio broadcast that Dontrelle Willis had met his father, and reporters rushed to the clubhouse after the game for a reaction. "I gave him a handshake and a hug and we just chilled," Dontrelle told them. "I didn't know what he looked like, but he knew what I looked like."

Harold also knew what he wanted, casually letting it drop that things were tight and he could use a little money if Dontrelle were so inclined. Joyce was enraged when Dontrelle related the incident and called Harold and warned him, "Just stay away from us." From that point on, Dontrelle's only contact with his natural father would come by phone. The Great Reunion story was poignant but brief, and like so many other events in Dontrelle's rookie year, it went by in a blur.

As July turned to August, then September, Dontrelle's air of invulnerability began to wane. Fatigue was part of the problem. As the innings piled up, Dontrelle's radar gun readings declined, and his stuff lacked the old bite. He peaked on July 30, beating Arizona's Randy Johnson 3–1 before a crowd of 37,735 in Miami. But by the end of the regular season he had thrown 197 innings—40 more than the previous season—and he was clearly spent.

In his teammates' eyes, the media crush and demands of Dontrelle-mania never gave him the requisite room to fail. "As veterans we told him, 'Say no sometimes. Say no to the media when they ask for interviews. Say no to the team wanting you to do an autograph session in the afternoon. Just say no,'" says Mark Redman, a Marlins pitcher who was traded to Oakland the following winter. "But he never knew how to say no."

Matt, as overwhelmed by the onslaught as Dontrelle, tried to say no in a protective way. While acknowledging that Jeffrey Loria and his wife had treated Dontrelle like "gold," he told the *Sun-Sentinel* that the demands of autograph signings and meet-and-greets were distracting Dontrelle from his goal of getting hitters out. "He's physically exhausted," Matt told the paper. "Dontrelle does nothing else except give interviews and pitch and sleep. It's really not fair. He has no personal time at all. He's shot."

In the first round of the playoffs against San Francisco, Dontrelle tired and failed to protect a 5–1 lead. The Cubs shelled him in the National League Championship Series, and by the time the World Series rolled around, he had assumed the role of Florida's designated lefty out of the bullpen. He made three appearances against the Yankees, contributing 3⅔ shutout innings, and he was warming up with closer Ugueth Urbina when Josh Beckett tagged Jorge Posada for the final out in the climactic Game 6. The Marlins, so bad in May that they cost their manager his job, were suddenly spraying champagne and making preparations for a parade.

Dontrelle Willis keeps a permanent mental snapshot of the final play and everything that unfolded after it. He remembers tiptoeing through the Yankee Stadium monuments so that he wouldn't slip, and looking into the eyes of a New York fan and getting nothing but a vacant stare in return. All those Yankee fans sat in silence, as if processing the news that there would no game tomorrow. A group of Marlins supporters was in the grandstand behind home plate, at the opposite end of the old park in the Bronx, and Dontrelle could pick out shadows of them jumping and hugging in celebration.

As Dontrelle sprinted through the outfield toward the infield scrum, running smack into good buddy Juan Pierre for a celebratory hug, he heard somebody screaming at the top of his lungs. It was him, Dontrelle Willis, unplugged.

Sosnick has to remind himself to keep his composure when he calls the Marlins before spring training for an update on the team's plans for

Dontrelle Willis, and Larry Beinfest and Michael Hill put him on the speakerphone and begin rattling off the particulars.

The Marlins, like most clubs, have a formula for contractually rewarding young players for special achievements on the field. A little of this for an All-Star appearance; a little of that for Rookie of the Year. And a little more for certain statistical achievements. They're just sweeteners, really, for kids who are precluded from cashing in big by the requirements laid out in baseball's labor agreement.

In Dontrelle Willis's case, the little things add up to a $353,000 contract for 2004. But things could be worse: Miguel Cabrera, who drove in 62 runs in 314 at-bats as a rookie and batted cleanup against the Yankees in the World Series, receives a nominal bump from the rookie minimum to $320,000.

Other second-year players fare better. The financially strapped Milwaukee Brewers reward outfielder Scott Podsednik for his .314 average, 43 stolen bases, and 100 runs scored with a raise to $400,000, then tack on a 2-year extension. And Kansas City shortstop Angel Berroa, the reigning AL Rookie of the Year, will make $372,500 in the first year of a 4-year, $11 million extension.

Matt feels the room spinning for an instant when he hears the figure, and he feels the need for a cold compress. Then he makes his displeasure known to the Marlins' execs. "This is insulting," he tells Beinfest and Hill. "It's insulting and it's embarrassing."

He's not alone in that opinion. In a story headlined, "Key Marlins Get the Shaft," the *Sun-Sentinel*'s Berardino points out that Jeffrey Loria gave six-figure bonuses to a number of front-office employees and treated many of those people to an all-expenses-paid vacation. But the team gave only a token raise to Willis, who, Berardino observes, "made more school visits than McGruff the Crime Dog."

The Marlins, according to Sosnick, also renege on a promise by Loria to send Dontrelle on an all-expenses-paid trip to Las Vegas in the off-season, an oversight that pleases neither agent nor player. But outwardly, at least, the agent takes greater offense than the player.

Matt also represents Scott Olsen and Josh Johnson, top pitching prospects for the Marlins, and Josh Willingham, a highly regarded catcher in the minors, and he files away the Dontrelle negotiation for future reference. The Marlins' biggest mistake, he concludes, was lumping him in with more established agents who instinctively try to squeeze a team for every buck once they have leverage. Matt's not like that, he insists. He wants to build a relationship.

"Dontrelle and I are all about goodwill and trying to do the right thing," Matt says. "When I felt like they sort of punished me and my client, I have absolutely no loyalty to them anymore. I mean, can you imagine them ever asking me for a favor to do anything? I'll tell them to screw themselves."

Dontrelle, in contrast, reports to spring training in Jupiter, Florida, in sunny-side-up mode. He still considers himself an ambassador for the franchise, and he vows not to withhold a signature or a smile out of spite. "That's bogus, dude," Dontrelle says from his locker stall at camp. "That would be like payback, like vengeance, and I'm not about that. I've never been about that."

Joyce has always marveled at Dontrelle's knack for putting things in perspective—a trait he inherited from his grandfather, Frank Guy Sr. "Even if I'm the worst player in the major leagues, I'm only the worst of 740," he would tell his mom. Or he'd wax philosophical about money. "If they don't pay me now, they're gonna pay me later," he said, and Joyce wondered how her baby got so smart.

The blow is eased somewhat in April, when the Marlins receive the most enduring reminder of their World Series triumph. Loria, an art dealer by trade, has designed a ring with 228 diamonds, 13 rubies, and a special teal diamond in the center. The rings weigh 3½ ounces each, and the Marlins make a production of the ceremony by having a Brinks trunk drive into Pro Player Stadium and back all the way to the infield to unload them. The ring is so gaudy and has so many bells and whistles that it borders on unwearable. "They look like something out of a Mr. T starter kit," says a former Marlins scout. Show it off around town, the scouts joke, and people might mistake you for Liberace's son.

Beckett, the World Series hero, doesn't mind wearing the ring. But Dontrelle decides to stick his Marlins jewelry in a case with his All-Star ring and a ring from the Carolina Mudcats, who won a Southern League title after he left Zebulon. He plans to take them out for special occasions.

Joyce Guy-Harris travels to Florida for the World Series recognition ceremony, and she is moved to tears when Dontrelle gives her a pendant modeled after the Series ring. He doesn't want to see her cry, so he sends the trainer to give it to her in a waiting room outside the clubhouse. When Joyce sees the back of the pendant and the inscription, "I love you Mom. Thanks, Dontrelle," she busts out bawling, just as her son suspected she would.

Joyce spends her spare time in Florida hanging out at the dog track with her son's agent, the self-professed reformed gambler. Matt refers to Dontrelle's mother as "Mama Joyce," and jokes, "I'm the white kid that the family keeps hidden under the table and takes out for special occasions." But for all their happy banter, they've discovered it's not easy navigating the road to fame, with all its pitfalls and opportunities for quick scores. Joyce insists that her brother, Dontrelle's Uncle Frank, be consulted about every contract or marketing venture negotiated on Dontrelle's behalf. She's extremely fond of Matt, Paul, and Steve Reed, the San Francisco business manager who handles Dontrelle's financial investments. But business is business, and family is family. Joyce trusts Matt and Paul implicitly, but she doesn't want her boy to be one of those sad stories people read about in the papers.

"They're all great people," Joyce says, "but they don't have the same understanding and plights that we have because we're Afro-American people. Sometimes you see people with four Hummers and five Jags and no furniture in the house, but we think differently economically as a family. That's why you need good checks and balances. You don't want to wake up some morning saying, 'Where did all the money go?'"

Matt has a big heart and is fun to be around, Joyce concedes. When Dontrelle made the All-Star team and was told he could buy an extra ring for a family member, Matt picked up the tab and purchased one for Joyce. "Dontrelle loves Matt," Joyce says. "He really does. He loves Matt dearly, and Matt's been a great asset to our family."

In some ways, though, Matt's just a big kid himself, in need of direction both literally and figuratively. Shortly after the ring ceremony in Florida, Matt is driving around in circles looking for a baseball game at Laney College in Oakland, where he plans to check out Jeff Marquez, a junior college pitcher that the Sosnick-Cobbe agency will be advising in the June draft. After 15 minutes of wrong turns, he phones Joyce at her job at the Alameda Trade Council and asks, "Where the heck am I going?"

With Joyce's help, Matt finally finds the ball field, and he's mingling with scouts when she arrives carrying a stack of photos from the Florida trip. Joyce hands the pictures to Matt, and they gaze in amazement at the size of the new addition to Dontrelle's jewelry collection.

"That ring is so big," Joyce says, with wonder in her voice. "It's *ghetto* big."

Chapter
TEN

The resolution—a personal pledge to alter behavior for the better—is often triggered by a milestone or a flip of the calendar. Another New Year's Day passes, or a birthday ending in zero approaches, and the more introspective among us decide to view life in a new light. Or maybe you wake up one day in the throes of an epiphany, and you have no choice in the matter.

Matt is keenly aware of his imperfections through his relationship with his therapist, Jacob. A friend turned him on to the guy several years ago, and Matt was pleasantly surprised to find that Jacob wasn't one of those robotic types who'd sit upright in a leather chair, flanked by a mahogany desk and a wall full of diplomas, and take notes and nod vacantly while you cut open a vein and bled all over the couch. Jacob was more the interventionist type. He'd listen intently, and when was Matt finished spouting some rationalization, he'd call, "bullshit," and they'd start over and get to the root of the problem.

The arrangement was so productive that Matt began seeing Jacob regularly, to the tune of $10,000 a year in therapy bills, and he considered it the best investment he ever made. Jacob helped Matt view the world in shades of gray, and he became a valuable sounding board on matters of the heart.

"He's sort of like my guru," says Matt, who eventually referred several friends and family members. Before long, Jacob's appointment calendar was chock-full of referrals from Matt Sosnick.

Paul Cobbe, who knows Matt better than anyone, has never seen a person more aggressive in the quest for self-improvement. Matt attacks his shortcomings and isolates them the way a scientist might isolate a virus, so it's doubly painful when an observer notices a flaw in Matt's character, because that means Matt has failed to spot it first.

On April 23, the day of Sosnick's 35th birthday, the desire for personal betterment grips him like a low-grade fever, and he decides it's time for a healthier outlook. There are flowers to smell and sunrises to watch, women to date and cell phone calls to make, and the emotional capital spent dwelling on setbacks is sapping his zest for life. He goes for a morning run at the Crystal Springs reservoir, as a prelude to a day that will end with an elaborate birthday cocktail party at the Ritz-Carlton this evening. And when the endorphins kick in, he realizes it's not worth obsessing on the baser aspects of his profession. His mission is to stay calmer and less frazzled, and to avoid the highest highs and lowest lows.

"I want to have a more mellow attitude," Matt says. "If I lose a player, I'm going to be fine. If I get a player, it's great. Whatever happens, happens."

He is not about to look for problems where they don't exist. Early in the 2004 season, *Sports Illustrated*'s Tom Verducci writes an interesting and foreboding note on the hazards of overworking young pitchers. Verducci observes that Dontrelle Willis and the Chicago Cubs' Carlos Zambrano might be candidates to break down physically because they've been subjected to such an onerous workload at an early age.

Matt shrugs off the magazine item. He has his job—to get Dontrelle endorsements, be Dontrelle's confidant, and shower Dontrelle with love because he genuinely feels it in his heart. The Florida Marlins, in turn, have theirs. They needn't worry about him calling their offices as a self-appointed surrogate coach and bitching about pitch counts.

"I have enough trouble finding the can when I wake up in the middle of the night," Matt says.

Dontrelle's season gets off to a fast start in more ways than one. He wins his first three decisions, and he attracts even more attention by hitting safely in his first six at-bats. Manager Jack McKeon compares him with Lou Gehrig, and teammates joke that it's time for him to move up in the batting order, from ninth to cleanup.

Dontrelle recently bought a condominium on Williams Island, between Miami and Ft. Lauderdale, and he has a sweet view of the Intracoastal Waterway from the 26th floor. He has also broken off his engagement to his girlfriend, Kim, after only a few months. "They're both really good people," Matt says. "But I think they realized they have a lot of living to do before they're ready to take care of anybody else." Perhaps there's a chance down the road, but not now.

In the gossipy, backbiting agent grapevine, speculation persists that Dontrelle's fame will eventually prompt him to sever his relationship with his agent. But if anything, he and Matt seem to be drawing closer in both a personal and business sense. Dontrelle finally concludes that his family is so wrapped up with the daily updates of his endorsements and other ventures, it's a recipe for stress, so he sits down with the entire crew and makes it clear that Sosnick is running the show and will keep everyone apprised if something significant is in the works.

After overextending himself in his rookie year, Dontrelle feels free to pick and choose from a smorgasbord of opportunities. During an off-day he signs autographs at a Circuit City store in Miami, where there's no security and the event drags on 2 hours too long. Then, fans follow him into the parking lot on the way to his car. He decides a few thousand extra bucks aren't worth the hassle, and it's okay to be selective.

"As long as I have enough money to put some rims on my whip and get some gas and something to eat, I'm straight like an Indian hair," Dontrelle says, in a head-spinning lingo all his own.

As Opening Day comes and goes, it's Paul Cobbe, rather than Matt, who is suddenly hit with a string of crises. Spring is traditionally a time of rebirth and anticipation in the baseball world. But it can also bring upheaval in the life of an agent, as players adjust to new teams, new towns, conflicts with managers, and the usual array of problems linked to uncertainty and relocation. In Sports Agent 101 class, this might qualify as a worse-than-average week:

• Cincinnati minor leaguer Phil Dumatrait wakes up one morning with his left elbow swollen to obscene proportions, and a magnetic resonance imaging test determines that his ulnar collateral ligament is shredded. He calls Paul at 4:00 P.M. and says that the Reds have booked him for surgery at 7:00 A.M. the next day.

• Kory Casto, a third baseman in the Montreal system, is raking the ball in spring training when he takes a bad-hop grounder off the eye and suffers a crushed orbital bone. The Expos initially expect him to miss 6 weeks, but the good news is he'll only miss 2.

• Travis Hanson, a third baseman in the St. Louis chain, is called into the front office and told he's being moved to second base. The Cardinals like Travis, but they think a shift is wise given the franchise's long-term commitment to Scott Rolen.

• Zach McCormack, a pitcher with Florida's South Atlantic League affiliate in Greensboro, North Carolina, is doing some rudimentary stretching with rubber tubing when he suffers a freak accident. The tubing is faulty, snaps in two places, and hits him in the face. He's temporarily blinded in one eye and has lost 70 percent of his vision in the other.

"I don't think it's permanent," Paul says, "but he's walking around blind right now and he's shitting his pants because of it. It's amazing. We've had these freak little injuries and weird stuff. It seems much more prolific this year than in the past."

Cameron Crowe, apart from being a brilliant writer and talented director, is a stickler for authenticity, as evidenced by his detail work on the movie *Jerry Maguire*. The 22-page "mission statement" that Tom Cruise slipped into the office mailboxes at Sports Management International is a real-life document, filled with purged emotions and insights into what makes a sports agent tick. It's available on eBay for $9.99.

Jerry Maguire, as part of his awakening, laments the corrosive effect of money on his profession. For inspiration, he quotes Dicky Fox, the original sports agent and author of the book *A Happy Life*. Before Dicky died of a heart attack in front of Gate B at a Chicago Bulls playoff game, he spoke the words that Tom Cruise, as Jerry, believed should be the mantra for all agents.

"The secret to this job," Dicky Fox liked to say, "is personal relationships."

Matt Sosnick's personal relationships are governed, in many ways, by a desire for approval—a trait that isn't necessarily well-suited for the agent game. His friends and the women he dates say he sometimes tries too hard in his quest to be loved. "His expectations of himself are incredible," says Rochelle Eskenas, the Los Angeles-based psychologist who dated Matt for several months. "He wanted to be the perfect boyfriend."

Matt divides his business acquaintances into two categories: moral and not quite moral enough. Early on, when Matt was a complete zero in the profession, Jim Hughes of Rawlings was respectful to him and generous to his players. Matt concluded that Hughes is the "nicest, most honest, direct, and fair" guy he knows in the glove business, so he steers his players toward Rawlings instead of Wilson.

He is also quick to acknowledge good-hearted competitors. John Boggs, a San Diego agent who's universally well-liked, struck gold when one of his advisees, Adrian Gonzalez, went to the Marlins first overall in the 2000 draft and another, Mark Prior, went to the Cubs with the second pick in 2001. Boggs was surprised after the Gonzalez selection to receive a message on his answering machine from an agent he had never met.

John, you don't know me, but my name is Matt Sosnick. Congratulations. I understand you're a wonderful guy, and it's nice to know that good people can get guys at the top of the draft.

Matt's inherent sense of right and wrong, which tells him that caring and personally investing in a player should count for a lot, makes it that much harder to reconcile severed relationships. In 2000, he represented a St. Louis kid named Bob Keppel, who went to the New York Mets as the 36th overall pick in the draft. Sosnick later had a falling-out with Keppel's father, who fired him, and agent and dad aren't fond of one another. But Bob Keppel has nothing but good things to say about Matt and even recommends him to teammates who might need representation.

It's when the kids themselves turn on him and pejoratives fly that Matt has problems. He's trying to come to grips with the realization that for every Dontrelle Willis or Mike Hinckley who pledges loyalty for eternity, there's bound to be an Adam Stern or Bobby Jenks, who view him less kindly from afar.

Adam Stern was a hustling little outfielder at the University of Nebraska when Sosnick first encountered him on a recruiting trip to the school. Matt picked up three Nebraska players in the 2001 draft, and he negotiated Stern's $347,000 bonus as a third rounder with Atlanta—taking a $17,350 cut. He was excited over the fact that Stern, while not a practicing Jew, had a Jewish father.

"You're my favorite Jewish player," Matt joked with him.

Things apparently went fine until Stern came to San Francisco and spent 2 days watching his agent talk on the phone. At one point, according to Stern, Sosnick promised to take him on a tour of the city, to show him the docks and the Giants' new home at Pac Bell Park. They hopped in Sosnick's Jaguar, drove past the park, and Matt pointed over and said, "There's Pac Bell," and just kept driving and talking on the phone.

"I might as well have taken a tour bus and gone past it," Adam Stern says.

Adam Stern eventually grew dissatisfied with pretty much everything about Matt and Paul's business model and service. He thought that his equipment came late and was substandard when it finally arrived, assertions that Matt disputes. He became convinced that Sosnick and Cobbe had too many clients and failed to give him the attention he deserved. And their orientation as non-ball guys bugged him no end.

"I don't like guys who don't know anything about baseball," Stern says. "I don't want a business guy coming up to me and saying, 'Your swing looks good,' when they don't know A-Rod from the friggin' Pee Wee League."

Adam Stern also felt ripped off paying a 5 percent draft commission, especially when he found another agent, Michael Watkins, who said he negotiates bonuses for free. The concept made perfect sense to Stern, who figured he had enough exposure at a Big 12 school and there was nothing Sosnick could do to put him on the map. Nothing that justified a $17,350 fee, anyway.

When Stern called and fired Matt, things were as testy and personal as he feared. "He thought we had this tight bond," Stern says. "And I was like, 'You thought so, but I don't know where you got it from.'"

So they parted ways, and to this day Matt believes that their falling-out reflected Adam Stern's ill-conceived notion of what an agent is supposed to provide. Stern was unpopular with his teammates at Nebraska, Matt says, and he was warned that the kid might be trouble.

"He fired me and then said, 'I'll un-fire you if you give me back the money from my signing bonus,'" Matt says. "It was totally about the money. I'm still not sure what triggered him being so pissed off. I don't understand why he's so venomous, because I always thought there was a closeness there."

Lincoln, Nebraska, where Matt hooked up with Stern, is downright cosmopolitan compared with Spirit Lake, Idaho, where Sosnick traveled to find Bobby Jenks in 2000. Spirit Lake is a mere 15 minutes from Hayden, where white supremacists congregate, and it's just a hop, skip, and a few burning crosses north of Coeur d'Alene, where the Rev. Richard Butler's Aryan Nations group paraded through the middle of town in 1998.

Bobby Jenks left California's San Fernando Valley as a teenager when his father, "Big Rob," took a job in Idaho as a roofer. The family lived in a ramshackle log cabin, and Bobby dropped out of high school in his senior year. But what he lacked in social graces and academic credentials, he made up for with his ability to pop a mitt. He was clocked at 96 mph in American Legion ball, loud enough to attract a slew of pro scouts to Spirit Lake—along with a single agent by the name of Matt Sosnick.

When the Angels selected Jenks with the 140th pick in the 2000 draft, he considered it a new beginning. Matt invited him to San Francisco for the event, and Bobby hugged everybody in the room, tearfully calling it "my chance to start over." His $175,000 draft bonus was gravy.

Bobby Jenks was the type of personal reclamation project that Matt lives for, except that he couldn't be reclaimed. One day Bobby showed up with several nasty, quarter-size marks, the result of burning himself with a cigarette lighter. He lied to the Angels, telling them he suffered the burns while working on his car, and he continued to light up radar guns. On another occasion, Matt received a call telling him that Bobby had gotten drunk at a team pool party, fired a basketball, and accidentally hit the child of one of the team's coaches.

Matt claims that Bobby Jenks began referring to him as "D. J.," short for Dirty Jew, an assertion that Jenks denies. But Bobby's drinking and capacity for self-destruction were harder to deny; they soiled just about everything he touched. He became an agent's nightmare—the type of player who constantly tests management's patience and rarely takes responsibility for his actions. One of Matt's principle contributions was easing the fears of Bobby's wife, a sweet girl who privately confided that she was scared of Bobby because he would get angry at times and his temper would spin out of control.

In 2002, Bobby Jenks confronted his manager with a drunken outburst on a bus, and he was punished with a demotion from Double-A

Arkansas to Class A Rancho Cucamonga. Not long afterward, he called Matt and said he was leaving Sosnick-Cobbe for the Scott Boras Corporation because Boras never would have allowed him to be demoted.

In June 2003, Tom Friend of *ESPN Magazine* wrote a story on Jenks, he of the million-dollar arm and tragic tendencies, in which Sosnick played armchair psychologist. Matt spoke of Jenks's inner demons and predicted a downward spiral to come. "If Bobby gets to the big leagues, he'll free-fall," Matt told Friend. "He can't handle success."

The characterization hurt Jenks, who says in hindsight that he never had a beef with Sosnick. Firing Matt was such an emotional ordeal for Bobby, he needed 3 or 4 days to muster the courage to make the phone call.

"I was getting closer to the big leagues and I just didn't think he was doing enough for me, so I decided to make a bigger move," Bobby Jenks says. "I was more surprised than anything—why would he say this stuff? Of course, I was a little pissed off as well. But I wasn't gonna stab back at him. Whatever he's got to say is his business, just him showing his true colors right there."

Jenks went on to suffer a series of elbow problems, and his off-field misadventures convinced Sosnick and Cobbe that he's a wonderful player to have as a former client. In the spring of 2003, he drank too much at an Arizona bar, misplaced his wallet, and began shaking down customers, accusing them of stealing it and forcing them to empty their pockets on the table.

By that point, Bobby Jenks wasn't even Scott Boras's problem anymore. He had decided Boras wasn't doing enough for him either, and he'd moved on to Tommy Tanzer's group.

"There was an endearing side to Bobby when he wanted to be endearing, and I conned myself into thinking he was going to be on my side and his normal pathology wasn't going to come out," Matt says. "But it did." If Bobby Jenks can find a way to pull his life together, it will have to be with the help of an agent other than Matt Sosnick.

At the end of spring training, Arizona Diamondbacks reliever Brandon Lyon is scheduled for elbow surgery and understandably antsy. In a bolt from the blue, he calls Matt and says he's thinking about switching to another firm.

Lyon, a young Mormon, is as low-key as Sosnick is hyper, but they have a nice, complementary dynamic. They first became acquainted when Brandon was pitching at Dixie State College in Utah in 2000, and Matt called to introduce himself. Lyon wasn't in the market for an adviser at the time. But at the end of his first professional season, he flew to San Francisco for a visit on Matt's dime. They hit it off just fine, and Brandon told himself, "Why not?"

One winter, Matt took Lyon and his wife on a trip to Hawaii, and Brandon, who never had trouble unwinding, laughed at the way his agent sat by the pool with the cell phone surgically attached to his ear. *If he's this much of a workaholic, I guess he must be doing a good job for me,* Brandon thought.

On autumn weekends, Brandon will be driving along and his cell phone will ring, and it's Matt telling him the New England Patriots are a great pick giving seven points in the Monday night game against the New York Jets. Or maybe they'll just shoot the breeze for 5 minutes before Matt returns to his list of 15 morning errands.

Brandon Lyon is shy by nature, with a sleepy-eyed demeanor and a goatee so lame that it's a stretch to refer to it as facial hair. But he's competitive and blessed with athleticism. He's a scratch golfer, and he was one mean snowboarder before separating his shoulder in a wreck in 1997. The accident ended his snowboarding career, but he went 15–1 and made All-America in baseball at Dixie, then signed with Toronto for a $100,000 bonus. In 2001, Lyon joined Dave Stieb as the second pitcher in Blue Jays history to sign one year and pitch in the majors the next. He beat Baltimore 2–1 in his first start, making history as the first player named Brandon to win a major-league game.

His manager, Buck Martinez, noticed that there were no signs of fear in Brandon Lyon's eyes in his big-league debut. Tim Huff, the young scout who signed Lyon, called him a cross between Tim Hudson and Greg Maddux. But to Sosnick, he was just a fun-loving kid soaking up life in The Show. Matt went to visit Brandon in Anaheim before his second start, and it was as if Brandon had clicked his heels and realized that he wasn't in Utah anymore. "We asked him who his roommate was," says Matt's friend Eric Polis, who also made the trip. "Brandon told us, 'This is the major leagues. I have my own room.'"

The Jays, as part of a purge prompted by front-office turnover, waived Lyon in October 2002, and he was claimed by the Red Sox. Brandon got a shot at closing, saving nine games in 2003, before Boston traded him to Pittsburgh in July.

But the deal hit a snag for medical reasons. Pittsburgh's doctors looked at an MRI and found fraying tendons in Lyon's elbow, while Boston's medical staff regarded it as simple wear and tear. The Pirates gave Lyon an arthrogram—a procedure that involved shooting dye into the elbow to detect possible tears that an MRI might have missed—and were sufficiently concerned to void the trade.

In the Boston front office, some people questioned whether the players union or Sosnick and Cobbe, as Lyon's agents, should have been more vigilant in protecting his rights by questioning the necessity of such an invasive test. "We didn't think they were attentive enough," says a Red Sox executive.

Matt and Paul consider it more a question of integrity than expediency. What if Lyon had pitched two games for Pittsburgh, then blown out his elbow? Wouldn't the Pirates have filed a grievance and tried to nullify the trade anyway? Weren't they within their rights to ensure they didn't trade for damaged goods?

"The bottom line is, I want to protect my player," Matt says. "But I also want to do what's morally right. Pittsburgh deserves to get the player they thought they were getting."

Lyon ultimately left Boston in November 2003 in a five-player trade for Curt Schilling. In the spring of 2004, he began to feel soreness in his right elbow, but he said nothing to his agent. When they finally spoke, Brandon revealed the extent of his injury and chided Matt for being out of touch. He also carped, uncharacteristically, about a shipment of baseball shoes that failed to arrive.

To the agent, this smells like a kiss-off. Players make decisions to switch agents primarily on emotion, Paul Cobbe has learned. The justification comes later. If Lyon believes it's time for a change, the reason is almost irrelevant.

For Matt, the prospect of personal rejection is more crushing than the potential lost income. If Brandon Lyon tops out as a serviceable middle reliever in the majors, he'll never make Sosnick-Cobbe rich on commissions. But 2 days after their conversation, Matt has a dream in which he's walking up a hill with Lyon and the rest of his 40-man roster players, carrying a torch. Freud or even Jacob might have trouble discerning the relevance of *that*.

"It's a horrible feeling," Matt says. "Your initial gut reaction is the shame and humiliation of losing a guy and having everyone know about it." Then comes the pain of knowing that Lyon might think someone else can do a better job representing him. How could he, given Matt's emotional investment?

Brandon Lyon's revelation makes Matt question his commitment to the business for the umpteenth time, and he wonders what it is about human nature that makes players so susceptible to being lured. Lots of kids profess their undying loyalty in Savannah and Dubuque. But when the checks get bigger and the ballparks suddenly have two decks instead of one, players always feel compelled to go shopping.

"It's Human Behavior 101," Matt concludes. "Guys are only as loyal as their options."

"Matt's very grandiose about birthdays," says his father, who should know. Five years ago, when Ron Sosnick turned 55, Matt called with excitement in his voice and the promise of a wonderful surprise. He picked up his father and they drove to the tony community of Atherton, where they passed through a gate and up a driveway and knocked on the door. After a brief wait, they were greeted by Hall of Famer, cultural icon, and Ron Sosnick dream date Willie Mays. "Nice to meet you," Mays said, extending a hand.

The three of them drove to Chantilly, a Palo Alto restaurant specializing in French and Italian cuisine, where Mays has a table at a private dining room upstairs away from the crowd. For 3 hours, they sat and talked baseball, just Matt and his dad and the Say Hey Kid. They discussed Pete Rose's gambling ban and racism in baseball and the final game of the 1951 season, when Mays was 20 years old and standing in the on-deck circle as Bobby Thomson went deep off Ralph Branca to win the pennant for the Giants. The Shot Heard 'Round the World, indeed.

They reminisced about the 1962 World Series with New York, and Ron asked Mays why the heck the Yankees chose to pitch to Willie McCovey in the ninth inning of Game 7 with first base open and Orlando Cepeda on deck. "Boy," Willie replied, "you really *are* a fan." Mays has a reputation as a guy who wouldn't walk across the street if compensation weren't involved, but Matt swears that a cent never changed hands—that he's just a loving son who wanted to do something nice for his dad's 55th birthday. That something was tracking down the phone number of the man many people consider the greatest player in history, and talking him into a 3-hour dinner.

Matt is grandiose about his own birthday, too. When he turned 30, more than 50 friends flew into San Francisco from around the country to share in the celebration. Now that No. 35 is here, he's decided another gathering is in order, so he rents the Presidential Suite at the Ritz-Carlton in San Francisco and does the night of April 23 up right.

Isabella Sikaffy of Flora Bella event planning has spent 3 months putting the party together, and 50 to 60 guests have come from near (Sausalito and San Ramon) and not-so-near (Chicago; Washington, D.C.; Vermont; and Jerusalem) to celebrate Matt's 35th. They arrive at 7:00 P.M., to the accompaniment of Dave Matthews and Counting

Crows selections on the stereo system, and enjoy a sumptuous display of food. The menu consists of tenderloin of beef, pesto-stuffed mushrooms, Mediterranean chicken skewers, steamed prawns with orange cilantro dipping sauce, a marinated olive display, an assortment of cheeses from France, and, of course, Matt's favorite, sushi.

The Presidential Suite is 1,980 square feet, with a Steinway grand piano, and rumor has it that Prince recently stayed here. The party guests munch and mingle and periodically step outside onto a massive balcony for a view of the Coit Tower and the San Francisco Bay. It's a quintessentially brisk and beautiful northern California evening.

Matt collects interesting friends—doctors, writers, a golf pro, and a self-made Internet millionaire, to name a few—the way most people collect stamps or rare coins. Yet many of them regard him as the most fascinating, complex person they've ever met.

Eric Karp works in Hollywood for MGM Studios and deals with agents all the time, and he's found that when you scratch the surface, most of them are complete dicks. But Matt is different. Sure, it's important to Matt to appear intelligent and be the center of attention. But Matt is ethical to a fault, Eric has learned, and fearless in a way you can't help but admire.

Most people start a business and spend months reading books and surfing the Internet for background. Matt wanted to be a sports agent, so the next day he started a sports agency. "He has something hardwired into his genetic makeup that you can't teach in a business school," Eric says.

Several years ago, Eric accompanied Matt to a Tom Petty show at Shoreline, a popular concert venue south of San Francisco, and played spectator as they blew off the opening act in a quest for better tickets. They arrived with a pair of 12th-row seats and swapped them for a single in the first row. Then, Matt exchanged the single for eight seats 30 rows up on the side. And on it went, Matt's mind whirling, the transactions flying, until the moment he and Eric settled in for Petty's opening number. They had missed the warmup act, Los Lobos, and were five rows closer than when they started.

Eric Karp was amazed at the way that Sosnick could instinctively pick people out of a crowd in his wheeling and dealing. "To watch him in his element, that's as much of a show as going to the show," Eric says. "He'll change his cadence and the way he operates depending on whether it's an inner-city kid holding two tickets or a middle-age guy doing this for a living. He can tell who's legit and who's not legit, who really has something to offer and who doesn't. It happens every time we go to a show."

Matt's party is scheduled to run until midnight, but around 11:00 P.M., Paul Cobbe calls the room to order. He shares a personal recollection from March 2003, when Sosnick-Cobbe Sports survived its biggest crisis to date. After a series of player defections, Paul and Matt met in an Arizona hotel room and wondered whether they could ever make it. Were they destined to be nothing more than a feeder system for the big groups? They dissected everything about their business model and their approach, and debated whether it might be time to sell the agency and abandon the dream. But in the end, they couldn't do it, because they had a good business and an even better friendship. Quitting simply wasn't an option.

Victoria Zackheim pays tribute to her son's gentleness and natural empathy for others. When Matt was 5, she tells the other guests, he saw a man sitting alone in the corner of a restaurant and was so concerned he asked the lone diner to join the Sosnick family for a meal. It became something of a tradition—little Matt picking out stray males at dinner and approaching them with invitations. "I should have brought you with me once I was divorced," Victoria says, eliciting laughter from the other partygoers.

They all agree that Matt passes the "3 o'clock in the morning test." If you had a crisis and called him at 3:00 A.M. and roused him from a sound sleep, he'd be the first one at your house to help. And he enriches their lives with his antics and supersize persona. Who else takes a trip to Paris and dribbles a basketball all over the city in search of a place to shoot hoops? Who else gives his old teacher two round-trip plane tickets to Italy, as Matt did with John Devincenzi upon his retirement from Burlingame High?

"If you just went off face value, Matt probably wouldn't seem like the most trustworthy person," says Mark Mintz, an old college friend from USC. "The truth is, he's a more loyal friend than you'll find anywhere."

Before they dig into the Niagara Falls cake and fantasy tortes, Paul pulls a piece of paper from his jacket pocket. Matt's clients are scattered all over the country at ballparks tonight, but they've taken time out to send along their birthday wishes:

Jon Pridie of the Minnesota Twins: The first time I saw Matt in Cedar Rapids, in the stands pulling his hair out on the cell phone, I would have said that he would burn out before 35. Since then, he has become a very special friend to me. Everything that he has done for me has been more than I ever expected. Slow down a bit, so that I can be with you for another 35. Hope you have a great birthday—and I love you.

Tripper Johnson of the Baltimore Orioles: You are more interested in me as a person than [as] a client. It's nice to have a friend who really cares about me and my family. It is always that before we ever talk about baseball or business. Happy birthday.

Darrell Rasner of the Montreal Expos: As time has gone by, I have realized that Matt is one of my true and loyal friends. He really cares.

Mike Hinckley of the Montreal Expos: Our relationship is more than that of a player and an agent. It's a friendship, like family. He is like one of my brothers. We discuss each other's problems and try to work them out. It is a great connection and I absolutely love the guy. I couldn't imagine anyone else taking care of me. Have a great 35th.

Dontrelle Willis of the Florida Marlins: I have so many stories to share, but the day I got into my car accident and he picked me up stands out for me. The funniest thing about the whole situation is that we ran together all off-season. And I swear I have never seen a man run as fast, in jeans and T-shirt, as he did out of his car that day. . . . It showed the love and the sincerity he had for me, and it was mutual. The way that he hugged me showed that nothing else mattered but me being okay. From that day on, I vowed to work as hard as I could to help him as much as he helped me. I love him. Happy 35th—and get a woman in your life so you can stop calling me so much.

Three weeks after his birthday party, Sosnick gets an unexpected present. Brandon Lyon, still recovering from ulnar nerve transposition surgery on his right elbow, is now vacillating over his decision to switch agents. They agree to meet in Phoenix the following week, and over lunch at a Ruby Tuesday's, Matt lays his emotions bare.

"Obviously it makes me feel insecure to think you're meeting with another agent, and it'll play on my craziness," he tells Lyon. "But you certainly have a right to be with another agent if it's going to make you feel better. I won't get in the way, and I won't drive you crazy about it."

The meeting goes well, all things considered, and it appears that Brandon might not leave after all. He has one more meeting left, with veteran Chicago agent Barry Meister, and he promises to call Matt when he's made his decision.

Sosnick flies home to San Francisco and shortly thereafter comes up with a theory not at all dissimilar to Jerry Maguire's epiphany when he banged away on a typewriter at 1:00 A.M. in the Miami Hilton. Matt calls his the "conflict of conscience."

Sosnick holds himself up as a moral person who's good to his parents, loyal to his friends, courteous to waitresses and Bed Bath & Beyond cashiers, and ethical and truthful in his business dealings. It's convenient to categorize him as a salesman based on his ability to talk fast and exercise persuasion, but what he craves most is the relationships without the selling.

Wouldn't it be nice, Matt asks himself, if you could just level with prospective clients and dispense with the selling? Or grow your business without giving a second thought to what Scott Boras has cooking down there at his shiny corporate offices in Newport Beach?

If you agree to let me represent you, I'll attack this job with my heart and soul, and I'll do the very best I can to be a good agent and help you in any way I can. No promises. No indulging. No sucking up to 19-year-olds who've been accustomed to the star treatment for most of their lives because they can throw a ball hard or hit it a long way. Just one-on-one, candid, honest, and 100 percent spiel-free.

Matt allows the thought to hang in the air, like a San Francisco morning fog that will surely lift when the sun comes out. Then he laughs.

"You wouldn't get a fucking player that way," he says. "Nobody could."

Chapter

ELEVEN

The University of the Pacific, a private school
located in the central San Joaquin Valley in Stockton, California, has
produced an array of high-profile alumni from all walks of professional
life. The list includes actors Robert Culp and Darren McGavin,
actresses Janet Leigh and Jamie Lee Curtis, musicians Dave Brubeck
and Chris Isaak, San Diego Chargers owner Alex Spanos, and Theodore
B. Olson, the 42nd solicitor general of the United States.

Scott Dean Boras, baseball agent and lawyer by trade, stands atop the
list alphabetically. Where he ranks as a contributor in his chosen field
is subject to debate. Even his detractors, from agents who fear and envy
him to club executives who dread his phone calls and interminable
"World According to Scott" soliloquies, respect him for his intellectual
motor and attentiveness to detail.

And for better or worse, depending on your philosophy on whether
wealth is a commodity to be hoarded or shared, he's left an imprint on
the game. Jim Bouton, former big leaguer and *Ball Four* author, once
observed that the owners screwed the players for 75 years and the

players have screwed the owners for 25 years, so the players have 50 years left to get even. Few people have done more to advance the timetable than Scott Boras. In 2050, when Alex Rodriguez III is contending for a Triple Crown and Seoul and Taipei are duking it out in the American League Far East, Boras will be remembered for breaking salary records for big leaguers and draft picks alike.

Perhaps the best thing about Scott Boras, says Gene Orza of the Players Association, is that he doesn't care whether teams like him, provided his players are well-served. "I've had disagreements with Scott," Orza says. "We've had our fights. But the criticism of him, as I see it, is borne out of jealousy. I've said it before and I'll say it again: If I had a son and he was a premier high school baseball player, I'd pick Scott Boras to represent him."

Andrew Zimbalist, a Smith College economics professor and former adviser to the players' union, calls Boras a "go-getter and an innovator." In 1994, Zimbalist encountered Boras at a meeting, and the agent explained how he had assembled a technical staff to compile statistics and incorporate hardcore number-crunching into negotiations. Boras had also hired an economist, who was doing work on regression analysis and estimating marginal revenue products.

Boras pushed and prodded and exploited so many holes in the system, he spurred the owners to band together and embrace several largely socialist initiatives in self-defense. "Project yourself 50 years into the future and then look back and say, 'Here's this guy Boras—what did he do to the game?'" Zimbalist says. "Maybe it was, accelerate the trend toward high salaries for superstars in a way that pushed the owners more rapidly toward embracing a revenue sharing system and a luxury tax system. So, he actually may have catalyzed the reform of the baseball labor market."

Big-league teams were naturally averse to signing aging pitchers to long-term contracts because it was deemed too risky. Yet there were the Los Angeles Dodgers, introducing 34-year-old Kevin Brown as the game's first $100 million player at the 1998 winter meetings in Nashville. To seal the deal, the Dodgers even paid for 12 flights a year from Macon to Los Angeles on a private jet for Brown's family. It was a proud moment for Boras. But he still had to listen to Sandy Alderson, a representative from the commissioner's office, stand in a corner of the Opryland ballroom and rip the Brown deal as a monument to excess. This was the same Sandy Alderson who gave Jose Canseco a record 5-year, $23.5 million contract with Oakland in 1990, and who signed Todd Van Poppel—whom Boras had advised—to a $1.2 million deal in the draft that same year. Who was Alderson to talk?

Boras discusses market forces and safeguarding the interests of players with such zeal, he sounds like a man who aspires to a lofty, noble calling, like curing cancer or eliminating world hunger. He's puzzled by writers who parrot the owners' shtick about the game being in economic peril when the numbers clearly show that it's thriving. Why, Boras wonders, does baseball insist on trashing the very players it should promote? Does the Safeway manager pull the Campbell's soup off the shelf, stomp it, dent it, then place it back on the shelf to be sold? Of course not.

Boras can't understand why inept owners get a pass to run their franchises ineptly in perpetuity. "If a player hits .200, he's not in the league long," Boras once said. "And if you don't win something in 10 years—just one division—you've got bad management and you're not a good partner. I'm giving them 10 years, and you know what? That's it." So long, you serial bumblers in Pittsburgh and Milwaukee. Don't let the turnstile hit you on the way out.

Boras is friends with Robert Wuhl of *Arli$$* fame, and he has been approached by Hollywood types to represent people in the entertainment industry. But he wants to keep it strictly about baseball. He resisted selling out to a big public company, the way Jeff Moorad and Arn Tellem did, and becoming an afterthought for the marketing arm or the financial services division. He was repulsed by Moorad's annual All-Star Game parties, which featured hot women and great food and looked like nothing more than a front to solicit other agents' clients. He suggests that the players union throw a party and give away free hot dogs, and leave the Playboy stuff to the carousing agents.

As a lawyer and a former professional ballplayer, he prefers that his players address him that way, to distinguish him from the creeps, hucksters, and salesmen who debase the profession. "Early on, he made it very clear with me that when I was talking to a club and referring to him, he was my adviser, my legal counsel, my attorney," says Tim Belcher, a long-time Boras client. "I think he's softened up on that a little bit, because a lot of agents now are attorneys."

His agency is reminiscent of a major-league front office, with scouts and field personnel and divisions of duty leading up to a strong and decisive leader at the top. He has his own "sports training institute," hitting consultants to help players with their swings, and a psychologist, Dr. Harvey Dorfman, on retainer to help them with their heads. He claims that the full-service approach helps players maximize their potential, but some baseball executives think it drives a wedge between players and clubs. Why should a player trust the team physician when Scott's doctor has his best interests at heart and advises him to rest that hamstring for an extra week or two?

There's no question who's in charge at the Scott Boras agency. When the big man strides through the lobby of the winter meetings hotel, carrying a leather satchel holding more powerful secrets than Marsellus Wallace's briefcase in *Pulp Fiction*, his company lieutenants walk dutifully behind him. If there's a newspaper interview to be done or a photo opportunity to be capitalized on, only one face and one voice will matter.

The skeptics in Major League Baseball consider Boras a general manager wannabe, with control freak tendencies. And it's true that Boras likes to dissect trades and signings while opining that some teams don't know their assets from their elbows. At the general managers' meetings, he's been known to gather his guys in a suite, invite a couple of L.A. writers up and play "rank the GMs" over pizza and a few beers.

Stan Kasten, who once ran three sports franchises in Atlanta, believes that most agents secretly yearn to run professional teams. Boras, in Kasten's estimation, is the rare exception. "He's so dyed-in-the-wool, believing in his particular mission in life, that he may not rather be doing that," Kasten says.

Boras detests the notion of agent-as-salesman, but he's quick to use salesmanship to make his case. While the mom-and-pop groups are winging it, his company churns out artful brochures in black or blue binders. *Alex Rodriguez: Historical Performance* ran more than 70 pages and cost a reported $35,000 to produce. Boras's presentation for Barry Bonds included laudatory quotes from Todd Helton and Dusty Baker and comparisons to Ted Williams. It also projected that Bonds would have 802 homers by the end of the 2006 season, in case you didn't know.

Boras is adept at making figures sing—shaving 6 months off a player's age in idle conversation or using semantics to make his deals look better. Instead of reporting Greg Maddux's contract with the Chicago Cubs as 2 years and $15 million, with a vesting $9 million option for the third year, he insists on calling it 3 years and $24 million, with the third year *voidable* if Maddux fails to achieve certain thresholds for innings pitched. It's pure verbal gymnastics, and general managers claim there are only two reasons for doing it this way: It feeds Scott's ego, and it makes him look good for recruiting purposes.

Pat Gillick, one of baseball's most respected executives, speaks for many front-office types when he says, "Scott's totally committed to his clients, and totally committed to what he has to do and how he has to do it. He's almost obsessed with it. But sometimes he has a tendency to fluff a little more than necessary. All agents fluff their clients. That's just normal. Sometimes maybe he overexaggerates the fluff."

Convincing people to believe something when all evidence points to the contrary is a skill. In March 2003, Alex Rodriguez tells *Baseball America* that young players should exercise caution in choosing an adviser. "I don't want agents coming to me promising a house or a limo or a car, all that BS," A-Rod says. "Tell me about your arbitration record. Are you a lawyer? How close do you work with our union?"

At that very moment, A-Rod's man Scott Boras has a 1–9 record in his previous 10 arbitration cases. He fared better in the 1990s, but people in the commissioner's office think that time and technology have caught up with him—that he's prone to filing extravagant numbers and getting testy in hearings when he thinks he's been challenged personally.

Too many cases turn into a referendum on *his* skills rather than the player's. But Boras continues to sell himself as an arbitration master.

Boras refers to so many of his clients as "special" or "premium" players that the designation elicits snickers in the business. Sure, Greg Maddux and Bernie Williams are special. But Darren Dreifort and Chan Ho Park? An American League executive says Boras has become baseball's equivalent to Donald Trump, making grandiose proclamations with no forethought to their credibility.

Sometimes, Boras exceeds even his own lofty rhetorical standards. At the 2002 World Series in San Francisco, he sat in the stands before a game and gave reporters the scoop on his then-prize client, Barry Bonds. "Barry Bonds isn't Superman," Boras told the press. "He's a 'He-Man.' The *H* is for Herculean. The *E* is for Einsteinian.'"

When his skills of persuasion are exhausted, Boras has discovered there are more forceful and efficient means to make people bend to his will. In October 1991, a *Baseball America* story titled "Boras' Clients Break the Bank" detailed how the agent helped fuel a surge in bonus money for draft choices. The article included a spicy comment from then-San Diego Padres general manager Joe McIlvaine about Boras and the NCAA rules governing the draft.

McIlvaine received the obligatory arm twist from Boras's office, and three issues later, a small box appeared at the front of the magazine with the headline "McIlvaine Retracts Comments."

"I completely retract all statements regarding Scott Boras attributed to me in the October 10–24, 1991, issue of *Baseball America*," McIlvaine said in the two-paragraph follow-up. "I do not agree, however, with the tactics employed by Mr. Boras in his representation of amateur athletes."

Front-office people see Boras's tempestuous side. He can smell weakness over the phone lines and will go off if he feels wronged. In March 1997, the Anaheim Angels released Boras client Todd Van Poppel on the last day of spring training. Van Poppel, who believed he had been guaranteed a roster spot, allowed 15 runs in nine Cactus League innings and imploded in his final appearance. So the Angels cut him, and Tim Mead, Anaheim's assistant general manager, was on his way to a Phoenix Suns game when he had the unfortunate timing to be at the other end of the phone from Scott Boras.

"Let's just say if the phone had space for a hand to come through and grab the throat, I'd have been victimized," Mead says.

Most front-office personnel find a way to slice through the posturing and sermonizing. In 2002, the Florida Marlins used their third-round draft pick on Trevor Hutchinson, a senior pitcher from Cal-Berkeley. Hutchinson held out until the following spring before signing for a $375,000 bonus.

Stan Meek, Florida's scouting director and a former minor-league teammate of Scott Boras, handled the negotiations for the Marlins. Meek considers Boras a friend even though some of his scouting colleagues might disapprove. But he gets exasperated sometimes with Boras's penchant for hyping his assets.

"At times Scott and I disagree on the fact that most of his guys are 'special' guys," Stan Meek says. "We're all special to somebody. I'm special to my mother."

The backdrop for Scott Boras's life story reads like a John Steinbeck creation. He was born in 1952, grew up on the family farm in Elk Grove, California, near Sacramento, and spent mornings working the fields and afternoons listening to Russ Hodges call Giants games over the radio. Young Scott rigged up an earplug and, the story goes, was so dizzy with joy when Willie McCovey homered to beat the Dodgers that he drove his tractor into a ditch, prompting his father, James, to smash his radio as a punishment.

Baseball was his passion, and he was good at it, but his contribution was best appreciated over extended viewing rather than in bits and pieces. Boras was dangerous in both the batter's box and the infield, but for entirely different reasons. "The kid swings the bat okay, but he can't catch a cold at third base," Buzzy Keller, his former manager at Double-A Arkansas, once said.

He attended Pacific to study chemistry and walked onto the baseball team, where he quickly endeared himself to coach Tom Stubbs. "He was the type of individual you just love to have on a baseball team, because he worked as hard as anybody," Stubbs says. "He had a love for the game and he was an outstanding citizen."

Boras believed in the sanctity of training rules: no drinking, smoking, or succumbing to other temptations that might negate his competitive advantage. "I don't want to say 'straight arrow,' because it wasn't exactly that," Stubbs says. "But he was the type of person who believed that when he stepped across the chalk line, he had to be in as good a shape as possible." Scott Boras was named Pacific's team captain, and he still ranks sixth on the school's career list with 92 walks. He was, according to Tom Stubbs, the "ideal college player."

During college summers, Boras played ball for Guild Wines, a local winery. Ed DeBenedetti, head of the Lido Parks and Recreation Department, had a cousin, Reno, who was a scout for Cincinnati, and they tried to push the Reds to take a look at the hard-driving kid with a flair for a quip.

"Oh, he could be funny as hell," DeBenedetti says. "He could come up with some beauties." It was Boras, for example, who coined the nickname "Fat Rat" for Tony Zupo, a portly coach with the Guild Wines squad. During a trip home from San Jose, the team passed a radio station in Stockton where one of Boras's college buddies was moonlighting as a disc jockey. Boras got out of the car, dropped his pants, and mooned his friend, who busted out laughing on the air.

Boras had a single-mindedness that ensured nothing would get in his way. He would do anything to play at a higher level, and he went to Ed DeBenedetti, who told him it might be in his best interests to switch from third base and the outfield to second base. "Show up at the Parks and Rec tomorrow at noon," DeBenedetti said, "and I'll work with you on it."

Informal pacts of this nature were commonplace: Kids would be all hepped up for extra instruction and quickly lose interest. But not the Boras kid. He showed up every day for a month, always at noon or a little before. DeBenedetti threw him batting practice and hit him grounders until they were both soaked with sweat and had to drag themselves off the field. "Never once in his mind did he think he wasn't going to play professional baseball," DeBenedetti says.

Boras signed his first professional contract with St. Louis in 1974 for an $8,000 bonus, and he entered an organization with hard-and-fast rules and a focus on fundamentals. George Kissell, the beloved field coordinator, quickly grew fond of the young infielder with the scrappy persona and scrap-metal hands. On Sunday mornings in spring training, Kissell would pound on Boras's door as the sun was coming up. "Boras, you've got to get up and go to church with me!" he'd shout through the door. "You need more help than anybody in camp."

Boras had a knowledge of the strike zone and a firm grasp of the game, but he made his pitchers nervous. With St. Petersburg in the Florida State League, he was part of a double-play combination with Garry Templeton, who went on to play 16 seasons in the majors.

"Scott had a pretty athletic approach at home plate, yet it didn't seem to transfer to the other side of the game," says Stan Meek, a pitcher on the St. Pete team. "He wrestled with his defense. I remember looking out there and seeing Templeton at shortstop and Boras at second base. *You* figure out where I tried to direct the ball."

Boras was more mature than many of his teammates and less inclined to go carousing after games. He was also more curious about the inner workings of pro ball. Today, a player who's spent 6 years in the minors with the same organization is free to sign elsewhere. Back then, you could be stuck with one club for eternity. "Most of us really didn't give it a lot of thought," says Jim Riggleman, a Boras teammate who later managed the Padres and Cubs. "But Scott and a teammate or two used to talk about the system not being right."

Boras hit .275 in 88 Texas League games in 1977, but his knees and hopes finally gave out. After he doubled off future big leaguer Bob

Welch in his last professional at-bat, the Cubs released him. He returned to Pacific for his law degree, then worked as a medical litigator for a big firm in Chicago. He'd already helped boyhood friend and minor-league teammate Mike Fischlin with a contract, but his big headline deal came in February 1985, when he negotiated a 5-year, $7.5 million contract with Toronto for another former teammate, pitcher Bill Caudill. It proved to be awfully good for business.

Boras immersed himself in the mechanics of his profession, learning the labor agreement from every possible angle and boning up on historical precedents. Many of the new agents wouldn't know Marvin Miller from Marvin Hamlisch, but Boras was aware of the sacrifices Miller had made in laying a new foundation. He was astonished to learn that some so-called agents didn't even like watching baseball. Even as his clientele expanded and his time grew precious, Boras made a point of arriving early to games at Dodger Stadium or the Big "A" in Anaheim. Once there, he'd watch BP and infield practice and glean insights that only a former player could discern.

Even after setting records for Kevin Brown and A-Rod and advising more than 50 first-round picks at the amateur end, Boras stayed true to his ball roots. It wasn't unusual for him to return a writer's phone call on the fly, while ordering a Big Mac or the No. 4 special from the counter at Taco Bell. His whole approach—hiring nothing but former ballplayers, basking in the ballpark atmosphere—gave the impression of a man who couldn't relinquish his major-league dreams.

Boras still has a wristwatch given to him by Hall of Famer Stan Musial for his exceptional play as a Cardinals farmhand in 1976. Stan Meek made the mistake of kidding him about it once, and Boras reacted testily. "He can say what he wants, but I'm never fooled by the fact he would have liked to play in the big leagues like a lot of guys," Meek says.

There's a startling dichotomy in assessments of Scott Boras then and now. People in baseball front offices can live with Boras constantly pushing, pushing, pushing. The Hendricks brothers and Jim Bronner and Bob Gilhooley were tough negotiators too. But major-league executives shared too many stories about Boras floating phantom offers, or neglecting to convey information to players. First he took their money. Then he wore them out with sanctimony, condescension, bullying, and brinksmanship, and they determined *en masse* that they really didn't care for him a whole lot.

Agent Ron Shapiro, author of *The Power of Nice*, is often praised for understanding that Cal Ripken Jr. and Kirby Puckett were better off taking less money to remain in cities where they were loved. In Shapiro's world, a negotiation is most successful when both sides win. In Boras's world, it almost invariably comes down to Scott and his principles, whether he's protecting the sanctity of the "market" or setting another salary record. Team officials didn't see a lot of graciousness in Boras as he scrambled for a front-row seat at the press conference. He might bring the game to its knees, but he'll never have the reverence that he craves.

"Scott has an agenda and he's got an ego, and those two things together are a lethal combination," says a National League general manager. "And you know what? He's had so much success. The game has given him so much. It's given him fame and fortune. I mean, he's got a ton of money. He's established an agency from nothing and turned it into one of the most powerful things in professional sports. What more does a guy need? I mean, somewhere along the line don't you take a step back and say, 'Gosh, you know what? This game has done a lot for me.' Or, 'Why don't I have more friends in the game?'"

At the other end of the spectrum are the people who knew Boras back when and who speak of him with the utmost warmth. Maybe it's Stanford athletic director Ted Leland, Boras's old fraternity buddy at Pacific. Or perhaps it's his college coach Tom Stubbs, who appreciates that Scott Boras has never forgotten his roots. The school inducted Boras into its sports Hall of Fame in 1994, and several years later, Boras contributed $250,000 to the Pacific baseball program.

Tom Stubbs nearly busted with pride when he read a magazine article listing Scott Boras as one of the 25 most powerful people in baseball. Conversely, he's angered when he hears that "Most Hated Man in Baseball" talk.

"I heard something on sports talk radio recently," Stubbs says. "It was a negative comment about Scott Boras. You know, 'You sure don't want Scott Boras as your agent because nobody's going to be interested in signing you.' They said he was a cheat and liar, and I know that's not true from my experience. Scott is a very fair-minded individual, and it hurts me deeply when I hear negative comments about him."

Don't blame Scott Boras, Ed DeBenedetti says, when teams choose to pay his clients gargantuan sums of money. He seethes when people say that Boras is greedy.

"Oh, bullshit!" DeBenedetti says. "He's doing his job! He didn't give A-Rod $25 million. He just throws a figure at 'em and they start to negotiate. How do you blame him for that?"

Doug Melvin's most memorable encounter with Scott Boras left him with a baseball-size knot in the middle of his stomach.

Melvin, a native of Canada, spent six relatively undistinguished seasons in the minor leagues as a pitcher before moving on to front office jobs with the New York Yankees, Baltimore, and Texas. He believes strongly in the concept of team-building through player development, and he helped bring the Rangers their first three postseason appearances that way. Yet in the winter of 2000–2001, he was almost an innocent bystander when Scott Boras convinced Texas owner Tom Hicks to spend $252 million over 10 years for free-agent shortstop Alex Rodriguez.

When the Rangers announced the signing on the ballroom stage at the Wyndham Anatole Hotel in Dallas, Melvin seemed out of place and vaguely embarrassed. He attended a general managers' meeting before the announcement and felt the animosity in the air, as if his colleagues suddenly regarded him as some form of traitor. He felt the onset of a headache, as if he were hung over when he hadn't had a drink.

"You know this deal and you know it's going to happen, and word got out and everyone was just staring," Melvin recalls. He could *feel* the eyes boring in on him.

That was another element of Scott Boras's strategy: Find an owner you could belly up to, and skirt the chain of command. If San Diego general manager Kevin Towers claimed the Padres couldn't afford to pay Greg Maddux $12 million a year, Boras might throw a paternal arm around his shoulder and ask, "Kevin, do you want me to talk to John Moores?" It was as if Boras thought he could make an extra $5 million a year magically appear through his powers of persuasion.

Charisma had certainly worked wonders in Los Angeles, where Boras held so much sway over chairman Bob Daly and GM Kevin Malone that it's a wonder he didn't have a branch office at Chavez Ravine. The story is told of how former L.A. manager Davey Johnson wanted to move Darren Dreifort to the bullpen, and Boras and Malone opposed it, and Boras spoke to Johnson for an hour in full view of the media. Shortly thereafter, Johnson changed his mind and said that Dreifort would remain in the rotation. His general manager couldn't convince him, but Scott Boras apparently could.

Boras later become a sort of horsehide Svengali in Texas. Under the Hicks regime, the Rangers signed pitcher Chan Ho Park to a 5-year, $65 million deal and had nine Scott Boras clients on their 2002 spring roster. The Rangers' infatuation with Boras became such an industry joke that Pete Gammons suggested that Hicks, vice chairman of Clear Channel radio, start a comedy show called *How Scott Takes Tom's Money*.

Melvin encountered the Boras influence with amateurs as well as pros. In the seventh round of the 2001 draft, Texas selected Clemson outfielder Patrick Boyd, who'd played one game as a senior because of back trouble. Boyd's adviser, Scott Boras, called him a legitimate high-rounder who had fallen through the cracks and deserved at least $600,000. Melvin and scouting director Tim Hallgren held firm at $200,000, even as Hicks questioned their judgment.

"Scott says this guy is worth $600,000," Hicks told them both, and Melvin and Hallgren replied that a $600,000 investment in Patrick Boyd would be insane.

On October 7, 2001, after Texas finished last in its division, Melvin's 7-year run as Rangers general manager ended. He'd produced more winners than losers, but had failed, Hicks said, to develop enough talent on the farm. Rumors immediately surfaced that Melvin had been pushed out by Boras, but Hicks denied the speculation. "That's not the way the world works," he told the Fort Worth *Star-Telegram*.

Hicks replaced Melvin with John Hart, former Cleveland general manager, and turned over the development system to former Oakland scouting director Grady Fuson, who had a big admirer in Scott Boras. Hicks gave Fuson a 3-year, $1 million contract, a huge payday, after Boras said he was one of baseball's most astute talent evaluators and deserved to be compensated handsomely.

Coincidentally or not, the Rangers signed Scott Boras advisee Patrick Boyd 2 months after Grady Fuson took his job. Boyd's signing bonus: $600,000.

Baseball people wonder when Boras is going to run out of owners to charm and teams to compete for his high-rent clients. For a while, Texas and St. Louis seemed to be guaranteed fallbacks. The Yankees supposedly hated him, and then Brown and A-Rod became available and George Steinbrenner climbed back on board.

In Seattle, Scott Boras will never be confused with Mr. Congeniality. Mariners officials claim that when A-Rod filed for free agency, Boras told them that the franchise's best hope was to go "short" and make an offer in the 5- to 6-year range. So the Mariners offered 5 years and $90 million, with an understanding that they'd revisit the terms if necessary. CEO Howard Lincoln and President Chuck Armstrong asked Boras if it would help their cause to travel to Miami to see A-Rod personally, but Boras assured them that it wasn't necessary.

Then Rodriguez signed with Texas, and the Mariners heard that Boras was telling A-Rod that Seattle management didn't care enough to travel to Miami to see him.

Armstrong, understandably, will not be featured on Scott Boras promotional material as a celebrity endorser anytime soon. "My problem with Scott is not that he's difficult to deal with necessarily, or that he doesn't tell the truth on a regular basis," Armstrong says. "In my opinion, I don't think he represents the best interests of his clients. I think he represents the best interests of Scott Boras."

The Mariners got their revenge in the summer of 2001, when they set an American League record with 116 victories. Texas, with marquee acquisition Alex Rodriguez, went 73–89 and finished 43 games behind Seattle in the AL West.

As the Mariners celebrated their accomplishment late in the season, a reporter asked Armstrong for reasons why the team had played so surprisingly well.

"Because we didn't have any Scott Boras guys," Armstrong said. The writer waited for Armstrong to laugh. But he never did.

That's the thing about Scott Boras the agent. You either buy into his philosophy or you don't.

Tim Belcher bought in, with some persuasion. As a high school shortstop in Ohio, Belcher wasn't even drafted. He attended Mount Vernon Nazarene College close to home and developed into a hot commodity as a pitcher. By his junior year he was moving up the draft board, and scouts and agents began showing up at his games. Belcher initially planned to handle the negotiations with help from his coach and his father. Then one day, the coach, Sam Riggleman, told him, "I just talked to a guy that I think you need to talk to." For Sam to give a plug, well, Tim Belcher figured this guy must be special.

The Belchers had their first meeting with Scott Boras at the Columbus airport, came away impressed, and told him, "Thanks. If we need you, we'll call." That call came sooner than expected. Minnesota selected Belcher as number one in the nation, but Twins scouting director George Brophy was a ball-buster, and the team held firm at $60,000 even when the going rate was $125,000. Belcher called Boras and said, "You're in," then headed overseas with the Pan-Am team. When he returned, the Twins were just as intransigent. He refused to sign, reentered the draft, then signed with the New York Yankees for $125,000.

Scott Boras guided Tim Belcher through the draft and represented him until his retirement in 2000, and Belcher considers Boras a close friend to this day. Not that they didn't have their battles. In 1995, after the strike, Belcher was unemployed and forced to audition for clubs at a free-agent camp in Homestead, Florida. He drifted from Seattle to Kansas City and was on his way to a career-high 15 victories when he told Boras he wanted to stay with the Royals.

But now that they had leverage, Boras started waxing on about the possibilities. "You really could command a lot if you went out on the open market," Boras told Belcher. "I really think the Royals are low-balling you." Belcher conceded that, yes, he understood. But after playing with five teams in 4 years, he craved stability even if it meant taking less money.

Eventually, Belcher had an angry exchange with his agent, dropping several profanities before slamming down the phone.

"Who was that?" said his wife, Teresa.

"Scott," Belcher said.

"You talk to him awful."

"Fuck him," Belcher said. "He works for me. He's laid out what he thinks my market value is. I understand it. I know if I stay here I'm going to take less than if I went out and pushed the market to the limit. But I've told him repeatedly that I'm not interested in that. Not this year. Not this time.'"

It's said in baseball circles that many Scott Boras players are too soft, too malleable, too readily inclined to let the agent run their lives. But Belcher wasn't soft. After growing tired of the negotiating dance, he walked into Kansas City general manager Herk Robinson's office intent on a resolution.

Belcher picked up the phone and called his agent. "Scott, I'm in Herk's office and we're going to work this out," Belcher told Boras. And Belcher agreed to a 2-year, $4 million deal, fully aware that he could have gotten more on the open market.

Sometimes, Belcher found, his agent was right and the market really did know best. At age 37, Belcher was almost consumed by a desire to pitch in the National League, and he banged on that theme incessantly with Boras. "National League, National League," he insisted. Then Scott would call back and say, "I talked to the Angels today," or "I talked to the Rangers," or some other American League club. When it came decision time and no National League teams stepped forward, Scott Boras got Tim Belcher, an aging right-hander, a 2-year, $10.2 million deal with Anaheim that included an option for a third.

Belcher still regards the negotiation as a work of art. "It was a hell of a contract," Belcher says. "He did great work for me, he really did."

Belcher concedes the imperfections in Boras. They clashed at times because he knew Scott wouldn't keep him informed of every development in talks. He knew that many people regarded Boras as arrogant. But he admired Boras's strong will to win.

"Deep inside him there's that former player who played professionally and competed on the field for a living," Belcher says. "The going back and forth with club officials—that's his competition now. Trying to one-up them. It's as if he's saying, 'My data is better than your data, and I'll prove it.'"

Dozens of other players swear by Boras, too. Jay Bell stayed with him forever, and Greg Maddux was with him out of high school through his 300th career victory and beyond. Outfielder J. D. Drew speaks of Boras in reverent tones. "People don't know him the way we do," Drew says. "He's a great person and a great friend."

Of all the players Boras represented through the years, Jim Abbott might have touched the deepest nerve of all. Abbott, born without a right hand, was an All-American at the University of Michigan and became a symbol of determination and a role model for the handicapped. He accomplished more with a single hospital visit than in his 254 career starts, and Scott Boras showed a genuine affection for him while navigating the unusual circumstances dictated by his handicap.

"I was always believed that Jim Abbott took a bigger piece of Scott Boras's heart than any of his other clients, including Greg Maddux and all of the Hall of Famers he's got," says Angels front-office man Tim Mead. Abbott began his career in Anaheim, left, and then returned as a free agent in 1996. When he suffered through a 2–18 season, Boras wondered if he put too much pressure on Abbott by bringing him back to the city where it all began. He showed enough concern over Abbott's emotional state that Mead later joked with him about it.

"If you keep doing some of these things, you're going to screw up your reputation," Mead told Boras.

Mead admired Boras's efficiency and take-charge approach. A lot of agents would indulge their players, but Boras worked with the Anaheim club and told players what needed to be said. He was there for damage control when pitcher Jarrod Washburn was accused of sexual assault—a charge that was eventually dropped—and advised Scott Schoeneweis to tone down the rhetoric after Schoeneweis ripped Anaheim fans for throwing trash onto the field during a period of labor discord in 2002.

"Scott is very passionate about what he does, and he has a tremendous ability to balance a lot of things," Mead says. "I think he's driven against himself more than he's driven against other agents. I think he really believes—and I'd be hard-pressed to argue—that he gives the best full service to his clients. I believe that when he sends out that bill, he knows he put everything into it."

Almost invariably, when things don't work out for Boras and a client, he'll attribute it to some character flaw or shortcoming on the part of the player. Joey Hamilton and Jaret Wright failed to show the requisite dedication and commitment, Boras will say, so it was inevitable that they would gravitate to other agencies. If Chan Ho Park is a $13-million-a-year bust in Texas, it's not because he failed but because Rangers management was negligent in recognizing that he has his own "special" workout program and approach.

The same logic applies to the amateur draft. If a year passes with no first-rounders advised by Boras, it's only because no one qualified as "Boras-worthy." Boras claims that he knew that Jose Canseco was not for him when Canseco, as a high school senior in Miami, fell asleep in the middle of their predraft interview.

Sometimes, the agendas just don't mesh. When San Diego pitcher Jake Peavy left Boras for Barry Axelrod before the 2004 season, he switched from a hard-liner to a perceived "nice guy" agent who plays golf with general manager Kevin Towers. Peavy wanted the security of a multiyear contract, while Boras traditionally likes to go one year at a time with younger players.

It takes a tough-minded individual to fire Scott Boras, but Peavy was resolute enough to make the switch. He has nothing bad to say about Boras in hindsight, except that their styles clashed.

"A lot of times, an agent speaks for you to the team and other people, and he'll make you come across the way he comes across," Peavy says. "Scott Boras is a great match with a lot of his other players. I just didn't think me and him were a good match."

Conventional wisdom holds that Boras is the best for superstars but not so hot for players at the back end of a roster. As Boras amassed more clients and built his operation, some fringe guys felt as if they were falling through the cracks. Bernie Williams or Kevin Brown never had trouble getting the Big Guy on the phone, but Joe Schmoe the typically average major leaguer might have to be content with a Boras associate.

Former Cincinnati catcher Joe Oliver saw the dynamic from both ends of the spectrum. In 1993, Boras won Oliver a $1.2 million award in salary arbitration, and Oliver felt as if he had a front row seat to watch Leonard Bernstein. "It was incredible," Oliver says. "His delivery and preparation were so far and above the other side's preparation, you couldn't even compare apples to apples."

But as Oliver suffered through injuries and his career prospects ebbed, Boras still talked him up like a front-liner, and some teams said the heck with it because they didn't want the trouble. Oliver finally left for Randy and Alan Hendricks; he feared clubs were avoiding him because of Scott Boras.

"I don't know if it was because of his reputation as a hardballer, but a lot of teams didn't want to talk to me," Oliver says. "I made my change and Scott dealt with it and I dealt with it and we moved on. It was nothing personal. I think Scott is one of the best in the business when the player has all the chips."

In 1997, when reporters asked Oliver why he had continued to retain Boras even as his salary declined from $2.5 million to $375,000 over three seasons, Oliver uttered one of the classic lines in player-agent breakup history.

"After all those years, I felt I owed him the benefit of the doubt," Oliver said. "It turns out he got all the benefit and I got the doubt."

Sandy Alomar Jr. and his brother Roberto were both Boras clients as minor leaguers in the San Diego chain. But Robbie dropped Boras early in his career, and Sandy followed suit, he claims, because Boras's agency was growing too quickly and he was afraid of becoming an afterthought. "Scott represents a lot of superstars, so when it's time to negotiate a contract, he has to take care of those guys first," Alomar says. "I'd rather have a guy who might not get the best deal in comparison with Scott, but at least you have his full attention."

Alomar's contract with Boras included an option year that Cleveland declined to exercise. When Jaime Torres, Alomar's new agent, negotiated a new deal with the Indians, Boras claimed that he was entitled to a chunk, and he filed a grievance through the union. "He tried to intimidate me," Alomar says. "He told me, 'I'm going to take you to court.' He thought I was going to cave in and say, 'Okay, I'll give you the money.' But I said no. It was all about principle."

Alomar spent $25,000 on legal fees, won his grievance, and has since made his peace with Boras, but Gary Sheffield's animosity lingers. When Sheffield first struck up a business relationship with Scott Boras in 2001, he was one embattled star. Fresh off a 43-homer season, Sheffield wasn't pleased with being the fourth highest-paid Dodger behind Shawn Green, Kevin Brown, and Darren Dreifort. He wanted the Dodgers to tear up his contract and sign him to a new one, and he trashed the team in the *Los Angeles Times* on a daily basis before the start of camp.

Sheffield made up his mind before spring training that he was going to fire Jim Neader, his agent of 14 years. Neader, Sheffield had determined, was too nice a guy for the cutthroat games that lie ahead. Big money was at stake, and he wanted a wartime *consigliere.*

Kevin Brown and some of Boras's other Dodger clients got involved after expressing concern that an unhappy Sheffield might undermine the team's season. And Sheffield, knowing that Boras was in tight with Los Angeles ownership, was perfectly willing to be wooed.

It was a productive partnership for a time. Sheffield turned the fans' boos to cheers with a game-winning homer on Opening Day, and at the urging of Boras, he stopped ripping chairman Bob Daly in the papers. Boras did his part with some skillful contract machinations. He negotiated Sheffield out of a 2004 contract option in exchange for Sheffield agreeing to drop Atlanta from a list of places where he wouldn't accept a trade. The Dodgers sent Sheffield to the Braves for Odalis Perez and Brian Jordan before the 2002 season, and Sheffield became a free agent a year earlier than scheduled.

But Scott Boras doesn't cut his fee for anybody—not Barry Bonds, not Gary Sheffield, not anybody—and Sheffield decided he'd just as soon have that extra 5 percent in his pocket. He had a business manager and a public relations woman, and he believed that better things were in store in light of a religious conversion.

Sheffield initially wrote a letter to fire Boras, because he thought that was the professional way to handle it. *He's got plenty of clients,* Sheffield told himself. *Who am I to worry about?* But Boras wasn't going to be dumped that easily. In the spring of 2003, he traveled to Miami to try to persuade Sheffield to remain part of Team Boras. When Boras walked into the room and found lawyer Rufus Williams sitting with Sheffield, he had difficulty concealing his displeasure. "Scott's problem is, he can't deal with rejection," Sheffield says.

Like Curt Schilling, who worked out a 2-year contract extension with Boston, Gary Sheffield decided that he was smart enough to be his own agent. He negotiated a 3-year, $39 million deal with Yankees owner George Steinbrenner that included some twists and turns, a few angry broadsides in the paper, and some apparent confusion over the precise meaning of "deferred money."

The transaction leads to Sandy Alomar redux. In the spring of 2004, Boras files documents with the Players Association claiming that he is entitled to a 5 percent cut of Sheffield's $39 million deal with New York, 5 percent of the $11 million option that Atlanta dropped to facilitate the 2002 trade, and $200,000 for a booklet that the Boras group prepared in anticipation of Sheffield's free agency. That's $165,000 more than the reported $35,000 Boras spent for his Alex Rodriguez brochure 4 years earlier.

The dispute doesn't prevent Sheffield from leading New York to a division title and finishing second in the American League MVP balloting. But the experience has left him with mixed feelings on the role of agents. One in particular.

"There are good ones and bad ones with everything in life," Sheffield says. "I'm not going to say Scott is a good or bad one. He just has an ego the size of L.A.—that's about all I can say."

Chapter
TWELVE

Tim "Rock" Raines, Mike Hinckley's manager with the Class A Brevard County Manatees, is the easygoing sort, with a cackle that resonates up and down the bench. They play a round of golf together, and Raines tells Mike that he'd be in the big leagues already if he weren't just a babe in his fourth professional season. The observation lifts Mike's spirits, since Raines spent 4 decades in the majors and knows talent when he sees it.

After Mike pitches seven innings of one-hit ball in his 10th Florida State League start, Raines spots him in the clubhouse and says, "We have a flight for you to go to Double-A after the game tomorrow."

"Really?" Mike says.

"No, man," says Raines, busting out laughing. "I'm just kidding."

But he's not kidding. The following night, Raines and coach Andy Skeels call Mike into the manager's office and tell him that he's headed for Harrisburg of the Double-A Eastern League. "Just go get 'em, and keep doing what you've been doing," is all Raines says.

At 21, Mike Hinckley is on the fast track. Earlier this year, he began seeing a sports psychologist at the recommendation of his 2003 minor-league manager, Joey Cora, and now he's embraced the art of positive visualization. Mike begins mapping out each start 2 nights in advance, picturing himself as an All-Star throwing to Albert Pujols or Chipper Jones. After every strikeout, he asks himself how Pujols or Jones might have fared against the same pitch. It's easy to stay grounded that way.

Chris Rojas, still a faithful Sosnick-Cobbe client 3 years after watching Dennis Tankersley check out, is pitching for San Diego's Mobile farm club in the Double-A Southern League. On the day of Mike Hinckley's callup to Harrisburg, Chris loses control of a fastball and plunks Prince Fielder, Milwaukee's prize prospect, in the helmet. Fielder brandishes his bat on the way to first base, and suddenly both benches have cleared and there's a full-scale brawl. Chris is poised to dispense some Bedford-Stuyvesant street justice when he's grabbed from behind by a Huntsville Stars player and whiffs in his attempt to slug big Prince.

"The worst part is, it was such a great punch," Chris laments to Paul Cobbe over the phone. "I had him in my sights, and I came up 3 inches short."

Another Sosnick-Cobbe client, pitcher Dusty Bergman, is summoned to the majors by the Angels for the first time at age 26, and Matt takes him shopping for a suit when Bergman passes through San Francisco en route to Anaheim. Dusty's mother is a blackjack dealer and works a roulette wheel in Reno. He talks to the casino operator and explains his situation to the pit boss before delivering the news to her personally.

"That's awesome!" Dusty's mother shouts into the phone, in a display of emotion that piques the gamblers' curiosity.

"What, are you a grandma now?" a casino patron asks her.

It appears that Matt and Paul might have a sleeper this year in Richie Gardner, a former University of Arizona pitcher who's making quite an impression in the Cincinnati chain. After going 8–3 with a 2.50 ERA for Potomac in the Carolina League, Richie earns a midseason callup to the

Double-A Chattanooga Lookouts. With a strong July and August, he can put himself in position to win a big-league job in 2005.

Gardner, a northern Californian, is a happy-go-lucky kid who personifies *mellow*. He has spiky, blondish hair and is partial to jeans, T-shirts, and flip-flops. After he received his $160,000 draft signing bonus from the Reds, he ran out and bought a surfboard to celebrate. It bums him out that the Reds train in Sarasota, because the waves are a lot smaller on the Gulf Coast than on the eastern side of Florida.

Richie feels a kinship to Paul Cobbe, who showed faith in him when he was basically a nobody. But now that he's sailing through the Cincinnati system, everyone is on board. First, a representative from SFX approaches him at the ballpark. Then, he gets phone calls in his hotel room from the Scott Boras group and the Beverly Hills Sports Council, inviting him to lunch.

Richie doesn't want to go to lunch, so he says he's not interested. Then he calls Paul to give him the scoop.

"This whole thing is insane," he says.

"Richie," replies Paul, "you haven't seen anything yet."

The Major League Baseball Players Association regulations governing agents, written in 1988 and revised now and then to reflect changing times, run 16 pages and address topics ranging from agent conduct to the grievance procedure. The rules give the union sole power to certify agents to negotiate contracts and conduct business, and they duly note that certification is not meant as an endorsement of the quality of an agent's performance.

Aspiring agents who have engaged in embezzlement, theft, or fraud need not apply, and those who try to lure talent with bribes or inducements are asking for trouble. Section Three says that an agent can be decertified or disciplined for "providing . . . money or any other thing of value to any Player (including a minor-league player or amateur athlete), the purpose of which is to induce or encourage such Player to utilize the Player Agent's services."

In 1990–91, the Players Association investigated Dennis Gilbert of the Beverly Hills Sports Council for allegedly giving cash and other inducements to players, but it cleared him of wrongdoing. The image of Gilbert as Sugar Daddy didn't exactly put a crimp in his business. Seven months after the union disposed of the matter, Gilbert client Bobby Bonilla signed a 5-year, $29 million contract with the New York Mets to become the game's highest-paid player. In 1993, a *Sports Illustrated* feature hailed Gilbert and Scott Boras as baseball's reigning Agent Kings.

Baseball agents generally believe that bribes are less blatant in their sport than in, say, football or basketball, because the payoff is less certain. A 7-foot center or hotshot quarterback can step off a college campus directly into a starting lineup—or a soft drink commercial—far more easily than can a third base prospect with great "tools." Even the most hyped Class-A player might spend 3 more years in the minors polishing his skills. And once he gets to the majors, it'll be 2 or 3 years after that before he's eligible for salary arbitration and a seven-figure contract. Why invest good money now in something that might prove to be a losing proposition later?

Still, that doesn't deter agents from playing ethical limbo ("How low can you go?") with prospects. Andy Sisco, a pitcher in the Chicago Cubs chain, recalls the case of a teammate who was caught "between a rock and a hard place." The player was living with his wife and their baby in a one-bedroom apartment when the wife had an accident and totaled the family vehicle.

"He was screwed," Sisco says, "and then all of a sudden he switched agents, and he had a new Mustang and a new Expedition. And I was like, 'Shit, unless he signed a new contract in the last week, that stuff's not free.'"

The horror stories are more prevalent in Latin countries, where ballplayers come from meager backgrounds, sign as free agents rather than through the June draft, and are more susceptible to being lured. David Rawnsley, the former Sosnick-Cobbe draft recruiter who once ran Latin American operations for the Houston Astros, says a $25,000 car was once considered the going rate to represent an elite Dominican prospect. In baseball circles, that benchmark was informally known as the "Ruben Mateo rule."

Most agents equate conduct rules for the profession with following a road map through the desert. They compare it to TEGWAR, the card game that the New York Mammoths play in the Mark Harris novel and baseball movie *Bang the Drum Slowly*. TEGWAR is an acronym for "The Exciting Game Without Any Rules."

Many agents wonder: Is there a moral distinction between slipping a player $5,000 in a manila envelope and giving him a laptop computer? What the heck—Paul Cobbe once lost a player to another agent because of a free cell phone. If you can bump into a competitor's client at a restaurant, why not call him in his hotel room six times and hound him into having dinner? And is hitting on another agent's 40-man roster player, who's covered by the major-league labor agreement, different from pursuing a kid in the low minors who's not covered?

Jeff Frye, a former major leaguer who now runs an agency, once asked his agent which players are permissible to approach under the rules. "Basically, if the guy can talk, then you can talk to him," the guy told Frye.

While it's convenient—and warranted, to a degree—for agents to trash the union for its inattentiveness to client-stealing, the "he said/he said" nature of disputes can be problematic. During agent update meetings, startups occasionally gripe about bigger firms stealing their players. But the Players Association often encounters the same problem when investigating complaints: First, the agent accused of stealing denies any wrongdoing. Then, the player who was allegedly stolen says, "I don't want to discuss it."

It's one thing to have opinions, says Gene Orza, and something else to commit the Players Association to a course of action based on those opinions. Institutions, like it or not, must adhere to a higher standard.

"There were all sorts of prosecutors who knew something was fishy at the Fulton Fish Market years ago, but when you act on behalf of the

Federal Government, you better have your ducks in a row," Orza says. "I know there's a lot of stuff going on out there, and I'd bet my life. But I'm not going to bet the Association's life, because the Association is bigger than just my hunches."

Sometimes when the howling gets loud enough, the union can't help but get involved and make an effort to sift through the damage. And it's not always the poor, outgunned little guy who's crying foul.

In late 2003 the Reich, Katz, and Landis group (a big agency) initiated a grievance against Jim Lindell (a little agency) with the Players Association. The grievance accused Lindell of "improper, disloyal, and deceitful conduct" and of a "plot" to take clients from RKL. It also called for Lindell to compensate the firm for both a loss of income and damage to its reputation.

Jim Lindell, a Washington native, resembles your next-door neighbor more than a deceitful client-stealer. He's tall and lean, with wavy hair and a fresh-scrubbed look straight out of an L. L. Bean catalog. "He has a look that says, 'You can trust me because I go fly-fishing,'" says Andy Sisco, one of his clients. Lindell is married with three children, and he worked as a certified public accountant before giving athlete representation a whirl.

In the fall of 2003, Jim Lindell reached what is commonly known as a career crossroads. He'd worked for Tom Reich's group full-time since 1998 and had recruited pitchers Ryan Dempster and Adam Eaton, among others, to the firm. He made a base salary of $84,000, plus commissions on new clients he brought to the agency.

But in August of that year, company president Adam Katz came to him with a new world order. Revenue was shrinking, and the agency needed to make significant changes. Among them: a new contract for Lindell that called for a 23 percent decrease in salary and a 33 percent reduction in commissions. According to Lindell, the group also proposed that he spend less time on the draft and more on major-league recruiting (i.e., taking players from someone else).

Lindell enjoyed working for the Reich guys. He considered them excellent agents, if not especially astute businessmen, and he was particularly fond of Adam Katz. But personal allegiances didn't mean much when you were about to have a $19,320 pay cut crammed down your throat. After reviewing the proposed contract with an attorney and determining that it wasn't to his liking, Jim called his clients with a stock speech.

"I'm leaving RKL for economic reasons," he told them. "You're free to choose whether to stay with Reich and Katz or select a different agent. If you decide to leave the firm, I would love the opportunity to win your business."

A total of 16 players—including "high-ceiling" prospects Jeff Francis, Luke Hagerty, Andy Sisco, and Ty Howington—followed Lindell out the door. Two months later, Adam Eaton called and said that he wanted to come along as well. When Eaton signed a 2-year, $5.25 million contract with San Diego in January 2004, company chairman Tom Reich had even more reason to go ballistic.

Just a week after Jim's departure, he received a letter from in-house counsel Jack Kincaid. "To say that the partners at RKL are extremely disappointed by your actions these past months is an understatement," the letter began, and went downhill from there.

Reich and Katz then enlisted the help of former agent and players' union honcho Dick Moss to pursue a grievance against Lindell. In early 2004, letters from Moss began arriving at the office of Jim Lindell's lawyer, accusing him of any number of unethical actions. A hearing before an arbitrator was scheduled for June, only to be postponed until November, then put off until January 2005. "This is so far down the list of the union's priorities, it's ridiculous," Jim says.

Jim Lindell takes heart in the advice of his attorney, who tells him the grievance is baseless because he never signed an agreement pledging not to take clients from Reich and Katz. In the meantime, Jim has amassed more than $15,000 in legal bills to help put this entire business behind him. He believes it's dragging on only because his former employer wants to make an example of him.

"I think this is Tom Reich telling the rest of his employees, 'You better not try to leave and take players,'" Lindell says. "The difference is, I never had a noncompete agreement, and everybody else there does."

Jim Lindell finds it mildly amusing that Tom Reich probably regards him as a "terrorist." Only in the agent business can a CPA with a closetful of Dockers and oxford shirts suddenly morph into a guerilla warrior.

Jeff Moorad suffered his first client defection in the mid-1980s, when Indians outfielder Cory Snyder left him for Ed Keating's agency. Moorad was so distraught that he broke down crying on the stairs in front of the Berkeley office where he worked with partner Leigh Steinberg. Then Steinberg gave him a pep talk and exhorted him to win Snyder back, and Jeff Moorad summoned the fortitude to get the job done.

Moorad's massive clientele and station in the industry are proof that he's not afraid to mix it up, whether battling with Scott Boras over Pudge Rodriguez and Juan Gonzalez or taking Travis Hafner away from Paul Cobbe. He sure seems like a congenial guy in person, but other agents have grown wary of what he might be doing out of earshot.

At Moorad's All-Star Game party in Seattle in 2001, he threw an arm around Jim Lindell's shoulder, told him he was quite a fine fellow and doing a bang-up job for Reich, Katz and Landis, and that it was great to finally meet him in person.

Two days later, Jim got a phone call from Ty Howington, a minor-league pitcher in the Cincinnati chain, who reported he'd been hit on by none other than Jeff Moorad.

"Who's your agent?" Moorad said.

"Jim Lindell of Reich, Katz and Landis," said Howington.

"I think I can do better. Let's go for coffee."

"I don't drink coffee."

"Well, let's just hang out."

"I don't hang out," Howington said, and that was the last he heard from Jeff Moorad.

Like many of the big agents, Moorad makes it a practice to use "runners," or "street agents," whose sole purpose is to recruit talent from competing firms. While the runners aren't certified to negotiate contracts, they have energy and ambition and can make a comfortable living enticing players to switch representatives.

Orlando Cepeda Jr., son of the Hall of Fame first baseman, is a runner for Moorad. So is Brian Peters, a former tennis player who began his career in the International Management Group mailroom. Peters is an able self-promoter, adept at cultivating the media, and so relentless it's almost charming. He's also what you might call a personality "chameleon," someone who works across racial lines and is equally at home recruiting an inner-city kid or hanging out with the country club set.

Brian Peters is smooth enough to talk a cat out of a tree—or through the front door of the city dog pound, if necessary. And he doesn't lack for self-confidence. At the 2000 Area Code Games, Peters walked up to Scott Boras and said, "I can outwork and out-recruit anybody at your company." "No thanks," Boras replied, but he made sure to convey the message to the guys at his agency, both for kicks and as a motivational tool.

Richard Justice, a Houston Chronicle columnist, witnessed some classic Brian Peters salesmanship at a Cypress Falls High School baseball game in the spring of 2002. In an effort to generate buzz for pitcher Scott Kazmir—who was about to be represented by the Moorad group in the draft—Peters took out his mobile phone between innings and called scouts with a blow-by-blow account of Kazmir's radar gun readings. "Hey, they just got my boy at 96," Peters told one scout after another.

Big agencies looking to expand their client base can cut down on mileage and phone calls by simply recruiting somebody else's runner, who'll bring along a passel of talent in the process. When Moorad hired Peters away from IMG, he got Vernon Wells, Adam Dunn, Brad Penny, and several other players as part of the package. In response, IMG filed a grievance with the union against Peters.

During spring training in 2004, agent Kenny Felder left Tommy Tanzer's group. His departure raised the possibility that he might take along several players—including Milwaukee outfielder Geoff Jenkins—to his new job with Moorad.

The timing was awkward, to say the least. Tanzer officially learned of Felder's intentions as the Brewers prepared to announce Jenkins's new 3-year, $23 million contract in Arizona. Shortly before the press conference, media members were treated to the sight of Jenkins's two agents spraying invectives at each other. The incident was even more bizarre given that Tanzer is a diminutive bull terrier, and Felder, a former Florida State University outfielder, stands 6'4" and somewhere north of 240 pounds. Yet there they were, going nose-to-nose—or chest-to-nose—until the Brewers asked them to take their dispute outside to the parking lot.

"A couple of coaches walked in and heard them fighting and yelling and walked out," says a Brewers official. "We were worried that the deal was going to fall apart. I swear they were going to punch each other."

Scott Boras has a message for would-be agents who've been hammering away for 5 or 6 years and are frustrated because bigger groups keep taking their clients and they can't make any headway in the business.

I've been there.

Boras was there in 1985, when all he had was his law degree and his baseball background and a single major-league client, Toronto pitcher Bill Caudill. The big agents pounded on him too, but Boras threw himself into the business with a frenzy, spending the better part of 3 years on the road, staying in cheap hotels to keep his overhead low, and running his agency with the help of a lone secretary. It took 8 years before he first turned a profit, and even when the big public companies threw gobs of money at him to sell out, he resisted because he didn't want to do it somebody else's way.

"Bill Caudill had a real good season, and all of a sudden, all these agents started coming in and saying, 'This Boras guy—he's inexperienced, he's young, he's never done this, he's a small-timer,'" Boras recalls. "But I stayed in the minor leagues and I went from league to league assessing talent, and that's all I did. And I went and I watched amateur players, and I didn't make a penny.

"I climbed the mountain because I passed the same litmus test that everybody has to go through. Your ability to survive in the system comes with showing your clients that you're competent in what you're doing. It's an arduous and difficult battle, and it's not much different than playing ball, because you have to prove yourself every day."

Most competitors assume that Boras pursues other agents' players for pragmatic reasons, because he has a business to run, with office space and travel costs and employees in Venezuela, Puerto Rico, and the Dominican Republic. It stands to reason that he must maintain a steady pipeline of talent and income, if only to pay his bills.

But Boras makes it sound more like a public service—that he's helping aspiring big-league ballplayers who might otherwise be victimized by raging incompetents. He's sensitive to the perception that his group preys on weaker agencies, to the extent that he engages in delicate verbal gymnastics to dispute it.

Scott Boras employees who track other agencies' players aren't *runners*—they're *former ballplayers*. And they don't *recruit* but rather *dispense information in an effort to educate young players*. Boras wants talented athletes in the Texas or California Leagues to notice his guy sitting in the stands every night, because that distinguishes his firm from the hit-and-run artists who pop in for a few days, hand out some goodies and make a few hollow promises, and then leave town.

But it's the zeal with which Boras's underlings pursue their assigned tasks that leads to anger and recriminations. When Scott Boras reps follow players from town to town and stand outside the bus handing out business cards like Halloween candy, then everybody notices, and the word spreads.

"Scott's people stay on a kid until he agrees to meet with Scott," says Tommy Tanzer. "Then he fills their heads up with what a great negotiator he is, and what a great arbitrator, and how he's the only one that understands this process and has never sold a player out. He tells the kid he's the only one who'll fight for him, and is really the only 'true' agent.

And whether or not he's successful, he does damage to that person's relationship with their current agent, because people are affected by what they hear."

Scott Olsen, a Sosnick-Cobbe client and top prospect with the Florida Marlins, got the hard sell during the 2003 season, when a Boras field rep named Terrence Smalls tracked him all over the South Atlantic League. Smalls was known as a hustler when he played for the Citadel as part of a double-play combination with his little brother, Tavy, and that trait served him well in his new line of work.

Scott Olsen struck out 129 batters in 128⅓ innings in Greensboro, North Carolina, and Terrence Smalls was in the stands for the last five or six starts. He would watch Olsen's games and then call him—every 5 days or so, for an extended period—until Olsen finally stopped taking the calls.

When Smalls finally reached him over the winter, Scott Olsen reiterated that he was happy with his agent, Matt Sosnick, and had no plans to switch. Terrence was cordial and seemed willing to take no for an answer. But 2 days later, he called back with a Boras superior, whose identity Olsen can't recall, and the higher-up was more persistent.

"He wanted to know how I felt and why I chose who I chose," Olsen says. "So I told him. He said I made the wrong move because Matt is a small corporation and he doesn't think he can do the same things the Boras people can do for me."

Scott Boras draws a clear distinction between minor leaguers, who need to be educated on what his group can provide, and big leaguers, who presumably are already aware. "In the major leagues, we do not solicit other agents' clients," Boras says. "That's very clear." When Barry Bonds, Gary Sheffield, and other top players left competitors for his group, Boras insists that it was entirely their initiative and that they called him unsolicited.

But that assertion rings hollow among many in the business. "It's BS," says Andrew Lowenthal, who works for the agency that represents Phillies closer Billy Wagner. "Players don't call agents in this business and say, 'Will you represent me?' That just doesn't happen."

During the 1980s, when Boras was still making his way and not nearly as contemptuous of the agent fraternity, Tommy Tanzer regarded him as a friend and an ally. Scott was incredibly bright, and he was willing to give Tanzer advice on marketing ventures and such. Tanzer, in turn, put in a good word for Boras with kids who didn't fit his own profile. "If you want somebody who's consistent and will really push for you, Scott's the guy," Tanzer would say.

But the two agents had a falling-out several years ago when Tanzer became convinced that Boras stole first baseman David Segui from him. After a snippy exchange in the hotel lobby at the 2000 general managers' meetings, Tanzer followed Boras to the parking lot, taunting him and challenging him to a fight before Boras got in his car and drove away.

Larger rivals and smaller targets all regard Boras with a degree of wariness or fear because of his resources and reach. But the aftermath is almost as painful. First you lose your player to him. Then he tells the world that the player left because you were too pathetic to keep him.

"I would respect him if he were honest and said, 'Look, I'm going to go after the best players, and if you can stop me, do your best,'" Matt Sosnick says. "But he's deluded himself into feeling that he doesn't have to steal players, because they're all dying to go to him. Everybody in the business knows that he stalks players and bullies them into switching to him. He facilitates disloyalty."

Says another veteran agent, who prefers anonymity: "Scott Boras is a guy who's pissed on a lot of agents' shoes, then told them it was raining."

Jay Franklin worked as a recruiter for the Scott Boras Corporation from 1998 to 2000 and never once offered a player money or inducements to leave another firm. But he was certainly persistent. And as a former minor-league ballplayer and Cleveland Indians scout (and the brother of Seattle Mariners pitcher Ryan Franklin), he was adept at relating to players and drumming up business, an endeavor that was encouraged by his superiors.

His introduction to Boras was an eye-opener because they seemed to have so much in common. Jay was just a country kid from Spiro, Oklahoma, as earthy as a puddle of tobacco spit. Scott had grown up on a farm in California, and they were linked by small-town sensibilities and a fondness for ball.

The Boras group hired Jay as a form of contract labor, on a 6-month "trial" basis to prove that he had the right stuff. The trial led to a 2½-year stint, during which Jay helped convince 11 players to leave other firms for the Scott Boras Corporation. The list included Carl Crawford, Marlon Byrd, Felipe Lopez, Gookie Dawkins, Ben Broussard, and the crown jewel of the lot, Los Angeles reliever Eric Gagne.

For his drive, skill, and ambition, Jay Franklin received the nickname "Hitman." That was sort of ironic, given that Jay spent his entire career as a pitcher, first at Oral Roberts University, then as a minor leaguer with Texas and the Cubs, and finally in Mexico and Taiwan.

There was a cachet to working for Boras, for sure. Scott surrounded himself with good people—former players such as Jeff Musselman and Mike Fischlin—and fostered an air of collegiality and singleness of purpose. Everyone spouted the company line, and the agency's resources, prominent name, and reputation for getting top dollar made recruiting relatively easy.

The ballyhooed Boras database, so renowned for spewing out player stats and historical comparisons, was also helpful. When Jay was pursuing another agent's player and needed an edge, he'd call the office in Newport Beach and get access to all the dirt. Maybe it was a newspaper story on how Agent A had screwed up this negotiation or Agent B had a poor relationship with that club's general manager. Every little bit helped. When the kid got up from the dinner table with a look that said, *Geez, I didn't realize my agent sucked that bad,* Jay knew that the meeting had gone well.

Some agents were easier marks than others. The Scott Boras Corporation compiled contact lists of potential recruits, with the kid's name, age, current ballclub, and present representation. "Weak agent—need to see again," it might say beside the name of a kid who was represented by some lightweight. The Boras guys even talked to minor leaguers who were represented by Ron Shapiro, Arn Tellem, and Randy and Alan Hendricks, although they were the furthest thing in the world from lightweights.

Jay knew lots of people from his playing days, so he'd call ahead and let a manager or coaching friend know that he would be in town, and most kids were at least amenable to a free meal. The toughest part was knowing how hard to push. Jay believed in taking things just so far, in putting himself in a player's spikes. If a kid said he was happy with his current agent, Jay would hand him a business card and say, "If you need anything down the road or you want to talk, just give me a call." That would be that, except when his bosses made it known that he should try harder.

The only thing that prevented Jay Franklin from staying with Boras for eternity was the lack of opportunity for advancement. For all the income Jay generated, he was making barely $40,000 annually. At his evaluation meeting in 2000, Jay recalls, Boras told him that he could recruit Eric Gagnes by the dozen and he would never surpass $100,000 a year. He wasn't going to negotiate contracts or do the "real" work that agents do. He was destined to be the relationship guy, the "runner," the rainmaker. In the end, that was all he needed to hear.

The Boras guys thought Jay was bluffing about leaving, because the Scott Boras Corporation is like the CIA—no one ever leaves. But Jay went to spring training in 2000 and had a long talk with his old buddy, Jeff Frye, and they talked about starting their own agency. Jay subsequently signed a noncompete clause, which legally bound him to keep his mitts off any Boras players for a year, and set out on his own.

If Jay Franklin is going to make it post–Scott Boras, he'll have to exercise better judgment than he has in the past. As a scout in Cleveland, Jay clashed with his boss, ran up more than $20,000 on his expense account in a show of defiance, and was eventually fired. And before leaving the Boras group, Jay charged $310 to a company credit card at a gentleman's club as a parting shot. Given a second chance, he might reconsider that one.

Maybe Jay Franklin was just too naïve for his own good. In 2003, Jay, his brother Ryan, and some other Seattle players were scammed by a local con man named Eddie Rivera, who passed himself off as an entertainment agent looking to segue into the sports world. Rivera conned players with promises of bogus "appearances," bilked investors out of more than $100,000, and was charged with several counts of theft.

Jay Franklin, understandably, wants to put all that behind him and build a successful agency with Jeff Frye. They've added a new partner, Seattle car dealer Mike McCann, who's helping to minimize the financial growing pains. And as former ballplayers, they believe they can relate to the kids they represent, because they know what it means to be benched or released, or, in Jay's case, to have Tommy John surgery.

"We're going to use an honest, blue-collar approach," says Jay Franklin, now a reformed Hitman. "I can't go in and blow smoke up people's ass and try to get them to sign with me for no reason. I want the people to want us, too."

Chapter

THIRTEEN

In late May, Matt Sosnick encounters a crisis of sorts: Toby Trotter has caught wind that the Jeff Frye–Jay Franklin agency is talking to players who have already committed verbally to Sosnick-Cobbe for the upcoming amateur draft.

A pissing match was almost inevitable. Franklin and Frye recruit heavily in Washington, Oklahoma, and Texas—states where Sosnick and Cobbe have been busy in recent years. If a kid in Seattle, Stillwater, or Sugar Land has a prayer of going high in the draft, he'll probably hear from one or both groups.

Given the natural animosities in the agent business, it's a chore for either side to choke out much that's complimentary about the other. Mike McCann of the Franklin-Frye group admires the Sosnick guys for working hard. But they recruit too indiscriminately for his tastes. "We're like a rifle," McCann says. "Sosnick is a shotgun guy. He's like, 'Let's shotgun everybody in *Baseball America*, and see what sticks.'"

That characterization sticks in Toby Trotter's craw. "Ninety-five percent of the kids that I recruit are referrals from scouts," Toby says.

"If I'm going up against a group with a former major leaguer and I'm getting better referrals, I must be doing something right and they must be doing something wrong."

Jeff Frye, the former big leaguer, is hammering the draft because he knows no other way. When you stand 5'9" and 165 pounds, enter professional ball as a 30th round draft pick, and play 8 years in the majors, it's a testament to your unwillingness to take no for an answer.

In 667 career games with Texas, Boston, Colorado, and Toronto, Jeff Frye developed a reputation for plain talk and dirty uniforms. In 1995, when Rangers manager Johnny Oates gave Mark McLemore the bulk of the playing time at second base, Frye fired off on a Detroit radio show. And when the Red Sox released clubhouse favorite Mike Stanley in 2000, Frye ripped GM Dan Duquette, prompting the team to trade him to Colorado. Frye figured that someone had to have the guts to verbalize what the entire clubhouse was feeling.

Frye has been an agent for only a year, but he has lots of experience with the breed. As a player, he was represented by David Sloane, Jim Bronner and Bob Gilhooley, Don Mitchell, Scott Boras, and Pat Rooney of SFX. Frye fired Sloane, he says, because it bothered him that a guy who hadn't played pro ball was telling him he needed to hit more homers or steal more bases. He fired Rooney in the spring of 2002 because the agent told him he was too busy with arbitration cases to help find him a job.

"I remember his exact words," Jeff Frye says. "He told me, 'I'm pretty much out of bullets. Why don't you make some calls on your own?'"

Jeff Frye has only one big-league client: pitcher Darren Oliver. But he and Jay Franklin are making inroads with the type of humble, Texas-Oklahoma kid who has hunting and fishing in his blood. Their message is as straightforward as can be: "If you don't like the job we're doing," Franklin and Frye tell families, "then fire our asses."

Two weeks before the draft, Frye is sitting in the stands at a junior college tournament in Bartlesville, Oklahoma, when his cell phone rings. It's Matt Sosnick calling from San Francisco, and in Frye's estimation, he's picking a fight.

Recently, the two groups had a dustup over a Texas-Arlington pitcher named Mark Lowe, who ultimately chose the Frye agency. And now Matt receives word that the Frye group is courting another one of his guys, an Oklahoma high school outfielder named Brandon Timm. Is a pattern developing here? Sosnick calls Frye and wants to know.

"If you're going to go after my guys in the draft and bad-mouth me behind my back, I have no problem budgeting some of the money we've put aside for this year's expenses to target your guys,'" Sosnick tells Jeff Frye.

Frye denies that he's stalking Sosnick's players. And besides, it's a free country, and who says you can't listen to a kid who's having second thoughts about his current adviser?

Apparently, something else gets lost in the translation, because Jeff Frye recalls a completely different message than the one Matt recollects.

"He told me he's independently wealthy," Frye says. "He said he made over $30 million by the time he was 25 years old, and he doesn't even need to do this job. He said he does it as a hobby, and if we continue to go after his players, he'd spend every penny of his resources to go after our guys or make sure they leave us."

Matt shakes his head. "There's no way in the world I would tell anybody I had $30 million," he says. "First of all, I don't have anywhere near $30 million. If I did, Frye and Franklin would be working for me. And second, this is not a hobby for me. I don't know too many people who have a hobby that runs 80 or 90 hours a week."

What a world, Frye tells himself. He wanted to stay in baseball, but he had no desire to be a big-league coach because he's married with three children and couldn't hack all the road time. So here he is in Oklahoma, banging heads with some stranger over a kid who may or may not amount to anything. He clicks off his cell phone and is happy to resume watching the action on the field in Bartlesville.

At the other end of the line, Matt Sosnick clicks off his phone and gets back to preparations for the 2004 draft. Which most likely means another phone call. . . .

Toby Trotter is piling up the mileage and working his butt off this spring, but Matt and Paul know from experience that the draft is subject to wild swings in the months and weeks preceding the big event.

Sometimes, the scouting grapevine can make a hash of things right up until June. Several years ago, Sosnick and Cobbe were representing California junior college pitcher Jake Woods in the draft, and there happened to be another Woods in Florida who was seeking a $1 million bonus. The scouts got the two players confused, and Paul had to hit the phones and hustle to spread the word that *his* Woods was the one with reasonable expectations.

A group of scouts might be sitting in the stands watching a pitcher scratch a bug bite on his elbow, and the next thing you know, there's a rumor going around that he's a candidate for Tommy John reconstructive surgery. It sounds ridiculous, but Paul Cobbe actually saw it happen a few years ago with a pitcher named Jason Smith.

Matt and Toby's February recruiting trip to Houston, which appeared to be so fruitful, yields no immediate results. Brian Juhl, Mark McGonigle, and Jordan Dodson—the three high school seniors who committed to Sosnick-Cobbe earlier this spring—are upper-middle-class kids and good students. So, when it becomes apparent that they're not going to be drafted high enough to warrant the bonus money they desire, they all opt for college. Juhl will attend Stanford, McGonigle will go to Houston, and Dodson plans to play third base for the reigning national champions at Rice. The hope is that all three boys will remember their experience favorably and retain Sosnick-Cobbe if they're drafted as college juniors in 2007.

The closer teams get to the draft, the more major-league scouting departments obsess over "boards" projecting which players will go where. It's a fluid and constantly evolving process. Nick Adenhart, a Maryland high school pitcher who throws 95 mph and is considered a sure first-round pick, blows out his elbow in May and is suddenly out of sight and out of mind. At the same time, there's a kid somewhere who fits the "sleeper" designation and who will be picked higher than the conventional wisdom would ever suggest.

Sosnick and Cobbe, more than many agent groups, are tapped into the intricate intelligence network that links agents and scouts. If a team wants to pick a kid in the third round and wonders who else is interested, it certainly can't ask other teams, so the agents can be a valuable resource. While Scott Boras has a reputation for not talking to scouts, an accommodating group such as Sosnick-Cobbe can make inroads by diving headfirst into the information swap shop. *Sure, we'll tell you what we're hearing. But first, you tell us what you're hearing about our junior college lefty with the 89 mph fastball. What's the word out there on him?*

"I wouldn't hesitate to say that they get more information from scouts and scouting directors than any other agents," Minnesota scouting director Mike Radcliff says of Sosnick-Cobbe. Smaller groups, Radcliff says, are more inclined to look for common ground. The bigger agencies, like Boras or IMG or Octagon, represent elite players with the intention of "extending the envelope" financially.

At 10 days and counting to June 7, Matt can feel the sense of anticipation mounting. Sosnick and Cobbe have developed a reputation for productive drafts, but now that they have to spend more time taking care of the Willises and Hinckleys, they have a lot less time to recruit. So this year, Matt will have to trust in fate, good karma, and the efforts of Toby Trotter. "I only control what I control," he says.

The process of funneling talented amateur athletes into the play-for-pay realm—a.k.a. "the draft"—is now a celebrated piece of sports Americana. In football, arcane Web sites and "drugstore" publications devote months to speculative mock drafts, and Mel Kiper Jr., a Maryland native with lacquered hair and 512 megabytes of memory, has transcended the level of niche celebrity and embraced the designation of "draft guru."

Football, hockey, and basketball all parade their draftees on stage in televised events, before they lose all the cartilage in their knees, or sport gap-toothed grins, or begin traveling with their very own posses. Major League Baseball, in contrast, welcomes its newest talent under cover of apathy. Pittsburgh general manager Dave Littlefield calls the draft the "Super Bowl of scouts," but the national appetite for baseball draft information is negligible. People at ESPN and the commissioner's office have no interest in televising the baseball draft, because they recognize that log-rolling, spelling bees, and championship poker are more sure-fire ratings-getters.

The baseball draft is routinely labeled a "crapshoot," and the numbers support that theory. Along with players from Puerto Rico and Canada, about 140,000 U.S. high schoolers, collegians, and junior collegians are available for the taking each June. Of that total, roughly 1 in 94 American ballplayers is drafted by a big-league club each year.

Then the odds continue to narrow. *Baseball America* studied the drafts from 1965 to 1995 and found that 15,660 players were selected in rounds 1 through 20. Among first-round picks, 64.9 percent eventually played in the major leagues, and 48.7 percent lasted more than 3 years. In the second round, the percentages declined to 41.6 and 25.7. By rounds 16 through 20, only 3.7 percent hung around longer than 3 years in the majors. For every Keith Hernandez or Mike Piazza who makes it big as a draft afterthought, there are scores of picks who have a fun summer in Oneonta, then graduate to batting cleanup for the Smokey's Rib Pit slow-pitch softball team.

College baseball receives little national exposure, so even players from Texas, Louisiana State, and other traditional powerhouses are lacking in cachet. They're also destined to spend time on the farm; it's just a matter of degree. Mark Prior, a pitcher so polished and overpowering he was compared with Tom Seaver coming out of college, made only nine minor-league starts before his debut with the Cubs. Milwaukee outfielder Scott Podsednik, in contrast, spent parts of nine seasons in the minors before finally sticking with the Brewers in 2003. Bob Feller, Al Kaline, Mel Ott, Sandy Koufax, Catfish Hunter, and Dave Winfield are among the rarities who played in the majors without a day of minor-league seasoning. It's no accident that they're all Hall of Famers.

Unlike basketball, where a high schooler with a high vertical leap and low hoops IQ can spend 3 to 4 years absorbing from the bench and serving as practice fodder, baseball dictates that progress is achieved only by playing, then playing, then playing some more. It's a repetition game, and a vulnerability to curveballs can only be addressed by facing curveball after curveball, and learning to judge spins and speeds and pitching patterns, and adjusting accordingly. Pitchers who can't pitch inside learn to acquire that skill with time, and it had better occur in the minor leagues, where winning is secondary to long-haul thinking and teams can afford to lose games for the sake of development.

The vast majority of players selected in the draft are "organizational" types who fill out rosters and provide the competition that helps steel the Alex Rodriguezes and Albert Pujolses for the next rung. Most wash out with the realization that the dream, however romantic, is unattainable, and the understanding that persistence and a love of the game can only go so far. But the big mistakes make big headlines and have staying power in draft lore. Exhibit A of draft-as-crapshoot is Steve Chilcott, a California high school catcher who went to the Mets number one overall in 1966 and peaked in Double-A ball. Kansas City used the next pick on Arizona State outfielder Reggie Jackson, who went on to hit 563 homers and have a chocolate bar named after him.

In recent years, a debate began to rage, fueled by Michael Lewis's best-seller *Moneyball*, over whether teams were best served drafting high school players with raw skills or college players with more detailed statistical portfolios. The collegians might have lower upsides, but they're more predictable and, theoretically, less risky.

Scouts have always been fond of unpolished gems. In the early 1990s, Major League Baseball produced a video in which Hall of Famer Jim Palmer, clad in suit and tie and looking earnest in front of an old school building, reflects with pride on his shutout against Los Angeles as a 20-year-old Baltimore Oriole in the 1966 World Series.

The message to young ballplayers: *If you go to college rather than sign with a big-league team as a high school senior, you might miss out on your big dream.*

"I showed it to Gene Budig and he almost puked," says Gene Orza, recalling the day that he pulled out the tape for the former University of Kansas chancellor and American League president.

Scott Boras's enduring legacy, in Orza's estimation, was alerting high school players that they had an option. The option was college, which gave them a fallback for life in the event that they failed to make it in pro ball, and which enhanced their leverage. If you're a fastballing right-hander and a Stanford education awaits you, Boras knew, a team would have to invest more to make sure that you never set foot on campus in Palo Alto.

"Scott Boras was the first person to understand the degree to which a practice could be built on convincing high school draftees that college was a viable, worthwhile alternative which they could introduce into negotiations with clubs," Orza says. Boras's success in making millions for unproven players was ironic, given that the draft was introduced less as a talent equalizer than as a cost-containing mechanism. When Cowboy Gene Autry and the Los Angeles Angels gave Wisconsin out-fielder Rick Reichardt a $205,000 bonus as a free agent in 1964, it was a wake-up call to teams that they had better get a grip on the situation. The draft began the following year, and top pick Rick Monday signed for a more palatable $104,000 with Kansas City.

Bonuses generally stayed under wraps until the late 1980s, when Boras came along and made it clear that he would push deadlines, tax limits, and fray the nerves of club executives in pursuit of "fair market value." In 1988, Evansville pitcher Andy Benes set a record with a $235,000 bonus, and the payouts spiraled upward—from a $950,000 package for LSU pitcher Ben McDonald to $1.2 million for Texas high school pitcher Todd Van Poppel to $1.55 million for North Carolina schoolboy pitcher Brien Taylor, who hurt his shoulder in a fight after going number one overall in 1991 and never played a day in the majors.

Boras once compared baseball's traditional mindset to a cement block;

it could leave you with a stubbed toe if you insisted on kicking it, but it was more susceptible to change when attacked with a jackhammer. Boras was a lawyer, a former ballplayer, and a master jackhammer operator rolled into one, and he gradually made baseball conform to his will.

But he needed players to buy into his vision, and several obliged. In 1991, first-round picks Kenny Henderson and John Burke refused to sign and went back into the draft the following year. That showed teams there was a price for holding the line. Four years later, Georgia Tech catcher Jason Varitek signed with St. Paul of the independent Northern League, and Boras argued that since he was under a professional contract, he was no longer draft-eligible and should be declared a free agent. Varitek signed with Seattle before it came to that, but the message was sent.

Some of Boras's lab rats didn't fare so well. Henderson spurned a $650,000 offer from Milwaukee, then a reported $350,000 from Montreal before signing with San Diego for $55,000 out of the University of Miami. One newspaper called him the "Backward Bonus Baby."

High school pitchers Matt White and Bobby Seay, conversely, cashed in big-time in 1996 when Boras took advantage of a technicality to set them loose on the free market. The Tampa Bay Devil Rays gave White a $10.2 million bonus and Seay $3 million, and the message was clear: Scott Boras, Lord of the Loophole, would find a way.

He found a way by wielding absolute control over the process. If an elite Boras pick is anxious to play and thinking about softening his demands, the team will never know. After the draft, the kid's cell phone number changes and he might as well be in the witness protection program. And good luck trying to do an end run on Boras to find him.

Scouting directors began to slap a label on Boras kids. While no one ever accused Jason Varitek of being "soft," baseball people said that Boras players were easily influenced and had a sense of self-worth out of proportion to reality. "One of the common denominators is, there always seems to be a dominant parent," says a scouting director. "There's a dad who is really strong and has an overinflated view of his son, or a mother who is very protective and doesn't want her son to get shortchanged. I think Boras is able to connect with that one parent. He's able to reinforce what the dad believes: 'My kid is the greatest. He's special. He deserves this.'"

Boras's mere presence could alter a team's draft strategy. One American League team places a red, yellow, or green flag beside each player's name based on his representation. A green flag means that the adviser is upfront and interested in getting the player signed quickly. A yellow flag means that the adviser is generally straight, but not always reliable.

And a red flag?

"A red flag means, Don't go there, because you just know it's going to be a royal pain in the ass," the scouting director says. "Boras is an absolute, positive, red-flag deluxe."

Teams have learned to view information disseminated by Boras with a wary eye. Several years ago, Boras conducted a study of the 1983–1988 drafts and found that 48 percent of collegians picked in the first round had a big-league career of at least 6 years, while only 14 percent of high school players met that standard. The figures, trumpeted by Boras in a *USA Today* story, substantiated his theory that college was the best option for an aspiring big leaguer.

But when an American League club ran the numbers, it found that 48 percent of college first rounders played 6 years in the majors and 33 percent of high schoolers met the standard—well above the 14 percent figure cited by Boras.

Many front-office people won't discuss Boras publicly, because they dislike him intensely and see nothing to be gained from equivocating. But the assessments aren't all doom and gloom. "Scott makes you think," says Dan Jennings of the Florida Marlins. "You can also say anything to him, because he has thick skin. On the negative side, when you make valid points and you know they're valid, he refuses to acknowledge them. But you can always say no."

Paul Snyder, former Atlanta Braves scouting director, is revered throughout the game for having drafted Bob Horner, Tom Glavine, Steve Avery, David Justice, Ron Gant, and Chipper Jones, among others, in his tenure with the club. Snyder doesn't like the Boras gambit of pulling rank and bypassing the scouting director to speak directly with the general manager or owner. And he's aware of the orientation speech that Boras gives draft picks and believes that it demonizes teams in the eyes of kids and their parents.

"I didn't appreciate that he would get the families in this closed room and kick the organizations in the shin, right where he was making his living," Snyder says.

Nevertheless, Snyder's dealings with Boras were generally productive through the years—hardly the nightmare he might have expected. Atlanta allotted $1 million in 1999 for Florida pitcher Matt McClendon, a Boras pick, and signed him for $900,000. Deep down, Snyder believes that Scott Boras wants the best for his clients, even if they're a means to his own end. And he considers Boras a little sharper and more prepared than the fraternity at large.

"You have to respect him for what he's done for his clients," Snyder says. "You'd have to be half-blind not to. He's gotten better and better at his business and kept baseball on their toes. If you're gonna draft a Scott Boras client, you better go to bed and get your rest, because you're gonna be in for a long ballgame."

Boras's seminal draft negotiation came in 1997 in the person of Florida State outfielder J. D. Drew, who has the given name of David Jonathan but has gone by the ass-backward moniker of J. D. since he was a little boy. The oldest of David and Libby Drew's three baseball-playing sons, J. D. grew up in the one-yellow-caution-light town of Hahira, Georgia, which is known for its Honey Bee Festival. He aspired to play pro football until age 12, when he concluded he wouldn't see the ball enough as a wide receiver to stay engaged.

J. D. Drew's mode of speech includes liberal use of the expressions "Gol-ly!" and "I reckon," and he enjoys Bible reading, duck hunting, and pulverizing fastballs, in no particular order. His Florida State coach, Mike Martin, compared him to Joe DiMaggio for his understated approach, but Drew's compact frame and propensity for batting practice bombs reminded others of Mickey Mantle. Doug Mientkiewicz, Drew's former college teammate, marveled at his ability to take two straight curveballs down the middle for strikes, then pull an 0–2 outside fastball 400 feet. "The dumbest, best hitter I've ever seen," Mientkiewicz once called him.

After Philadelphia chose Drew with the second pick in the '97 draft, he was billed as the next Fred Lynn or Larry Walker. With the help of his adviser, Scott Boras, he became a round-the-clock nightmare for Phillies management. The fun and games began when the Phillies mailed a contract to the home of Drew's parents in Georgia, and Boras claimed they broke the rules by failing to send it to the player's "last permanent address" in Tallahassee, Florida, within the allotted 15 days. Major League Baseball denied Boras's requests to have Drew declared a free agent, but the folks at Federal Express enjoyed a bonanza of free publicity in the Philadelphia papers.

Drew spurned the Phillies' $2 million offer, held out a year, played in the independent Northern League with St. Paul, reentered the draft, and signed a deal with St. Louis in 1998 that was potentially worth $8.5 million. But he paid a price in acrimony and stifling expectations. The skeptics wondered how a self-professed Christian with an aw-shucks manner could seem so cannily mercenary in his objectives, and Philadelphia fans, who never take rejection well, reacted to being spurned.

In August 1999, J. D. Drew made his first trip to Veterans Stadium as a Cardinal, and the backlash was so pronounced, St. Louis bullpen catcher Jeff Murphy wore a jersey with "Drew" and the No. 7 on the back as a decoy to take some heat off the real thing. Fans waved signs with messages like "J Greed Drew" and "Greed Is a Cardinal Sin," and threw batteries onto the field in anger. When the Phillie Phanatic dropped moneybags in front of the St. Louis dugout, it was too much for Boras, and he became the first agent to bash a mascot for inappropriate behavior. "Whoever controls the Phillie Phanatic should be reprimanded," Boras said.

By waging an economic crusade on two fronts, Boras had to work overtime to keep his constituencies in order. Big leaguers who broke in when bonuses were smaller rejected the notion of aluminum-bat-wielding collegians becoming instant millionaires. During Drew's holdout, Phillies pitcher Curt Schilling challenged Boras to a televised debate on the issue. The atmosphere got so testy, Boras nearly walked off his remote location during a commercial break.

Even fan favorite Mark McGwire spoke out about J. D. Drew. "These kids have no right to ask for these amounts," said McGwire, who signed for $145,000 as a first-rounder in 1984. "It's sad. They should want to be able to play baseball, not make $10 million without ever stepping on a pro field."

Boras saw it as a matter of principle: If Orlando Hernandez could step off a boat from Cuba and be the focus of a bidding war, why should a "premium" home-grown player be limited by artificial restraints? The more successful Boras became, the more elite draft prospects had to decide whether to embrace his vision or flee from it.

Larry Wayne "Chipper" Jones, the nation's top prospect in 1990, decided he wasn't cut out for the Boras doctrine. As a high school senior in Jacksonville, Jones routinely took the field and saw 50 to 100 scouts and 20 to 25 adviser wannabes eyeballing his every move. The scouts were dreamy-eyed because Jones was a rangy switch-hitter with tools to burn, and the agents saw the lust in the eyes of the scouts and knew they would benefit by extension.

Boras was among the agents who made a pitch, and it was impressive. "He's a persuasive guy," Jones says. "He's good at schmoozing Mom and Dad. Coming from a middle-class family like myself, we didn't have a ton of money, and he tried to throw the dollar bills up in front of us." But the middle-class Joneses weren't biting. Atlanta sent two scouts into Chipper's house, and within a half-hour the two sides bridged the gap between a $300,000 request and a $250,000 offer to settle on a bonus of $275,000.

Chipper Jones broke his hand as a high school senior, but when the cast came off, he was on his way to Bradenton to play ball. He planned to earn his way to Atlanta one batting practice session at a time, rather than sitting at home waiting for his "fair market value."

More than a decade later, Jones has five All-Star appearances and 300-plus home runs on his resume, and he's convinced he made the right call. In 2000, when Chipper Jones signed a 6-year, $90 million contract with the Braves, he'd already won an MVP award and finished in the top 10 in the balloting three other times. True to his goal, he'd earned the big money, and the Braves loved him for it. A lot of old-time scouts loved him, too.

When Cleveland Indians scouting director John Mirabelli broke into pro ball as an area scout with Detroit in 1990, agents weren't nearly as prominent in the draft. "Maybe your first-round pick had one," Mirabelli says. "After that, you negotiated directly, from the area scout to the family and the player. Now, agents are involved with all top-10-round picks, and maybe more than that."

The National Collegiate Athletic Association has rules in place governing the use of agents in contract negotiations for draft choices. In a nutshell, a high school senior or college junior who's been drafted risks losing his college eligibility if he hires an agent to negotiate with a club. Players and their families can, however, talk directly with clubs and consult with agents who supposedly stay in the background as advisers.

The result is a system rife with hypocrisy, backroom dealings, and sporadic punishments meted out arbitrarily. Baseball expressly forbids "pre-draft" deals, but they're commonplace with number-one overall picks. And there's no rhyme or reason to NCAA discipline. In 2001, the Cincinnati Reds selected Kentucky high school pitcher Jeremy Sowers in the first round even though they lacked the $3 million required to dissuade him from going to Vanderbilt. Sowers did, indeed, go to school, and the next spring, the NCAA slapped him with a six-game suspension because his "adviser" at IMG had talked over the phone with a Reds official. It was the obligatory knuckle rap, intended solely to send a message.

"The NCAA selectively and randomly isolates guys who don't sign to make examples out of them," says an agent. "It's ridiculous."

Several years ago, Major League Baseball's scouting committee invited an NCAA official to come in and address the issue of "agent" versus "adviser." By the time the meeting ended, the assembled scouts were more confused than when it began.

"The hypocrisy is with the NCAA rules," says Florida's Dan Jennings. "We all know that once you go in and draft this player, you're going to deal either face-to-face or in the background with this particular agent. If that occurred in basketball or football, those players are declared ineligible. The NCAA says, 'Just give us proof.' Well, how in the hell do you get proof? Are you going to get an agent to sign a statement saying, 'I represent this player'? That's not the way it is."

Even sticklers in the Commissioner's office in New York concede that a balance must be struck. Should novice parents really be forced to negotiate directly with teams under the guise of some NCAA-mandated charade? In truth, a club would rather deal with a reasonable agent than directly with parents because it removes the emotional element from negotiations. But rules are rules, so the farce persists.

For parents, the process of picking an adviser is one in a series of anxiety-producing steps. Before the draft, teams routinely distribute tests and questionnaires to prospective draftees. If you're an aspiring big-league pitcher, a team wants to know whether you're an analytical Greg Maddux; a glowering, hypercompetitive Kevin Brown; or a free-spirited guitar strummer in the Barry Zito mold.

Teams also want to know whether a young man drinks or smokes, is neat or sloppy, and whether he values team accomplishments over individual statistics. And of course, they want to size up his financial expectations, to see if he'll be willing to sign for X amount if he's drafted in the second or fifth or eighth round.

The potential draftee and his parents must walk a line between being too coy and misleading teams, or offering too much information and blowing their leverage. It isn't easy.

"The first thing is, don't give them a price, because the minute you do, their job is to knock you down or tell the world," says Jerry Prior, father of former Cubs' number-one pick Mark. The only thing faster than the Internet, he's discovered, is the scouting grapevine.

Jerry Prior, a San Diego financial consultant, is an authority on parental draft etiquette. He went through the process when Mark turned down a $1.5 million offer from the Yankees out of high school. And then, when Mark was anointed the next Tom Seaver coming out of USC, things went completely insane. Jerry Prior thought that Tommy Tanzer's agency, in particular, had been excessively ardent in its pursuit of Mark over the years. The family tried to establish ground rules with USC coach Mike Gillespie, but it didn't prevent would-be advisers from calling and swarming, swarming and calling, enough to put all the Priors on edge.

In July 2000, Mark was playing for Team USA in an exhibition game on Cape Cod when everything came to a head. After a long day at the park in Chatham, the family was on the field taking pictures when Scott Boras Corporation representative Scott Chiamparino introduced himself to Jerry Prior and asked whether he might have a few minutes to chat.

Chiamparino's timing could have been better. Jerry Prior was already wary of agents, his wife was recovering from foot surgery, and the family was enjoying a classic bonding moment—laughing and chatting with friends beneath a Cape Cod full moon—before sending Mark off to Europe with Team USA.

"No, this wouldn't be a good time to talk," Jerry Prior told Chiamparino. "And by the way, would you please take a hike?"

As Jerry Prior recalls, he told Chiamparino to move away from the gate to create some space, but the guy refused to budge. Jerry's Irish temper kicked in, the old Vanderbilt football player came out, and he hit Chiamparino—flat-out smoked him—with a forearm smash.

"Mister, if you get near me or my family again, I'll turn you into fish food!" Jerry Prior shouted at the Boras recruiter.

Mark Prior, understated by nature, was mortified over his father's loss of self-control, and said so at dinner after the game. "What is it you want?" Jerry finally asked. Mark replied that he simply wanted to sign and play pro ball—not break a record or make a statement. He wanted an adviser who would help facilitate the effort and keep the process from becoming a circus.

Jerry Prior spent that evening nursing a cigar and a glass of bourbon while reflecting on the fiasco in Chatham, and the request seemed more than reasonable.

The Priors compiled a list of six agents, and they gradually winnowed the choices to John Boggs and Ron Shapiro. They ultimately settled on Boggs, the San Diego guy, and the Cubs signed Mark to a $10.5 million contract with a $4 million bonus in August 2001.

Jerry Prior, as a veteran in the process, gladly fields phone calls these days from anxious parents in search of help. But contrition isn't his thing. After whacking a Scott Boras representative on the Cape, he now revels in taking shots at Boras.

Jerry Prior did his homework and saw too many good college players that he believes were "screwed" by Boras's strategy. Taggert Bozied, a power-hitting first baseman from the University of San Francisco, turned down $800,000 from the Minnesota Twins as a second-round choice in 2000. He returned to school and signed the following year with San Diego for $750,000 as a third-round pick, but only after sitting out the entire summer and playing independent ball.

When amateur draft choices sign contracts, they get "on the clock" and begin amassing the service time necessary to force organizations to make decisions to propel them through the system. By delaying Tagg Bozied's debut by 2 years, how was Scott Boras helping him? And how was Boras helping Bobby Hill, a University of Miami infielder who held out, played independent ball, and turned out to be nothing more than a fringe big-leaguer? So many of the players hyped by Boras failed to meet expectations, and increasingly, more teams began shying away from them to avoid the hassle. Who was he really helping?

Jerry Prior saw Boras as the classic bully—a guy who scared teams with bluster and turned parents into "mushrooms" by talking over their heads and dazzling them with his brilliance. When he saw Boras smiling away at a press conference for A-Rod or some other superstar, he wanted to gag.

"He's an embittered ex-minor leaguer who's determined to get his pound of flesh from baseball," Jerry says. "We wanted no part of what we called hostage negotiators. And he is the number-one hostage negotiator."

In 6 years of mining the draft, Matt Sosnick has more parental stories than he can remember. He's dealt with salt-of-the-earth parents, nervous parents, interventionist parents, and parents with delusions of grandeur. One kid's father flew out from Oklahoma and stayed at Matt's house before the draft under the pretense of getting acquainted. They watched Barry Bonds hit his 500th career home run at Pac Bell Park, when just like that the dad decided he was going to fly to Las Vegas on a gambling jaunt. "This guy was so dumb," Matt says, "it took him 2 hours to watch *60 Minutes*."

Julie Bradley comes from a more sincere, heartfelt orientation. Her son, Jeff Marquez, is a pitcher for Sacramento City College, and it's an understatement to say that he's come from nowhere in the spring of 2004. Jeff stood 6 feet tall and weighed 145 pounds as a high school senior, and his friends laughed when he said he was going to play baseball at Sac City, one of the strongest junior college programs in the nation.

But Jeff proved everybody wrong. After redshirting his freshman year, he gained 2 inches and 35 pounds and added 10 mph to his fastball. He's now throwing 92 to 93, and scouts who wouldn't have considered him worth the gas and vehicle wear-and-tear necessary for a trip to Sacramento are suddenly showing up behind the screen with radar guns and serious expressions.

Julie, an oral surgery assistant who's divorced and remarried, is fretting every minute. If Jeff doesn't turn pro, big-time college programs at Miami and Long Beach State are interested. The Sac City coaches are telling him he should stay another year and get bigger and stronger. Jeff wants to be an architect one day, but if he enters pro ball, can he still go to school? And one team after another is sending questionnaires to the house. *Do you have any allergies?* they ask Jeff. *Ever been in an accident? Ever felt any pain in your elbow? And by the way, do you have any idea how much money you might want to sign?*

Scouts aren't fond of agents, and agents don't really care for scouts, Julie Bradley has learned. Some scouts tell Jeff that he should sign without an adviser, save himself the $30,000 or $40,000 commission, and give the money to his mom.

During the spring of 2004, Julie Bradley lost 15 pounds from worry—a real feat considering she weighed only 110 pounds to start. When Matt Sosnick arrived on the scene, 10 weeks before the June 7 draft, he looked the family in the eye and spoke with measured tones to put everyone at ease. If Jeff's a jerk, Matt said, he doesn't even want to represent him. But if things work out, he'll be a conduit with the clubs, a sounding board, and a friend for life.

"Matt was almost like an angel from heaven," Julie says. She buys into the Sosnick philosophy of working with teams rather than against them, and Jeff does too, and there's never any doubt that Matt's the one.

Over the next several weeks, Matt worked the phones and mined his contacts and discovered that the Yankees and Dodgers both had serious interest in Jeff Marquez. It became official the night before the draft, when Fay Thompson, New York's Northern California scout, called Matt twice in the span of 30 minutes and said, "We have to get this kid." During the second call, Matt recalls, Thompson was so excited that he was "hyperventilating."

Sosnick and Cobbe will be advising 15 picks in the 2004 draft, and they spend the night of June 6 holding a strategy session with Toby Trotter, their chief recruiter, and Jason Hoffman, the agency's newest employee.

Jason, a former high school baseball star in the San Francisco area, was selected by Montreal in the 22nd round of the 1996 draft. He played baseball for William Penn University in Iowa and once aspired to a career in sports journalism, but right now he fills a void in the

Sosnick-Cobbe recruiting scheme for several reasons: He's dynamic, has abundant connections in the Bay Area, and can help Matt and Paul make inroads with African-American athletes because he's black. Paul also gets a kick out of the fact that Jason, while black, has a Jewish last name.

In the pre-draft strategy meeting, Matt lays out three objectives for the big day: (1) facilitate the needs of the agency's clients; (2) make sure any questions that the ballclubs have are answered; and (3) pick up on any leads of players who have fallen through the cracks and might need an adviser after the draft. It's been known to happen now and then.

Matt and Paul have a couple of wild cards. Through their strong relationship with Garth Iorg, they're representing all three of the family's baseball-playing boys. Garth's oldest son, Isaac, is an infielder in the Atlanta Braves' system. His middle boy, Eli, is an outfielder at the University of Tennessee and a potential pick in tomorrow's draft. And the baby, Cale, is a high school senior who looks like the best Iorg yet.

But Cale has made it known that he plans to spend the next 2 years on a Mormon mission, and no team is interested in wasting an early pick on a player who won't commit to suiting up until 2006. The Devil Rays, however, are among several clubs intrigued by Cale, and it's possible they'll pick him in the 8- to 12-round range and offer second-round money to persuade him to forgo his mission.

It's known in the business as "an underdraft and an overpay." And everybody, religious obligations or not, has to keep an open mind.

Chapter

FOURTEEN

It's a blustery San Francisco morning, and Matt arises early and rubs the bleariness from his eyes. He's sleep-deprived, and his insides do flips if he forgets to take his stomach medication. His wardrobe—gray Polo T-shirt, blue Toronto Blue Jays workout shorts, and flip-flops—seems more suited to a frat boy gearing up for a fantasy league draft than an agent presiding over the future of 15 aspiring big leaguers.

The only certainty today is that Matt and the other members of the Sosnick-Cobbe contingent will order out for lunch. Matt keeps delivery menus from a local pizza joint and an area sushi restaurant handy, in much the same way an asthmatic keeps an inhaler within easy reach. His reliance on takeout food for sustenance is a running joke among those who know and love him.

When Matt's sister, Alisa, was in college, she broke up with her boyfriend and lapsed into a state of emotional disrepair. "Come on over and you can sleep at my house," Matt told her. Shortly after her arrival, Alisa told Matt she was hungry, and he replied that he had just gone shopping and she was welcome to anything in the refrigerator.

"I open the door," Alisa recalls, "and there's one Snapple."

Takeout pizza and sushi won't cut it this morning. Paul makes an early bakery run for a dozen doughnuts, and Matt lays the tools of the trade on the round glass table in his office. There's a *Baseball America* directory with names of front-office people and team phone numbers, and Sosnick's personal phone list with dozens of contacts for area scouts, cross-checkers, scouting directors, and general managers. Many of these talent evaluators are hunkered down today in their teams' draft "war rooms," where preparation is the buzzword and the air is charged with anticipation.

The air in Sosnick's duplex, in contrast, is filled with the flatulent off-shoots of Griffey, the amazingly lazy bulldog, who is constantly shooed from one room to the next so that he doesn't interrupt the collective train of thought. Wherever Griffey goes, a miasma is sure to follow.

A couple of years ago, Paul's wife, Ellen, suggested that the boys use yellow Post-It notes to track the progress of potential draftees. Today, that's Toby Trotter's job. He writes the names of 15 aspiring picks on 2-by 3-inch yellow squares and methodically sticks them on the wall atop a framed color photograph of Joe Montana.

Once the players are selected, Toby will peel the notes off the wall, mark the name of the selecting team and the round, and move them to a larger framed photograph of Larry Bird and Magic Johnson. For 15 kids, a potentially life-altering event is as simple as shifting 2 feet to the right.

Sosnick will spend much of the next 2 days on the telephone networking with baseball scouting directors, an endeavor in which he takes considerable pride. He enjoys negotiating with the no-frills baseball guys—people like Cleveland's John Mirabelli or Baltimore's Tony DeMacio—because they're so direct and free of pretense. The ball guys, in turn, speak favorably of Matt and Paul because it's common knowledge that clubs aren't going to select a Sosnick-Cobbe player and get bushwhacked by unreasonable expectations.

"They're up-front and all their players sign," Mirabelli says. "They're not out there grabbing for every last dollar they can get out of you."

If two parties want to resolve a problem, Matt believes, obstacles can be overcome. When the Cubs drafted Dontrelle Willis, it was with the understanding that he expected a bonus of $200,000 from whichever team selected him. But after the Cubs chose Dontrelle, they found there had been a team miscommunication and only $60,000 had been allocated for the spot. Jim Hendry, then Chicago's scouting director, did some digging, got to the root of the problem, and made good on the $200,000 promise. "Not only did he take responsibility for the team," Matt says, "but he totally honored his word."

Recent draft history has amplified the hazards involved when teams and advisers are at odds. In June 2000, the Colorado Rockies selected a California high school pitcher named Matt Harrington number seven in the first round. But the negotiations quickly turned sour, and Harrington refused to sign when his adviser, Tommy Tanzer, claimed that the Rockies had reneged on a promised $4.95 million signing bonus.

The Harrington family fired Tanzer, hired Scott Boras, and turned down a $1.25 million bonus from San Diego the next year. Matt Harrington began playing independent league ball and has since become something of a professional draftee, going to Tampa Bay in the 13th round, Cincinnati in the 24th round, and the New York Yankees in the 36th round, but the offers are now so meager and the expectations so low that he has yet to sign a contract. In the summer of 2004, he's pitching in anonymity with the Fort Worth Cats in the Central Baseball League and barely cracking 85 mph on a radar gun. He's washed up at 22, and he pays the bills working at a Target store in the off-season.

Everyone takes their lumps, it seems, in the Harrington affair. The family sued Tanzer for negligence and eventually received a sizable sum in a settlement through an insurance policy. Tanzer sued the Rockies for defamation of character, but he dropped the suit when the team released a statement refuting a previous claim that he was dishonest. Tanzer called the statement "vindication," but he knows the Harrington fiasco damaged his reputation, because he heard secondhand that other agents photocopied disparaging articles about the incident and used it to clobber him in recruiting.

Matt Harrington serves as a cautionary tale—that no matter how much time a team invests in scouting a player, it's meaningless if he doesn't sign. "It's like an old scout once told me: 'This is a lot like fishing—they only count if you get them in the boat,'" says Chris Buckley, a front-office executive with Toronto.

Sosnick and Cobbe don't have any Matt Harringtons in their portfolio, thank goodness, but they know what it means for a negotiation to go bad. Their nastiest one came in June 2002 when they represented two high school players, Jason Pridie and Wes Bankston, who were selected by the Tampa Bay Devil Rays.

Pridie, one of Matt's three tattooed clients, signed for $892,500 as the 43rd overall pick. The player, his family, and the team were all happy, Matt says, until the commissioner's office chastised the Devil Rays for giving Pridie a bonus exceeding the recommended amount for his spot.

Matt and Paul both accused Dan Jennings, then Tampa scouting director, of playing games with the disbursement of Pridie's bonus. Teams typically pay a draft pick half of his bonus 60 days after the signing date, and the rest 6 months later. Jennings, according to Sosnick and Cobbe, waited an extra 10 months to pay the final 50 percent. For reasons that Matt and Paul couldn't understand, he held hostage nearly $450,000 that rightfully belonged to the Pridie family.

Sosnick is also convinced that Jennings made statements that caused him to lose Wes Bankston as a client. So he left a message on Jennings's answering machine that made the Steve Canter message seem like a love sonnet.

"You are an amoral person," Matt said to Jennings. "You did everything you could to be disgusting and unethical and distasteful about this to serve your own needs. There was zero morality in either of these negotiations, and it makes me ill."

Jennings, a true son of the South, is regarded in the business as the consummate "scouts' scout." He has a love for the craft and a lingo forged through long, hot days at the yard on the trail of the next Griffey or A-Rod. It's not uncommon for Jennings to observe that a prospect looks better than, say, Shania Twain, or to remark that a pitcher who just got shelled was "rammy-cacked" by the opposition.

When Jennings checked his answering machine, his opinion of Matt Sosnick fell almost as much as his blood pressure rose. He believes the real reason for Sosnick's displeasure was that Tampa Bay scout Craig Weissmann, following the organizational mandate to get players signed quickly, negotiated Pridie's deal with the family while Sosnick was in San Francisco, out of the loop.

Jennings denies that he "caught crap" from the commissioner's office, insists that he said nothing to convince Wes Bankston to dump Matt (because he couldn't care less), and can't recall precisely how the Devil Rays distributed Pridie's bonus. When he picked up the phone and called Sosnick, they had a shouting match loud enough to rattle the dishes.

"As soon as you begin to pay me a salary, then I'll start conferring with you," Jennings said.

Jennings has since left Tampa Bay to work in the Florida Marlins' front office, but there's been no rapprochement. Sosnick, who stakes his business model on congenial relations with front-office people, flatly calls Jennings a "liar." And Jennings can't quite understand why this San Francisco agent whom he's never met regards him as a sort of scouting Antichrist.

"When things don't go Matt's way, it's someone else's fault," Jennings says. "Maybe that's part of his silver spoon upbringing."

Shortly before 10:00 A.M., Paul punches up the Internet broadcast of the draft on Major League Baseball's official Web site, MLB.com, and it's click-your-seatbelt time:

10:05 A.M. The 30-team roll call is complete, and Mike Wickham, San Diego's assistant scouting director, announces that the Padres have selected Matthew Bush, a high school shortstop from Mission Bay, California, with the number-one overall pick in the 2004 draft. It's not exactly a state secret. Hours earlier, *Baseball America*'s Web site posted a story with the headline "Bushwhacked," reporting how the Padres and Matt Bush agreed on a pre-draft deal for a $3.1 million signing bonus. Pre-draft deals are supposedly *verboten* under baseball rules, but they're commonplace among teams who want to ensure that if they draft a player, he might actually *play* for them.

10:14 Scott Boras has two crown jewels in this year's draft: Jered Weaver, a pitcher from Long Beach State and the younger brother of Los Angeles Dodgers pitcher Jeff; and J. D. Drew's little brother Stephen, a shortstop from Florida State. The Texas Rangers pass on both players to select Thomas Diamond, a pitcher from the University of New Orleans, and the Dallas media applaud the pick as evidence that the Rangers are trying to break Boras's hypnotic spell over Tom Hicks.

10:17 The Anaheim Angels select Weaver with the 12th pick in the draft, and the Arizona Diamondbacks, whose financial problems are well-known in the industry, can't resist the temptation to pick Drew at number 15.

Critics later suggest that these are prime examples of the flaws inherent in the draft—that losing teams, tired of haggling with Boras and finding they lack the money to sign one of his "premium" players, routinely pass on superior talent and allow the best players to slip to better clubs. Something is wrong, purists contend, when teams make selections on the basis of "signability" alone.

Mike Rizzo, Arizona scouting director, will have the unenviable task of spending a long, hot summer haggling with Scott Boras over Stephen Drew. He didn't exactly consider it a jaw-dropper that 14 clubs passed on Drew.

"The Padres can spin it any way they want to spin it," Rizzo says. "But if I have the first pick on the playground, I'm picking Stephen

Drew over Matt Bush 100 out of 100 times. If I'm going to pick a guy to win the championship, I'll pick Stephen Drew over Matt Bush and about 13 of the 14 guys that went before Stephen."

Mike Rizzo feels this way a week *before* Matt Bush makes national headlines for sneaking into a bar in Peoria, Arizona, getting nabbed for being underage, and biting the bouncer on his way out the door.

10:22 Sosnick's cell phone rings and it's Mark Newman, senior vice president of baseball operations for the New York Yankees. Newman, a former college baseball coach with a law degree, has drifted in and out of George Steinbrenner's favor, but he is currently back in the mix and playing a central role in the Yankees' draft.

The Yankees received two compensatory draft picks when the San Diego Padres signed former New York pitcher David Wells as a free agent, and according to Newman, they're interested in using one of the picks on Sosnick advisee Jeff Marquez.

There's a fine distinction here; Matt wants Marquez to go number 41, as the final first-round "supplemental" pick, rather than with the 42nd pick, which kicks off the second round, because it will mean something to Jeff Marquez and his family. And truthfully, it's not bad for Matt's ego or the Sosnick-Cobbe agency's prestige to say that they represent a first-rounder with the Yankees. Matt tells Newman he'll give the Yankees a $25,000 break on the price if New York takes Marquez at 41.

10:35 On the MLB.com broadcast, Cleveland outfielder Jody Gerut recounts his draft day experience out of Stanford. Gerut says it was probably a good thing that he used Reich, Katz, and Landis as his advisers, because he would have slipped lower than the Colorado Rockies in the second round if he had used Scott Boras.

10:40 The draft is breaking down according to form, and Paul Cobbe takes it as a good sign. "When you've got surprises, that's when a kid like Marquez gets screwed," he says.

10:45 It's Mark Newman on the phone again. New York likes Marquez but won't draft him without assurances that he'll sign. The Yankees have made a habit of loading up on big-name superstars in recent years and treating the draft like an afterthought, but they're not about to squander this high of a pick.

Now all that's left is settling on a figure. The advent of "slot money," a system of forced financial certainty decreed by the commissioner's office, has all but removed the art of negotiation from the process. If Player A receives an $840,000 bonus and Player C gets $800,000, Player B is all but locked into an $820,000 bonus if he falls directly between them.

The scouting director who wants to pay above slot must get approval from his general manager and possibly his owner, then outline his reasoning with a representative from commissioner Bud Selig's office, who probably will try to dissuade the owner from spending the money. Baseball teams can't share information when it comes to free agents, but they get away with price-fixing in the draft because amateur players aren't represented by the union and there are no repercussions.

The most notable exceptions to the slot money arrangement are Scott Boras's "special players," who often drop because of signability concerns and the threat that they'll hold out for as long as it takes. In 2001, Cincinnati gave Justin Gillman $625,000 with the 64th pick, and Detroit signed Matt Coenen for $620,000 at number 65. Stanford pitcher Mike Gosling, a potential first-rounder who fell because he was advised by Boras, received a $2 million bonus from Arizona as the 66th pick.

But Matt Sosnick isn't trying to revolutionize the draft or change the world; all he wants is to meet the Yankees halfway on Jeff Marquez. Cell phone in hand, Matt grabs the list of 2003 signing bonuses and scrolls to number 41: San Diego gave Daniel Moore, a University of North Carolina pitcher, $800,000 in that spot the previous season.

"How about $800,000?" Sosnick asks Newman.

"How about $775,000?" Newman responds.

Matt asks for $790,000, and when Newman suggests splitting the difference, Matt laughs. "Come on," he says, and they agree on the $790,000 figure. The Yankees will kick in an additional $60,000 so Jeff can take college classes at a later date and pursue a career in architecture if he fails to make it in baseball.

Later, Matt explains that the actual contract negotiation is "a zero thing," the most meaningless part of the process. What counts is product placement. By working the phones and networking with scouting directors and talent evaluators, Matt has determined that the Dodgers and Yankees are the only teams with serious interest in Jeff Marquez. If he pushes too hard and New York passes at 41 and 42, there's a chance that Marquez could slip to Los Angeles in the 58th spot. The Dodgers later select Louisiana high school pitcher Blake Johnson with that pick and give him $600,000.

So by negotiating reasonably and quickly, Matt appears to have made Jeff Marquez and his family an additional $190,000 at the very least. If Matt shortchanged the 41st slot a few thousand bucks, he considers that a small price to pay.

10:56 The Yankees go through the formality of selecting Jeff Marquez.

10:58 Brett Smith, a right-handed pitcher out of the University of California–Irvine, goes to the Yankees with the 42nd pick, but it's unlikely that he'll sign anytime soon. Smith is represented by Scott Boras.

11:34 The third round is under way, and Mark Newman calls and says New York has an interest in Grant Hansen, the 6'6" pitcher from Oklahoma City. The Yankees have two players ranked ahead of Hansen. But if both go off the board, they'll take him.

11:39 Toronto picks Sosnick client Danny Hill, a pitcher out of the University of Missouri, 87th overall. Hill stands 5'11", 202 pounds—squatty for a right-hander—and is coming off a mediocre college season. But he's a senior with no college eligibility left, and the Blue Jays, always on the lookout for ways to save money, figure they can sign him cheaply and have a serviceable middle reliever down the road.

In 2003, Kansas City drafted college seniors with five consecutive picks and gave each a $1,000 bonus. That's the hazard of having no leverage. When Toronto scouting director John Lalonde agrees to give Hill a $285,000 bonus—about 70 percent of slot—Matt is ecstatic.

11:40 Cory Dunlap, a graduate of Encinal High, Dontrelle's alma mater, unexpectedly goes to Los Angeles with the 88th pick. His selection creates a stir in the room, because the *Baseball America* draft projections and the scouting buzz have overlooked him. Does he have an adviser? Jason Hoffman, through his local connections, is familiar with Cory Dunlap. He'll try to hunt down the phone number for Dunlap's mother, in the hopes that a connection can be made before the vultures descend.

11:41 The White Sox, in a surprise, select Hansen with the 89th pick before the Yankees can grab him. Matt and Toby are on the phone with Grant and his mother, Diane, within seconds.

"I'd like to take the credit," Sosnick says. "But this is totally Toby networking it out with the teams."

After congratulating Grant and telling him how proud he is, Toby touches base with Diane. "Grant's mom is a basket case," he says, returning to the room. "She's bawling her eyes out."

11:57 Matt talks to Dunlap's mother, Clovis Burton, and learns that the family has yet to pick an adviser. Clovis has, however, heard good things about Matt through his affiliation with Dontrelle Willis. And by the way, what's his fee?

"Whatever anybody else is charging, we're 1 percent lower," Matt says.

12:02 P.M. Time to summon the cavalry. Matt gets on the phone with Dontrelle to see if his star client can't apply some World Championship cachet to convince young Cory to enlist with the Sosnick-Cobbe agency.

"Bitch, that guy is yours!" Dontrelle says, laughing. "He used to hang around my house and eat my scraps!"

12:08 Seattle selects Mark Lowe, University of Texas–Arlington pitcher, with the 22nd pick in the fifth round. Toby had invested dozens of hours in recruiting the kid. But after lots of soul-searching, Lowe changed course in late March. He told Toby that he'd prayed on his decision, and that Christ told him to select Jeff Frye of the Franklin-Frye agency as his adviser.

It breaks no one's heart that Mark Lowe lasted a while before being drafted. "I guess Christ told a lot of scouting directors not to pick him high," Paul says.

12:30 The group breaks for lunch—a bag of cheeseburgers via delivery boy. Toby is mortified to discover that the burger joint doesn't serve fries.

12:50 Dontrelle calls back and tells Matt the details of his conversation with Dunlap's mother. "I know you guys are buying drinks and cooking up fried chicken, but when you're done, call me back so I can whisper in your ear about my agent," Dontrelle tells her.

1:03 Tommy Lasorda, former Dodgers manager, assumes the ceremonial role of announcing the team's draft picks. When he proclaims that a player hails from the "great state of California," eyes roll in the Sosnick war room. Parliamentary declarations have been made with less bombast.

1:20 Matt receives a call from Boston scouting director David Chadd. The Red Sox are interested in Ryan Phillips, a pitcher from Barton Community College in Kansas. They'd like to take him in the 11th round. But it's clear that 11th-round money won't be enough to convince him to sign. So, what's it going to take? Matt says he'll find out for sure.

1:40 Troy Patton, the Texas high school pitcher who left his interview with Toby to attend a friend's pool party, goes to Houston at number 274 overall. Troy's father, David, is the guy who developed a questionnaire to screen agents before deciding who would represent his son.

Dave Patton, it's observed in the Sosnick-Cobbe war room, must be "shitting bricks" right now.

(But it's only a temporary condition. Troy Patton, who has a full scholarship to the University of Texas, signs with the hometown Astros in July for a $550,000 bonus. That's second-round money.)

1:45 The Red Sox call back. They'd like to sign Ryan Phillips for $100,000, but indications are they'd stretch it to $155,000—the equivalent of a fifth-round bonus—plus money for college tuition.

1:52 The daily double has come in: Matt Sosnick is frantically working two cell phones at once. The Red Sox are at the other end of one phone, and a nervous Ryan Phillips is on the other.

"Is it your dream to play professional baseball?" Matt asks Ryan a few minutes later, "because you would have to have tremendous balls not to do this."

2:04 Sosnick is a font of obscure draft information. When Los Angeles selects Chris Westervelt, a catcher from Stetson, with the 328th pick, Matt tells everyone in the room, "Hey, I recruited that kid out of high school." Chris Westervelt, Matt reveals, scored better than 1500 on his SATs.

2:08 Boston selects Phillips with the 335th overall pick and will pay him $155,000 plus money toward college, about four times what an 11th-rounder typically might fetch. Matt holds the telephone up to the computer speaker so that Ryan and his father can hear a Red Sox official announce the pick on MLB.com.

2:48 Matt calls Baltimore scouting director Tony DeMacio and tells him that the Sosnick-Cobbe agency has four players left on the board: Cale Iorg, Tyler Beranek, University of Michigan pitcher Derek Feldkamp, and Tennessee high school catcher Chris Kirkland. Matt has a proven history of working well with DeMacio, but good faith only counts for so much on draft day. Sorry, DeMacio tells him, but the Orioles aren't interested.

2:51 David Chadd of the Red Sox says the same thing.

2:53 Atlanta scouting director Roy Clark doesn't answer his phone. "Roy Clark is giving me no love," Matt says, impatiently.

3:00 John Mirabelli of the Indians doesn't seem interested, either.

3:05 Sosnick calls Joyce Guy-Harris and asks if she can put in a recruiting call to Cory Dunlap's mother on his behalf.

"If I have Dontrelle and his mother call and recommend me and I don't get the kid, I have a problem," Matt says.

3:10 Matt, on the phone with a scouting director, snaps when he asks Toby for the lowest number that Tyler Beranek will accept as a bonus and Toby struggles for a definitive answer. "Just give me the fucking number!" Matt shouts.

The agency is encountering a similar quandary with Aaron Mathews, an undersize Oregon State outfielder who's not generating as much interest as hoped. When it appears that Mathews might be drafted so low that he won't fetch a bonus of more than $50,000, he tells Paul he might return to school as a senior and take his chances.

"This is a lesson learned," Paul quietly tells Toby. "You need to know your player's bottom line."

3:20 Matt arranges dinner for tomorrow night with Jeff Marquez's parents in Burlingame. "Your kid is very rich," he tells them, then shares his negotiating strategy. "It came down to creating the thought that if the Yankees didn't pick him, they weren't gonna get another chance," he says.

3:26 Matt gets on the phone with Alex Slattery, the Chicago White Sox area scout, and talks about doing a quick deal for Grant Hansen. "Let's make this a loving negotiation," he says. "I'm tired."

3:33 The Braves complete the first day of the draft by selecting Brad Emaus, a high school shortstop out of Sharpsburg, Georgia. He's the 551st player selected, and it's taken 30 teams a total of 5 hours, 33 minutes to choose them. That's an average of 1.65 dreams fulfilled per minute.

For the adviser, of course, the work has not ended, will not end, never ends. There are joyful parents to be congratulated and anxious parents to be cajoled or consoled. Matt speaks with Grant Hansen's mother again and tells her to make sure to thank the area scout, Slattery, who pushed so hard for the White Sox to draft Grant.

Chris Kirkland, a good-field, no-hit high school catcher from Tennessee, is still on the board, and his father is getting edgy. The consensus is that Kirkland will be best served playing college ball at Alabama, where his bat will have a chance to catch up with his defense. If a big-league team picks him after his junior year, when he's eligible to reenter the draft, Matt hopes the family will still use Sosnick and Cobbe as advisers.

5:20 Matt talks to Derek Feldkamp, the Michigan pitcher who has also gone undrafted on day one. Matt suspects that Derek's college coach might have undermined the kid's draft prospects by putting out a bad buzz with the scouts. But they agree that it's probably best for Derek to return to school for another year.

6:50 While Matt watches the Tampa Bay-Calgary Stanley Cup final on his big-screen TV and takes a break with a tin platter of takeout fettucini, the silence in the next room is interrupted by the hum of a fax machine: The Chicago White Sox have agreed to pay Grant Hansen $430,000, plus four semesters of college at $6,000 a semester.

Throw in Ryan Phillips's bonus, a cut of the $65,000 bonus the group negotiated for Aaron Mathews as a 19th rounder with Toronto, and commissions for a handful of middle-round picks, and Sosnick and Cobbe generated about $100,000 in income from the first day of the 2004 draft. That sounds great, Matt says, until you realize that they probably spent $70,000 for Toby Trotter's salary and travel costs in the past year.

It's pointed out to Matt that some advisers, in the quest for clients, charge less than the 5 percent taken by Sosnick and Cobbe. Certain groups are so rabid to sign up players, they don't charge a cent.

"Yeah," Matt says. "There are also agents who don't comb the draft to get a 19th rounder a $65,000 bonus. There's no one in the country who does a better job working a draft than me. It would be impossible."

Cory Dunlap, selected number 88 in the draft by Los Angeles, definitely slipped through the cracks. As a high school senior, he scared off big-league teams when his weight ballooned to almost 300 pounds. So he enrolled at Contra Costa College and took control of his future. With encouragement from coach Marvin Webb and former big leaguer Willie McGee, Cory eliminated sweets and sodas from his diet, began running regularly, hit the weight room, and dropped 70 pounds. He transformed himself from junk food junkie to a relatively lean, mean, line-drive-hitting machine. And the scouts who had previously ignored him suddenly began to take an interest.

According to his mom, Cory also graded high in the all-important "makeup" category. He was 9 years old when his father, Charlie, a 20-year Navy man, died in a car accident. Three months later, his paternal grandfather died, but Cory never allowed himself a shred of self-pity.

"Baseball and my church family kept him focused," Clovis says. "Cory is a very outgoing, friendly, happy-go-lucky person. He doesn't meet any strangers."

Two days before the draft, Dunlap was among 35 prospects invited to Dodger Stadium to work out for scouting director Logan White and the team brass. He showed impressive power and uncorked some strong throws, and Tommy Lasorda offered him tips during batting practice. White, a respected talent evaluator, dissected Dunlap's swing and thought of Tony Gwynn, eight-time batting champion and future Hall-of-Famer. Gwynn had the ability to wait long enough to snap a single the opposite way just as the catcher was reaching out to snatch the pitch. White saw the same skill in Cory Dunlap, and the Dodgers quietly kept tabs on him during Contra Costa's season.

Something about Cory's personal story also touched Logan White's heart. Here was a bright kid from the Oakland projects who'd worked hard to pursue a goal and improve his family situation. Cory's mom, Clovis, suffers from fibromyalgia, a chronic arthritic condition, and has had back problems since a fall in 1991.

Cory has made a verbal commitment to attend California-Irvine in the fall, but he clearly wants to play pro ball. As a third-rounder, he stands to receive a bonus of at least $400,000. That's a lot of money, given that his mom is living off disability checks and finds it a chore to climb a flight of stairs.

Even though there's not much wiggle room for bonuses, Cory will pick an adviser to guide him through the process. Choosing one after the fact is the tricky part, because now that the Dodgers have selected Cory in the third round, agents are coming out of nowhere to court him.

That includes Dontrelle Willis's agent, Matt Sosnick, who drives across the San Mateo Bridge to meet with Cory in the sports bar at the Oakland Airport Hilton. Jason Hoffman, Sosnick-Cobbe's new associate, accompanies Matt to help with the sales pitch.

They order soft drinks and get down to business at a small table near the popcorn machine. Cory, a burly black kid from the East Bay, is wearing a Brooklyn Dodgers cap, a throwback jersey, and a stern look, because he knows he got drafted by the Dodgers without the help of an adviser. Heck, a few days ago, he was the Invisible Man.

Matt was among those who overlooked Cory, but now he wants a piece of the kid's future. The air is thick with a sense of misgiving that might be uncomfortable if Matt weren't so quick to acknowledge it. He speaks to Cory in a tone so candid it's disarming. He left his tap-dancing shoes at home.

Matt tells Cory that he typically charges a 5 percent commission, but will represent Cory for 1.5 percent because frankly, that's all he deserves. Matt acknowledges that he didn't call scouting directors on Cory's behalf, or schmooze Cory up a few spots, or tap into the buzz after Cory's Dodger Stadium workout. A few years earlier, it turns out, Matt met Cory at one of Dontrelle's basketball games. But he didn't give the overweight teenager a second thought.

"It's not like I'm trying to do you a favor," Matt tells Cory. "If you were a 12th-round pick instead of a 3rd-round pick, I'm sure I wouldn't even be talking to you right now."

Cory leans back in his seat, head cocked to the side, and eyeballs this exceedingly well-dressed white dude. For the better part of 10 minutes, he barely speaks. But as Matt later observes, Cory maintained eye contact the entire time.

"He's a street-smart kid," Matt says, "and he wasn't going to be bull-shit."

Cory's biggest problem, at the moment, is a previous commitment with another adviser. In the weeks preceding the draft, he began speaking with Miles McAfee, an aging black lawyer and former college baseball coach who represented Rickey Henderson, Chili Davis, and several other prominent big leaguers back in the day. McAfee has written a book called *Four Generations of Color*, and he helped rapper Master P make a foray into the sports agent business with his No Limit Sports firm several years ago. Miles McAfee has some stature in the black community—and goes by the designation "Dr. McAfee"—but he needs to attract some young talent if he wants to be relevant as an agent again.

In his zeal to land Cory Dunlap, McAfee has apparently gone too far. Just a few hours after the Dodgers chose Cory, McAfee showed up at Clovis Burton's doorstep with an authorization form to formally desig-nate him as Cory's representative. It was neither a wise nor ethical act on the part of Dr. McAfee, because an amateur athlete who signs with an agent automatically relinquishes his college eligibility. But Clovis and Cory, in a judgment made of ignorance, fear, or a combination of the two, sign the form. Now Cory doesn't have the option to play at UC Irvine even if he wanted. And without the leverage of college, he's vulnerable to being squeezed by the Dodgers if they learn of his predicament.

Matt and Jason make it clear they're not big fans of Miles McAfee. They question whether he really has kids' best interests at heart. "Good luck trying to contact him on the phone," Jason says. They tell Cory that Miles's best days have passed, and he has no juice with scouting di-rectors, shoe companies, or card concerns.

In exchange for acting quickly, for a 1.5 percent cut, Sosnick receives a commission of $6,450. More important, he now represents a promising first baseman with Tony Gwynn–like hitting tendencies. If all goes well, Cory Dunlap won't get picked off by one of the monster agencies when he joins Double-A Jacksonville or Triple-A Las Vegas, and Matt will still represent him when he arrives at Chavez Ravine in 2008.

Matt is happy, Cory's happy, and the Dodgers are happy when the kid boards a plane a week after the draft for Ogden, Utah, in the Pioneer League. Matt books a flight and hotel for Clovis, as well, and she makes it to Ogden for her son's professional debut.

The only person who feels slighted is Miles McAfee, who appears at Clovis Burton's doorstep the day after Cory signs and vows to file a complaint with the commissioner's office. McAfee, agitated by the current state of affairs after 25 years in the profession, promises that some "heavy controversy" is imminent.

"I've enjoyed the business," Miles McAfee says. "But it's one of the crookedest, most unprofessional things around. No one polices the situation. If you're an agent and I'm an agent and there's someone you want to go after, you just go after them."

FIFTEEN

Cory Dunlap isn't the only draft day stunner who falls into Matt and Paul's lap. With the 51st overall pick, the Texas Rangers select K. C. Herren, an Auburn, Washington, high schooler who plans to attend the University of Washington if he fails to go in the first three rounds. The Herren family books a suite at the Hyatt Regency Bellevue, and when the Rangers pick K. C. in round number two, you can practically hear the celebration in downtown Seattle.

K. C. Herren is an unpolished gem and requires some projection, but he's a fast runner and possesses a valued commodity in the form of power from the left side. Some scouts liken him to Hank Blalock, the Texas Rangers' All-Star third baseman. Since K. C. plays center field and has a strong, sturdy build, San Diego's Brian Giles might be a better comparison.

But that's down the line. At the moment, K. C. Herren has lots of earning potential and no one to advise him, and several firms will rush to fill the void.

Through a network of scouts, Paul Cobbe tracks down the family in Washington, calls, and introduces himself. Several days later, he hops a 6:45 A.M. flight to Seattle, and he's in the Herren family living room by 9:30 giving his pitch. The audience consists of Mr. and Mrs. Herren, their daughter, and K. C., who's sleep-deprived after a weekend of high school graduation festivities.

Paul's speech isn't unlike the one that Matt gave Cory Dunlap, except the parents are in attendance and they're not novices in the process. K. C. Herren's father, Dee, was a good enough athlete that the Minnesota Twins selected him in the 1971 draft. He went on to play baseball at Brigham Young University, and he wasn't chosen again. His only advice to his son: Follow your dreams.

Paul, like Matt, understands that bearing, cadence, and volume can have a major impact on a potential client. When people are expecting Fast Eddie the Previously Owned Car Dealer, honest and understated can be disarming. So Paul stows the fastball and begins the encounter with a changeup: He admits that Sosnick and Cobbe blew it with K. C. Herren.

"I pride myself on knowing where guys are going to go in the draft, but I didn't know with you,'" Paul tells the family. "I'm Johnny Come Lately."

Each adviser who enters the Herren home will wipe his feet on the welcome mat, then promise K. C. a glove deal because he's a second-rounder. That's no great feat. And while Matt and Paul have the necessary contacts to get the kid $5,000 in card deals, it's presumptuous to think that any other agents wouldn't. So the choice ultimately comes down to gut instinct and karma.

"If you talk to different people in this area, I think they'll tell you I'm a trustworthy guy who gets good money for my guys, and I take care of them," Paul tells the Herrens. "That's the bottom line. This is my life, not a business. So if you're looking for someone who lives and dies by their relationship with you and will absolutely break their tail to do everything possible for you, then that's great."

Paul offers to match the lowest commission, and since everyone else agrees to negotiate K. C.'s deal with the Rangers *gratis*, so will he. But he refuses to give ground on Sosnick and Cobbe's 15 percent marketing fee—the money that K. C. Herren will receive for appearances, signatures, and card deals—even though another firm has told the family it will handle the marketing for as little as 4 percent.

The Herrens hear from several other groups and take a day to digest the information. During a follow-up call to the house, Paul talks to Dee Herren, then spends 5 minutes listening to silence on the other end while waiting for K. C. to get out of the shower.

It's worth the wait. "I've talked with my family," K. C. says, "and I'm gonna go with you."

K. C. Herren is a nice late addition to a strong draft class, and in keeping with the agency philosophy, he signs quickly with Texas for $675,000. While Matt negotiates deals the way a fireman rushes into a burning building, Paul is more deliberate by nature. He believes that the cost of a prolonged holdout must be weighed against the potential benefits. If 3 weeks might fetch a draft pick an extra $100,000, sure, you're patient. A 3-month holdout for $10,000 fails to compute, if only for the emotional toll involved.

"There's nothing positive about a kid sitting on his ass at home, trying to find something to do and getting down on himself," Paul says. "With young people, it's a bad situation. Young players are all impatient when they know everybody else is moving ahead."

Scott Boras, who will never be characterized as an accommodator, might beg to differ. College pitchers Brett Smith and Matt Durkin, Boras guys who went immediately after Jeff Marquez in the draft, signed for $800,000 each, or $10,000 more than Marquez. But they also spent the entire summer holding out, and they won't throw a pitch in professional ball until 2005.

This is another example of the Boras approach that mystifies scouts. Neither pitcher had a history of arm trouble or overuse, so they appear to have gained nothing from the holdouts. "Teams will sign guys like that in July or even the first of August and give them 20 innings just so they get their foot in the door," says Mike Radcliff of the Twins. "Then they're on the clock. To drag it out and cost them a year so they get an extra $10,000 . . . I don't see the compromise there."

A week after the draft, Sosnick receives a surprise phone call from Dan Lozano of the Beverly Hills Sports Council (BHSC), the group that Toronto's J. P. Ricciardi affectionately refers to as the Sopranos. Lozano, like Matt, graduated from the University of Southern California and prides himself on his ability to work a room. Unlike Matt, he's already made it big in the business. Lozano's gold-plated clientele features Mets catcher Mike Piazza, Pirates catcher Jason Kendall, and St. Louis first baseman Albert Pujols, who just signed a 7-year, $100 million contract in the spring.

Even agents who are petrified of Scott Boras and his elaborate network of "scouts" profess a certain admiration for the way he built his company and keeps it all about baseball. The fraternity looks more askance at the Beverly Hills group because of its reputation for dazzling recruits with limousine rides and glimpses of the Playboy Mansion-type lifestyle.

Competing agents portray the BHSC sales pitch as one big White-snake video come to life. They claim that it appeals to the type of kid who thinks, *If I have the same agent as Mike Piazza, maybe I can date the Millennium playmate's twin sister.* Company founder Dennis Gilbert, who made a fortune selling insurance to Hollywood stars and began representing ballplayers in the early 1980s through an association with George Brett's brother, Bobby, was a guy you couldn't help but like personally. But his smooth approach and the company perks—from *Arsenio Hall Show* bookings to BHSC leather jackets to the 900 phone line for Jose Canseco—helped cultivate a certain 90210 cachet.

Gilbert left the business in 1999 and now works as a special assistant to Chicago White Sox owner Jerry Reinsdorf. As a former ballplayer, he spends a lot of time raising money to help down-on-their-luck baseball scouts. Most front-office people coexist peacefully enough with Lozano, Rick Thurman, Jeff Borris, and Dan Horwits, the four partners who now run the group. But the Sopranos make other agents nervous, because they've channeled so much energy into taking from the competition rather than trying to recruit talent through the draft.

"I accept it as a fact of life that other people in this business will talk to my clients or steal my clients," says David Sloane, Carlos Delgado's agent. "But there's one group in the business that I have no respect for whatsoever, and that's the Beverly Hills Sports Criminals."

The Sports Council and *brazen* go together like Rodeo Drive and mink. Through the years, Paul Cobbe has found that when a white business envelope arrives in your mailbox with your company name typed on the front and no return address, it's bad news: You've just been fired. If the envelope bears a Los Angeles postmark, chances are it's come from the office of Jeff Moorad, Scott Boras, or Reich, Katz, and Landis. And if the origin is New York, maybe the kid is leaving for Seth and Sam Levinson's firm, ACES.

The letter usually reads something like this: *I appreciate everything you've done, but I feel like my career will be better served by someone else. I've chosen to go in a new direction. Please don't contact me concerning my decision. I wish you all the best.* The only time Matt and Paul lost a player and the "fire letter" mentioned the specific destination was when Baltimore minor leaguer Doug Gredvig announced that he had chosen the Sports Council. "Beverly Hills is the only one we've seen do it that way," Paul says. "I think they get pleasure out of it."

A story makes the rounds among agents that Beverly Hills once took a player from a competitor, who called the company's offices in a rage. As the flustered agent vented on the other end of the line, Dan Lozano and his partners gathered in one room, turned on the speaker phone, and laughed at him in unison.

Before Matt goes on his dinner date with Lozano, Paul gives him a warning, like a mother telling her little boy not to play in the street. "Be careful when you meet with this guy," Paul says. "Maybe he's just trying to soften you up to get as much dirt as possible."

Matt is less judgmental toward the Sports Council bad boys, if only because they're true to themselves. They're ruthless and unrepentant, but at least they don't rationalize. The Beverly Hills boys disdain truces and hollow pledges, because it's simply not practical when another opportunity might be lurking around the corner.

And Matt finds that he really, truly enjoys Dan Lozano's company. They arrange dinner at the Grand Café, and they discuss the business and share their personal histories for 2½ hours over contemporary French cuisine. Matt learns that Lozano is Roman Catholic and devoted to his family back home in Dixon, California, not far from Sacramento. Lozano always wanted to be an agent, and he made a mark drumming up business as a young intern at the Sports Council out of USC. He collects wine, travels extensively throughout Europe on vacations, and projects a worldly aura that's disarming.

During the conversation, Matt shares one of his pet theories with Dan Lozano: that ballplayers who cheat on their wives and deceive their families are more inclined to take a cavalier approach about changing agents. Lozano nods in assent, as if impressed that Matt has made the discovery so early in the game.

Just why Lozano contacted Matt is the question. Beverly Hills' business took a hit in 2003 when Damon Lapa and Scott Leventhal, the agency's top "runners," left the company. And it didn't help when Eric Chavez, Oakland's Gold Glove third baseman, left and signed on with former big-leaguer Dave Stewart, who established his agent *bona fides* by negotiating a 6-year, $66 million deal for Chavez in spring training.

Most likely, Matt figures, the Sports Council guys want to feel him out, to see if he might be interested in folding his business into theirs or even going to work for the company as a recruiter. He's entertained the possibility of selling out during assorted weak moments, only to catch himself in time. That's the curse of the entrepreneur. If Matt has somehow worked his way onto the Beverly Hills radar now, well, it's both flattering and a little scary.

Matt finds Dan Lozano to be smart, worldly, accomplished, polished, and charming. *If a guy this smooth makes an effort to target my players and steal them, I might be in trouble,* he thinks, after Lozano has picked up the dinner tab and they've left the restaurant.

Shortly after the Sosnick-Lozano summit, Mike Hinckley is sitting in a New Hampshire hotel room during a road trip with the Harrisburg Senators when the phone rings. It's a representative from the Beverly Hills Sports Council asking whether he might be interested in a cup of coffee. Mike politely but firmly declines. A cup of coffee means getting acquainted. Get acquainted, and you start listening to the pitch. And if you actually seem interested, it can only lead to more phone calls in hotel rooms in New Britain and Trenton and Altoona.

A lot of time-share condominiums are sold this way. It's also how ballplayers become jaded and agents land in therapy.

"It probably won't be the last time this happens," Mike says. "I'm as firm as I can be. I tell them, 'I'm well-represented, and I have a good relationship with my agent.' I'll never leave Matt."

Mike Hinckley's fourth professional season has been extremely productive with the exception of a hiccup or two. In June he experienced fatigue in his shoulder, and the Senators shut him down as a precaution. But for some unknown reason, the team announced he was going on the disabled list with an ankle injury. The conflict produced a moral dilemma for Mike. After hemming and hawing with reporters, he told manager Dave Machemer that he would no longer fib about a phantom injury to cover for the club.

"As a man of integrity, a man of God, I can't lie," Mike says. "It became a bigger issue than it had to be. If I had a tired arm and I was going to miss a few starts, just say that. Don't say I'm hurt. I was never hurt."

While on the DL, Mike Hinckley finds that patience isn't his forte. He's selected to the Eastern League All-Star team and travels to Bowie, Maryland, to tip his cap during pregame introductions. He's disappointed when Major League Baseball names the rosters for the Futures Game, a showcase of top minor-league talent in Houston, and Montreal sends Clint Everts, a former first-round pick who's pitching for Class A

Savannah. But Mike uses the slight for motivation. *I'll be pitching in Houston soon enough*, he tells himself. *And it won't be in some exhibition game.*

The schedule calls for Mike to come off the disabled list on Monday, July 19, but the Senators bump him up a day because Omar Minaya, Montreal general manager, is in town for the weekend and wants to see him pitch. The Senators determine that Mike will start against the New Hampshire Fisher Cats, a Toronto affiliate, and throw three innings or 50 pitches—whichever comes first.

In some respects, Mike Hinckley isn't all that far removed from Moore, Oklahoma. He's still wiry at 6'3", 170 pounds, and he views the world with a schoolboyish sense of wonder. The word *awesome*, for example, is a staple of his vocabulary. One time he went to dinner with Matt, and he must have dropped six or seven "awesomes" while saying grace.

Everything about Mike Hinckley's bearing suggests that he's simply passing through Harrisburg on his way to bigger things. The Senators, 30 games below .500, try to change their luck through sartorial bonding. One day they wear Hawaiian shirts to the park, the next day camouflaged jerseys. Mike gladly takes part in the routine, except on the day he pitches, when he insists on wearing dress slacks, a dress shirt, and a tie to the ballpark. *If this is the way big-leaguers dress*, he tells himself, *this is the way I'll dress, because I'm going to be in the big leagues.* Yet in his relations with the fans, ticket takers, and hot dog vendors, he doesn't betray an ounce of big-league-itis. He's nice to everyone.

On the day of Mike's big audition for Omar Minaya, there's an 80 percent chance of rain. Since it's Sunday, Mike sits in the dugout for chapel service. He prays constantly, and not out of some self-serving ritual. "That's me," he says. "That's who I am. I don't want it to be a routine. I want it to be what I'm longing after, which is a relationship with Him. He's blessed me with this, and all I can do is give it back to Him."

The stands are largely empty, and the serenity is interrupted only by the occasional sounds of feet stomping on the metal bleachers. Mike's father, David, has driven all the way from Oklahoma with his wife and two younger sons for the weekend series with New Hampshire, and he sets a camcorder on a tripod behind home plate so he can record Mike's outing and have more to take home than a Harrisburg Senators cap and warm memories.

At 1:07 P.M., Mike takes the mound and stands at attention for the National Anthem. When he faces home plate, the first thing you notice is that his cap is slightly askew, like Dontrelle Willis's. "It's a left-handed thing," Minaya says. Mike also wears a white pooka shell necklace, and he exudes a sense of confidence that says it's *his* game and he's in charge. Maybe he was rendered jelly-legged by the radar guns in Moore as a high schooler, but that was a long time ago. He's close enough now that nothing will deter him from his mission.

Omar Minaya hopes to see good things because his team's pitching is a mess, and the Expos have long since become an afterthought in the National League East. Earlier today, in white flag mode, Minaya traded outfielder Carl Everett to the Chicago White Sox for a 6'11" pitching prospect named Jon Rauch.

Mike Hinckley and Clint Everts are the future of the organization, whether the team moves to Washington, D.C., northern Virginia, or parts unknown, and Minaya wants to sample the merchandise. He's made the 3½-hour drive from his home in New Jersey with his two boys, and he takes a seat five rows behind home plate next to Joe McIlvaine, the former big-league general manager who's now a Minnesota scout. As his star prospect takes the mound, Omar Minaya absentmindedly squeezes a toy rubber baseball that the Senators have given out as a pregame promotion.

Minaya typically prefers that young players don't know he's in the stands, because it might put them on edge. But Mike Hinckley immediately makes it clear that he's focused on the game. He plans to make every one of his 50 pitches count.

Mike needs only seven pitches to dispatch New Hampshire in the first. Aaron Hill, a former first-round pick by Toronto, ends the inning by grounding into a 6–4–3 double play.

In the second, Minaya scoots down a row and asks a scout for Hinckley's radar gun readings. They're in the 89 to 91 range, but that's fast enough considering Mike has missed 3 weeks and the opposing lineup has so much trouble picking up the ball against his deceptive motion.

Minaya, who signed Sammy Sosa for a $3,500 bonus as a scout with Texas in 1985, is conditioned to look for small signs. In the second inning, Mike gets ahead 0–2 on New Hampshire second baseman Dominic Rich, and he takes the aggressive approach and throws a fastball inside. Rich barely moves, and the pitch plunks him on the arm.

After going up 0–2 on first baseman Michael Snyder, Mike summons Jason Belcher to the mound for a conference and throws a paternal arm over his catcher's shoulder. "That's a good sign," Minaya says. "A lot of times catchers go out to the mound, but he told the catcher to come out there." This time, Mike goes with the breaking ball, and Snyder swings and misses for strike three.

Mike's third and final inning is the most telling. After he allows two baserunners, the Montreal general manager wants to see him work out of trouble. "A lot of kids get ahead in the count and they want to attack," Minaya says. "What you want to see is whether a kid can be soft—if he can back off and save that money pitch for later."

Almost as scripted, Mike drops a slow curve on Aaron Hill for strike three, and it's, "Have a nice day."

The final tally: Three innings, six strikeouts, and lots of encouraging signs. The Expos don't have to place Mike Hinckley on their 40-man roster until the off-season, but he's shown enough that Minaya wouldn't hesitate to summon him in September. The issue, of course, is whether it's Minaya's call. The Montreal franchise is owned and operated by the other 29 big-league clubs. If MLB decides that the Expos don't need reinforcements for the final month, it won't matter how ready Mike Hinckley is.

"A kid like that, you can tell he has a bright future," Minaya says. "The question is, how far away is he from the major leagues? It all depends on what system you're in. If you're the New York Yankees and you're in a pennant race, you don't want to count on this kid. If you're in a development situation, you're trying to build for the future. But based on what I've seen so far, I would not be afraid to bring him up."

Following his brief outing, Mike takes a 10-minute run and does his shoulder exercises. Then comes the reward: Minaya is leaving early, but first he stops by the cramped Harrisburg clubhouse to shake Mike's hand.

"I saw a lot of good things out of you today," Minaya tells him. "I'm just really excited with what you did."

Well, at least they know I'm here, Mike Hinckley thinks, but he refuses to get carried away. Before Minaya's visit, Mike applied the visualization technique that he's been working on with his sports psychologist, and he saw himself whiffing all nine New Hampshire hitters. He struck out only six, so there's room for improvement.

Mike's parents and his little brothers, Jeff and Chris, are waiting when he leaves the clubhouse, and they congratulate him on a job well-done. The twins play long-toss during the walk to the parking lot, and the Hinckleys decide they'll go to Outback Steakhouse, where Mike plans to conquer the biggest piece of beef on the menu.

Sometime tonight, he'll call his agent in San Francisco with news from the game. Other than Mike and his family, there's probably not a person in the world who wants to see him in the majors more than Matt Sosnick.

"Matt always tells me that when I get called up to the big leagues, he'll beat me there," Mike says. There's not a doubt in Mike Hinckley's mind that it's true.

The dog days of July and August result in a flurry of activity for several other Sosnick-Cobbe players, both on and off the field.

Chris Rojas, pitching for the Mobile BayBears, is chosen to start for the West squad in the Southern League All-Star Game in Chattanooga, Tennessee. He gets pounded, allowing seven runs in the second inning in a 10–6 loss. But the day isn't a total loss. Chris retires Prince Fielder, and on the way back to the dugout, Prince slaps him on the butt to let him know that everything is cool; he's not holding a grudge over that bench-clearing brawl in May.

In July, Paul Cobbe is prompted to take a stance on behalf of Freddy Sanchez. The Pirates have recently sent Freddy to the minors to rehabilitate an ankle injury, and when his 20 days are up, they decide that he's healthy and option him to Triple-A Nashville. But Freddy insists that his ankle still hurts, and Paul wants the Pirates to place him on the major-league disabled list, where he can continue to collect big-league pay and service time. "As his agent, I must err on the side of caution," Paul says. "What if he plays and suffers a career-ending injury?" When no middle ground can be struck with Pittsburgh management, Paul calls the Players Association and files a formal grievance.

Chad Qualls, a starter his entire career, initially resists when the Houston organization tries to convert him to a reliever in Triple-A. But he relents, and it proves to be a wise decision. In July the Astros summon Chad from New Orleans for his major-league debut, and Matt celebrates on the phone with him, then talks to Mr. and Mrs. Qualls in California. He remembers the magical moment in 1999 when Chicago White Sox pitcher Joe Davenport became the first Sosnick-Cobbe client to reach the majors. Matt was so euphoric he called Paul, who was fast asleep at 3:00 A.M. in Japan, and they whooped it up from separate hemispheres. "It's still really emotional for me," Matt says, "because whenever a kid lives it for the first time, I live it all over again." And when the Astros trade for Darren Oliver and send Chad back to New Orleans 3 days later, Matt begins pulling for the kid anew.

In Florida, Marlins catcher Josh Willingham hits his first big-league homer while Sosnick is watching on his big-screen TV in San Francisco. Matt calls Willingham's wife, Ginger, on her cell phone at the park and points out the section of the outfield stands where the ball has come to rest so that security can retrieve it. While Willingham's teammates in the bullpen have already tracked down the precious memento, he appreciates the effort.

Shortly thereafter, Matt will fly to Miami for client maintenance, and Josh Willingham has a chance to see the Sosnick-Dontrelle Willis dynamic up close. He's amused by the way Dontrelle busts on Matt for being Jewish and Matt busts on Dontrelle for being black. Josh is also slightly unnerved when Sosnick and Dontrelle hug and kiss each other on the cheek when they first see each other. "Don't *ever* try to do that to me," he tells his agent.

It's an up-and-down season for Dontrelle, who's hovering around the .500 mark with the Marlins. But Matt continues to be on the lookout for endorsement opportunities. He negotiates a deal with a company that sells ready-made answering machine messages from famous athletes. *Hey, this is Dontrelle Willis of the Marlins. Leave a message at the tone.* Dontrelle receives a $10,000 check for a minimal time investment, although Matt can't immediately recall the name of the company.

"I think the name of the company is, 'Give me my $10,000,'" Matt says.

By August, Sosnick is feeling pretty upbeat about things, even though experience has taught him that another emotional setback is always just a phone call or a fire letter away. The agency is sending more players to the big leagues and getting fewer players stolen, the perfect equation for success in the business.

And then it happens: Matt's puttering around the duplex in Burlingame and the phone rings. It's Brandon Lyon on the other end, and he has some news to share.

"Hey, I talked to my wife about it," Lyon says, "and I've decided I'm going to switch."

Barry Meister is in the sports pages a lot in July 2004, when his most prominent client, Arizona pitcher Randy Johnson, is the subject of a flurry of rumors before the trade deadline. The Diamondbacks have a Mt. Everest–size pile of debt. Manager Bob Brenly has already been fired, and with the team headed nowhere, speculation abounds that Johnson will be dealt.

Meister represents 35 big leaguers and 35 minor leaguers out of his office in Chicago. While his clients include such big names as Johnson and Denny Neagle, he takes pride in his ability to find jobs for players in the $600,000 to $800,000 salary club. Meister is the patron saint of Keith Lockhart, a .261 career hitter who made $4.1 million during his 5-year peak with Atlanta. Lockhart, who played 8 years in the minors and spent a winter selling stereos at Circuit City to pay the bills, will forever be grateful for Barry Meister's persistence.

So will knuckleball pitcher Steve Sparks. He went 0–6 with a 4.88 ERA for Oakland and Detroit in 2003, but Meister delved into the record books and found that since the 1940 season, 12 of 13 knuckleballers who switched from the American to the National League experienced a drop of at least 1.50 in earned run average. Arizona GM Joe Garagiola was sufficiently impressed to sign Sparks to a guaranteed $500,000 deal.

The first thing Barry Meister tells you is that he's no client stealer, and he has no interest in chasing players in the minors, who are locked into salary scales regardless of performance. Standard pay for a kid in Double-A ball is about $1,500 a month, and Marvin Miller himself couldn't change that. "Any chimpanzee with a cell phone can represent a player in Double-A," Meister says. "Providing shoes and gloves takes no intellectual or life experience."

But Meister can relate to life as a small, up-and-coming agent, because 2 decades ago, he was a target for bigger groups looking to fleece him of his clientele. One big-name guy took aim at his agency and Meister was so enraged, he picked up the phone and called the bully directly.

"Do you like to read?" Meister asked.

"Sure," the agent replied.

"Do you read the classics?"

"Yeah."

"Okay, do me a favor," Meister said. "Let's table this discussion for 2 weeks. Get a copy of 'Robin Hood.' If you don't want to read the book, rent the movie with Errol Flynn. Not the Kevin Costner version—the one with Errol Flynn. And after you read the book or watch the movie, let's talk."

"What's the point?" the other agent asked.

"I'll explain this to you in terms of Robin Hood," Barry Meister said. "You're the sheriff of Nottingham, and I'm Robin Hood. You may be bigger and more powerful and have more troops, but it's a big forest, and I know where all your men are stationed. And if you fuck with me again, I will make it my life's work to clean you out."

In the area of "client procurement," there are always judgments to be made and balances to be struck. Meister, as head of a one-man shop, draws a distinction between preying on small competitors and having new business land on his doorstep—between solicitation and attracting players through word of mouth. A positive endorsement from a client to a teammate means a lot in the hermetically sealed environment of the clubhouse. In the end, that's what helped convince Brandon Lyon to leave Matt Sosnick for Barry Meister.

Brandon claims he never faulted Sosnick and Cobbe for the whole Pittsburgh trade fiasco. Maybe Boston was miffed that the Pirates put Lyon through the medical wringer and the deal fell through, but Brandon took responsibility for giving his consent. *I'm a big boy,* he thought. *I could have said no if I wanted.*

His disenchantment took hold shortly before spring training, when they were on the phone and Matt announced abruptly, "I negotiated your contract today." Brandon Lyon, who'd been in the big leagues since 2001 and appeared in 75 career games, would make $330,000 with Arizona, or $30,000 over the rookie minimum.

The declaration was a red flag to Lyon. When he first met Matt at Dixie College, he'd never even talked to another agent. And it was true that Matt had taken him to Hawaii, and that they had become friends. But now friendship was getting in the way of what he really wanted from his agent, which was less emotional and more utilitarian in nature.

This salary business threw him for a loop. Matt explained there was no wiggle room with the D-backs because of Brandon's service time. But Brandon still would have appreciated being apprised of the situation before the news was dumped in his lap. Why was Matt in such a hurry? Brandon asked around and concluded that if they had waited a bit, maybe they could have squeezed an extra $5,000 or $10,000 out of the Diamondbacks. That seems like a trifle now, but wouldn't it give them a higher starting point when Matt negotiated his next contract?

Major League ballplayers, Barry Meister says, become "educated consumers" through osmosis. Once you click your spikes and you've departed Roland Hemond's Podunk for the big-time, you begin lockering next to players with heavier beards and heightened consciousnesses, and they pass along insights like a generational relay baton. A veteran with advice on how to avoid being screwed by management was doing you as big a favor as the guy who shared the secret to his sinker or slider grip.

Brandon Lyon was moving up in the world and wanted an agent to guide him through the economic maze, to educate him on the process. Coincidentally, several of his teammates were already represented by Barry Meister. First, there was Tim Wakefield in Boston, then Steve Sparks, Brent Mayne, Randy Johnson, and Casey Daigle in Arizona.

When spring training began and Brandon's elbow began to throb, he didn't need much reason to be out of sorts. A shipment of baseball shoes failed to arrive on time and Matt blamed the problem on an oversight by the sporting goods company. It sounded like a rationalization to Brandon, who talked to Steve Sparks, who talked to Barry Meister, and a phone conversation was arranged.

They discussed the elbow injury, and Meister advised Brandon of his right to a second opinion and what questions to ask the doctor. "Barry, nobody's ever mentioned any of this to me,'" Brandon told Meister. And when Meister trumpeted his productive working relationship with Joe Garagiola and the Arizona front office, he could point to Johnson, Sparks, Mayne, and Daigle as a testament to his clout and credibility.

Brandon Lyon wants a seasoned advocate for his upcoming salary arbitration, and Barry Meister fits the description. In 21 years as an agent, Meister has prepared about 250 cases, of which maybe 20 actually went to a hearing, and he knows what an ungodly grind the process can be. An agent might invest 125 man-hours in an arbitration case, pulling numbers, preparing exhibits, compiling game logs of players and game logs of comparables. Barry Meister is sufficiently skilled at the process that other agents routinely ask him for help with their cases.

All these factors weighed into Brandon Lyon's decision to change agents. He had initially planned to inform Matt in a letter, but ends up breaking the news over the phone.

Sosnick is beyond groveling, because his pride tells him to refrain and he knows it's a lost cause. "I care a lot about you and I'm disappointed," he tells Lyon, "but I'd rather see you have a new agent than have it held over my head."

When Matt hangs up the phone, he feels like a tropical storm victim sorting through smashed dishes and wrecked furniture. He scours his apartment for pieces of Brandon Lyon memorabilia, and finds old Red Sox and Blue Jays jerseys in the closet and dozens of Lyon baseball cards. They're all destined for the trash pickup.

In Barry Meister's estimation, the smaller agent who gets pilfered isn't necessarily a victim. "Some are clearly being set upon by the wolves, but some are losing clients because they don't have the experience to handle certain situations or because they make mistakes," Meister says.

Matt believes he made no mistakes while representing Brandon Lyon. But that doesn't minimize his sense of loss. "I hope if it shakes out that the grass isn't greener for you and you decide this isn't the way it should be, that you'll call me again," he tells Lyon. It's a longshot, he realizes, but he feels a need to say it regardless.

In August, Brandon makes an aborted comeback attempt from elbow surgery, then shuts it down for the year. But he expects to be eligible for arbitration in February 2005, and he's confident that his new representative is on the case.

Just a few months ago, Brandon Lyon swore by Matt Sosnick and Paul Cobbe and identified with their quest to build a business. By staying, he might have helped establish their credibility and assisted in the firm's growth. Now he's gone, and other agents will add him to the list of defectors they cite when disparaging Sosnick and Cobbe.

Brandon still believes his former agents can make a go of it, and he wishes them well, but he thinks they might have to tinker with the foundation upon which their business is based.

"I feel they can be very successful," Brandon says. "I just think they need to base their agency on a different idea. Maybe not so much trying to play the friendship-loyalty thing, but more about getting things done and wowing their players once in a while. You know what I mean?"

Chapter
SIXTEEN

It's a 6-hour drive from Fort Lee, New Jersey,
to Montreal—plenty of time for Omar Minaya to contemplate his options. The Expos have been buried since a 5–19 April, but that doesn't
preclude the general manager from thinking of ways to finish strong. At
the moment, he's mulling over call-ups in anticipation of the roster
expanding in September.

Mike Hinckley has continued to pitch well since his three-inning
audition for Minaya in July. He has an 11–3 record between Brevard
County and Harrisburg, and the Expos seem convinced that he's ready.
But practical considerations point to Mike's dream being deferred
through the winter. The Expos expect only three September additions,
and they're likely to come from Triple-A Edmonton. Minaya is
concerned that Hinckley, with his wiry build, might be feeling the strain
after pitching 150-plus innings—more than he's logged in any of his
four professional seasons.

"If we were in a big market, I'd probably bring him up to get his feet
wet," Minaya says. "But right now I'd say it's less than 50–50."

Those odds, it turns out, are charitable. A week later, the Expos make it official: Mike Hinckley won't be joining the club in September, but will have every opportunity to make the starting rotation in spring training.

Mike still has reason to be sanguine because he's young and talented and the Expos desperately need pitching. He'll spend the winter at home in Oklahoma, working out, attending Sooners football games, playing guitar at the Emmaus Baptist Church, and giving talks at Fellowship of Christian Athlete functions. Clint Everts, the other bright light in the Montreal system, has blown out his elbow and will need reconstructive surgery, substantiating Mike's claim as the franchise's top prospect.

The sports psychologist who helped Mike and two other Montreal minor leaguers with "positive visualization" exercises has faded from the scene after squandering his credibility with some dubious advice. Mike became alarmed when he felt discomfort in his left shoulder and the guy told him to go inside the shoulder mentally and *think away* the pain. They spoke less frequently as the season progressed, and on the drive home to Oklahoma after Harrisburg's finale, Mike calls and severs their ties.

Still, Mike and his two teammates have a problem. The visualization expert, who was recommended by former Expos Class A manager Joey Cora, wants compensation in the form of thousands of dollars in consultation fees. Mike calls Matt Sosnick, who gets on the phone with Montreal assistant GM Tony Siegle and lobbies for the Expos to assume at least part of the tab.

"You have an employee who was advising kids to do this," Matt says.

"Are you out of your mind?" Siegle replies. Last year, the Expos didn't have the money to retain star free agent Vladimir Guerrero. Now they're supposed to start writing out checks to subsidize Mike Hinckley's phone conversations?

So Mike writes the check himself, and chalks up the expense to experience. "I messed up, and I'm okay with that," Mike says. "This just showed me that I can't continue to put my trust or faith anywhere but in Jesus."

In late September, the Expos fly Mike Hinckley to Montreal to honor him as the organization's Minor League Pitcher of the Year. They also apprise Mike of their plans for his career: He will be added to the 40-man roster shortly, which means he'll be signing his first big-league contract before spring camp.

Several weeks later, it's announced that the team will move to Washington, D.C., in 2005, and be nicknamed the Nationals. If Mike adheres to his timetable, he'll leave Florida in April as a member of the big club's rotation. And if Matt Sosnick is true to his word, he'll beat Mike to Opening Day.

In September, Matt goes on a date and tells the girl that he makes his living representing athletes as a sports agent.

"Oh," she says. "So you're like Tobey Maguire?"

Griffey, the amazingly lazy bulldog, blows an Achilles tendon, and the injury costs $4,160 to repair. Matt regrets his decision not to buy pet health insurance, but then, what's the likelihood of a dog suffering a disabling injury when its most strenuous activities are (a) drooling and (b) licking a black leather couch?

For the rest of the Sosnick-Cobbe clientele, it's a mixed bag of setbacks and successes, of growing pains and heartwarming tales, in places where baseball is big business or merely a centerpiece to the fabric of a small community. That's the beauty of running an agency with 80 or so clients: Whether it's batting statistics or moving expenses incurred, there's a tangible way to chart each player's progress.

Tampa Bay outfielder Jason Pridie, he of the Sosnick-Cobbe tattoo, hits .276 with 17 home runs for the Class A Charleston RiverDogs in 2004, which puts him on track for a promotion to Bakersfield in the California League. His brother Jon posts a 3–6 record with a 5.44 ERA for Minnesota's farm club in New Britain, Connecticut. That's sufficient for the Chicago Cubs to sign him to a contract as a minor-league free agent.

Mike Rouse, who bought his fiancée an engagement ring through Matt Sosnick's Israeli diamond connection, gets married in the fall, as does Montreal Expos minor leaguer Darrell Rasner. Sosnick, naturally, attends both weddings.

And even kids who haven't paid a cent of commission remain on Matt and Paul's radar. The Devil Rays tried to sign Cale Iorg, the youngest of Garth's three sons, after picking him in the 16th round of the June draft. But the Rays couldn't seal the deal, so Cale headed to the University of Alabama, where he'll play shortstop in the spring, then embark on his 2-year Mormon mission. Toby Trotter will keep in touch with him throughout.

By the end of the regular season, a total of nine Sosnick-Cobbe clients will have played in the major leagues in 2004, most of them in cameos. Travis Smith, a journeyman pitcher who's 31 years old and looks like Harry Potter, appears in 16 games for the NL East champion Atlanta Braves. Mike Wood, acquired by Kansas City from Oakland by trade in late June, goes 3–8 in 17 starts with the Royals.

Chad Qualls, recalled from Triple-A New Orleans in August, has a stretch run to remember in Houston. He quickly warms to his new role in the Astros' bullpen, and manager Phil Garner's team goes on a 36–10 run to come from nowhere and make the playoffs as a wild-card entry.

Late in the season, the Astros travel to San Francisco, and Matt has lunch with Chad and his parents at a restaurant near the team hotel. Two men walk past, and Sosnick doesn't even notice until Qualls points them out. *Did you see who's here?* It's Scott Boras and his star free-agent-to-be, Astros outfielder Carlos Beltran.

Sosnick has spoken with Boras only once, behind the University of San Francisco stands in a dispute over Jesse Foppert several years ago. He tries to sneak a peak at the power lunchers on the way to the restroom, but he doesn't have his glasses, so he's squinting to pick them out when two high school friends at the restaurant blow his cover. "Hey, Sosnick!" they shout.

Boras is too engrossed in his nine-figure client to notice that Matt Sosnick, a young agent who once lost Jesse Foppert, Dennis Tankersley, and Bobby Jenks to the Scott Boras Corporation in a 2-year stretch, is eyeballing him from the other side of the restaurant.

"I thought about going over and giving Beltran my business card," Matt says.

Matt sends a nice bottle of Bordeaux to the Beverly Hills Sports Council's office after his dinner with Dan Lozano, and they exchange pleasantries once or twice over the phone. He also receives a call from Barry Meister, who wants to make sure everything is copacetic after taking Brandon Lyon. Meister tells Matt that he was once a young agent himself, and he knows how tough the business can be, and that it was nothing personal with Brandon.

Just a few minutes into their conversation, Sosnick tells him not to sweat it.

"You didn't do anything wrong or have anything to apologize for," Matt says. "If the reverse had happened and I had a chance to take one of your players, I'd do exactly the same thing."

Major League Baseball owners have endured eight labor-related shutdowns since 1972. They survived a $280 million collusion judgment in 1990, the stain of steroid use, and the fallout from the Marge Schott era in Cincinnati. But all of that pales in comparison with the assault on the game's integrity in the summer of 2004, and the pressing question that confronts owners:

Can they survive having an agent in their midst?

In August, the Arizona Diamondbacks announce that Jeff Moorad, who's negotiated more than $2 billion in contracts as an agent, will be taking over as the franchise's chief executive officer. The news generates a spate of reaction, ranging from amusement to consternation to despair. Players Association officials question whether Moorad was secretly transitioning out of the agent business while negotiating contracts—a sticky situation at best and a moral breach at worst. Gene Orza says that Moorad's career change "raises a lot of questions that have to be answered." For instance, when Moorad was negotiating long-term contracts for his clients, was it in their best interests, or a way for him to reach designated "earn out" targets that facilitated his departure from Loring Ward International?

Owners will have to vote to approve Moorad's hiring only if he assumes a 5 percent ownership stake or becomes the "control person" who casts votes on behalf of the Diamondbacks at MLB meetings. With or without a show of hands, it's clear that they're nervous having him around.

Baseball officials haven't forgotten the 2000–2001 free-agent shopping season, when an ESPN camera tagged along with Moorad during the Manny Ramirez contract negotiations and Yankees general manager Brian Cashman was outraged to learn that a seemingly confidential phone conversation with Moorad had appeared on television. The stunt presumably didn't win Moorad any points with George Steinbrenner, either.

"When Ted Turner stood up and tried to prevent Rupert Murdoch from buying the Dodgers, there was some personal history there," says an American League official. "Oftentimes, personal history plays a role. With Jeff Moorad it might be a question of how people feel about his conduct and his reputation. Do they want him as a partner?"

There are ironies galore to Moorad's switch. Arizona has yet to sign its number-one draft pick, Florida State shortstop Stephen Drew, who is being advised by Moorad rival Scott Boras. And while Moorad helped drive up salaries for years as an agent, he might now become an advocate for fiscal restraint, of all things.

In an ESPN *Outside the Lines* piece, Moorad says he switched to ownership because he got tired of the hand-holding required in the agent business. "I reached the point where I believed my expertise and experience were a better fit on the management side over the next page of my career and life," Moorad says in a subsequent interview.

Behind the scenes, Moorad's fellow agents wonder when the feeding frenzy for his players will begin. Moorad's former clients praise him for his intelligence and business savvy, and they predict that he'll assemble an All-Star front office cast to turn around the mess in Arizona. But it remains to be seen whether he's a trailblazer or an aberration.

"I'm sure a number of prominent current and former agents are envious as heck and would love to be in Jeff's position," says Eric Karros, a long-time Moorad client. "If I were those guys, I'd be rooting like heck for Jeff to succeed, because all that will do is open the door for everybody else."

Scott Boras is not among the cheerleaders. ESPN interviews Boras at his Southern California office, with his company logo in the background, and he speaks passionately of the obligation that an agent has to the players he represents.

"There's a legal parameter here," Boras says. "What rights does an individual have to represent someone one year, and turn around and be management or work for management the next? Philosophically for me, it would be a breach of my commitment. It would be something I could not do."

If there were ever any doubt about which agent rules the industry, Boras has dispelled it this off-season. Although his group took a hit when Barry Bonds left for the Beverly Hills Sports Council for undisclosed reasons in June, Boras has assembled a free-agent class of historically impressive proportions. It features Beltran, one of the game's best all-around players, and Los Angeles third baseman Adrian Beltre, who hit 48 homers and finished second in the National League MVP voting. The Boras group will also negotiate deals for Atlanta outfielder J. D. Drew, Boston catcher Jason Varitek, Red Sox pitcher Derek Lowe, and Phillies starter Kevin Millwood this off-season.

Just a year ago, when owners moaned about the game's grim economics, Boras boldly asserted that he could still get a $252 million deal for A-Rod. Now, baseball is coming off a killer season, with entertaining races, a marked increase in attendance, and a Boston–St. Louis World Series that produced the highest television ratings since 1999. Boras, with evangelic fervor, tells one media outlet after another that the clubs are brimming with cash and should feel free to spend it liberally.

He unveils a new term for his stars—"icon players"—and adds a cherry on top in October when he signs up Chicago White Sox outfielder Magglio Ordonez, who had been represented for years by the Reich, Katz and Landis agency. The process, Boras says, was initiated completely at the behest of Ordonez.

"I don't know Magglio Ordonez other than the fact that he contacted us," Boras says. "He wasn't happy with the service that he was receiving, and he just didn't feel the people who represented him had an understanding of baseball."

The Reich, Katz, and Landis people respond that the remarks are "scripted" and totally in keeping with Boras's M.O. Like major-league teams, Boras's fellow agents don't care for him a whole lot. But they've yet to figure out a way to beat him.

No matter how often agents play golf with their clients or want to feel like part of the "in crowd," they'll always be outsiders to an extent. Nothing drums that home quite like a firsthand encounter with Barry Bonds.

At the 2003 All-Star Game in Chicago, Matt Sosnick by coincidence found himself on the Westin hotel elevator with the San Francisco Giants slugger. He took advantage of the opportunity to introduce himself and share a heartfelt sentiment.

"Barry," Matt said, "my family lives near you in Hillsborough. My dad and I are big Giants fans, and I just wanted you to know how much we appreciate all the good memories you've given us over the years."

Matt proceeded to spend eight floors in awkward silence as Bonds stared vacantly at a spot on the elevator wall directly over his head. As the door opened and they entered the lobby, he couldn't help but recall the near–fist fight between Bonds and former Giants second baseman Jeff Kent in the dugout several years earlier.

Geez, maybe it wasn't Jeff Kent's fault after all, Matt thought.

Sosnick has never been much of a Kent fan—having heard through the grapevine that Kent was a pretty irascible guy during his tenure with the Giants—and in October, something happened to drive home the point. Matt was sitting in his living room watching Houston and Atlanta play Game 4 in the National League Division Series, and he died a little inside when Chad Qualls gave up a three-run homer to the Braves' Adam LaRoche. While Chad was kicking himself over grooving a first-pitch slider, Matt checked out the replay and seethed.

As the other Houston players stoically watched LaRoche's home-run ball clear the fence, Jeff Kent angrily bent over at second base and smacked the dirt with his glove in disgust. It's a gut reaction, perhaps, but to Matt, he was showing up a rookie pitcher. Not to mention a Sosnick-Cobbe client.

"I thought it was pretty self-centered and embarrassing," Matt says. "Kent's a veteran player making $9 million a year, and Chad had been in the big leagues for, like, 6 weeks. It's amazing to me that some people feel so comfortable being pricks, they'll do it in front of millions of people."

At least Barry Bonds is nice to Dontrelle Willis. Earlier this year they were bantering before a game when Dontrelle made Bonds a proposal: *If I strike you out, you give me an autographed bat.* Sure enough, Dontrelle whiffed Bonds in August with a fastball, and he arrived at Pro Player Stadium the next day to find an autographed bat at his locker.

Dontrelle's second season in Florida, as a whole, does not exude the same feel-good vibe as his rookie year. He goes 10–11 with a 4.02 ERA, for a team that finishes third in its division and has much of the final month disrupted by hurricanes. When the Marlins demote pitching coach Wayne Rosenthal, a local newspaper writes that Dontrelle had long since stopped listening to Rosenthal's instruction. Dontrelle is more puzzled than angered by the observation. But then, he's learned to roll with the notion that people will take their shots. He still hears rumblings that the Marlins should move him to the bullpen, and he chafes over the perception that he's too nice to bust hitters inside and keep them honest.

"I'll come in and scratch your numbers off if I have to," Dontrelle says.

When Major League Baseball approaches Dontrelle about going on a postseason All-Star tour of Japan, he quickly says yes. He'll spend early November in the Far East, then return to Florida and begin working out with his buddy Juan Pierre in preparation for 2005.

Endorsement-wise, he is not going the way of Jerome Walton just yet. Dontrelle and Marlins teammate Mike Lowell compare their off-field deals in a good-natured way on road trips, and time after time Lowell checks out Dontrelle's haul and says, "Damn, D, again?" Other teammates see the stack of gloves in Dontrelle's locker and hear about his card deals and occasionally make inquiries. He puts in a plug for his agents, and feels as if he has an even bigger stake in the future of Sosnick-Cobbe.

As a product of the Alameda streets, Dontrelle knows a hustle when he sees one, but he's also aware that an agent needs a certain confrontational edge when things get tough. He wondered if Matt possessed it, but his initial apprehension quickly passed. He hasn't regretted telling his family members to back off and let Sosnick do his job.

"I was worried because Matt's such a nice, sweet guy," Dontrelle says. "I was like, when everything comes down, is he going to fight or hit the fence? You always want people in your corner to be good people and kind-hearted, but if somebody throws a beer bottle at you, you want your group to be ready to mount up. Sometimes there's no time to be rational. Sometimes you just have to get it done."

If Dontrelle stays healthy and takes care of business on the field, the best is yet to come. Matt recently called the Players Association and learned that Dontrelle's service time is likely to qualify him for salary arbitration in February 2006, which means that he's on the cusp of making some real money. Even though Sosnick and Cobbe plan to farm out the case to arbitration consultant Rick Shapiro, Matt will be sweating the details.

A few days before Dontrelle leaves for Japan, they have lunch at a burger joint in Burlingame, and Matt outlines his vision for his star client's financial future. The Marlins had their chance to reach out and do the fair thing in February, but they squandered their goodwill with that meager $53,000 raise. If Dontrelle is meant to sign a multiyear deal now, that's fine. If Matt has to haggle with the team year by year until Dontrelle's free agency in 2008, that's fine, too. Dontrelle has a favorite line to describe himself, and Matt has since adopted it: *Do not mistake my kindness or goodwill for weakness, because if you do that, you're going to end up being very surprised.*

"I want to be known as a good guy, and so does he," Matt says. "I also want to get him a ton of money. I mean, we're talking about one of my best friends, and this really sets up his family. But it's also the deal that I'll be evaluated on by all the other players and the draft picks who are going to consider going with me or leaving me. This deal right here is going to be paramount to my business."

When Dontrelle sees Matt getting progressively more animated and it's clear that his agent is ready to fight—not hit the fence—he pronounces himself on board with the program.

"He's balanced," Dontrelle says, "and that's the key. He has his times where he's good, and he has his times where he wants to kill everybody, and that's cool. I respect that. It fires me up when I see that."

Matt and Paul are always on the lookout for nonbaseball opportunities to subsidize the agent business. They consider sinking some investment capital into a dozen Asian fusion restaurant franchises, only to reconsider when the cost of waiters and waitresses in the Bay Area makes the venture too expensive. Instead, they move forward with plans to start a marketing division in conjunction with the Sosnick-Cobbe agency. By partnering with importers in the Far East on products ranging from bobbleheads to computer bags, they hope to gain greater access to the advertisers, PR firms, and product line managers who can provide endorsement opportunities for their clients. It's the ultimate synergy.

Paul, adhering to a tradition of challenging himself mentally and physically with a major undertaking once a year, travels to the California wilderness and treks 14,494 feet up Mt. Whitney, the highest peak in the continental United States. He also becomes a father for the second time when his wife, Ellen, gives birth to a girl, Rachel Ann, who's 7 pounds, 13 ounces, and loaded with personality.

For most agents in the non–Scott Boras category, the winter brings a flurry of transactions that don't make headlines but are still life-altering to the people involved. Paul negotiates a minor-league free-agent deal with the Philadelphia Phillies for Chris Rojas, who will make $7,000 a month if he pitches in Double-A Reading and $8,000 a month for Triple-A Scranton. More important, Chris now has a fresh start and reason to hope that better things lie ahead. If he can learn to temper his emotions on the mound and harness his control, who knows? He has a strong arm, and he certainly won't fail because he's scared.

Paul receives some good news in the fall when word comes down on Freddy Sanchez's grievance against Pittsburgh. An arbitrator rules that Freddy wasn't healthy enough to play for Triple-A Nashville and should have been allowed to recover from his ankle injury on the major-league disabled list. As a result, Freddy recoups $32,000 and 25 days of big-league service time.

Paul Cobbe takes pride in the result because it means he was thorough in his preparation and gave the proper advice to a player in need. Isn't this what the business is supposed to be about? Not fending off predators, but protecting players' rights and safeguarding their interests. It's just the way Marvin Miller envisioned.

The process also gives Paul and Matt some credibility with the union and a little "street juice" in the clubhouse. When Pittsburgh teammates ask Freddy Sanchez about his grievance and he says, "My agents took care of it," it's the kind of word-of-mouth that goes a long way.

Paul finds it gratifying that Freddy Sanchez, Chris Rojas, Richie Gardner, and so many other players continue to make strides, and that he was around to watch them fight through injuries and setbacks and self-doubt. Even the dozens of players who washed out along the way have given him an education in the business and his personal motivation.

"A big portion of the effort we put into this is for clients who'll probably never make it to the big leagues," Paul says. "We'll never see a cent from these guys. So if that's the case, why don't we just drop them? Because we've made a commitment."

A year or two ago, Matt and Paul reacted to every departure with hand-wringing and introspection. *Is there something flawed with our business model? Do these other agents know something we don't?* Now, they've learned to anticipate bad news and intellectually adjust if need be. Sometimes, guys are going to leave for no other reason than that they're going to leave. In this job, lots of things just happen.

Departures are now coming in trickles rather than in droves. When a fringe Minnesota Twins prospect named Kevin West calls and says he's leaving Sosnick-Cobbe for the Reich, Katz, and Landis agency, Matt lapses into a funk for a day. Then he's up at 6:00 the next morning frantically writing out his list of 15 important errands to complete before noon.

He truly believes he's finding a balance through candor, conciliation, and Better Living through Therapy. Jacob constantly tells him his biggest problem is that he's overly earnest. But he knows no other way.

"What I really want is to live my life in as authentic a way as I can," Matt says. "Clarity to me is much more important than happiness."

What he really wants is to be a business partner *and* a friend. While his quest to find Mrs. Matt Sosnick endures, he's not lacking for a family unit. Not when dozens of baseball players need his help and guidance.

In early autumn, Matt receives a phone call from Clovis Burton, Cory Dunlap's mother, with a proposal of sorts. She's done her homework and found that Matt was a positive influence on Dontrelle Willis the previous winter, and she wonders if he might have a place in his spare room for Cory this off-season. There's a dual purpose to the request: The more time Cory spends in Burlingame, the more time he'll focus on baseball and avoid potentially negative influences in the old neighborhood in Alameda.

Matt is receptive to the idea of Cory moving in, at least on a part-time basis. While Cory seemed a bit stern in their initial meeting at the

Oakland Airport Hilton, Matt discovers that the kid is a hoot, with a generous side and a cornball sense of humor that's endearing.

In September, Sosnick and Cobbe invite their June draft picks to San Francisco for a 49ers game, the traditional Saturday night dinner at Izzy's steak house, and an outing at a comedy club. As they troll the streets of San Francisco in Matt's Jaguar, Cory takes great relish in rolling down the window and hurling a few wisecracks at passers-by.

"Hey, drop the zeros and get with the heroes!" Cory yells as they pass several attractive young women standing with their dates in front of a nightclub. And everyone in the car busts out laughing.

Cory's skills on the field are apparent for all to see. He hits .351 for the Dodgers' Ogden affiliate in the Pioneer League and shows a preternaturally advanced knowledge of the strike zone for someone so young. With a .492 on-base percentage in his first professional season, he's a *Moneyball* monster-in-training.

The Dodgers reward Cory with a trip to the Florida Instructional League, but they send everyone home early in advance of Hurricane Jeanne. When Cory's mom broaches the possibility of him moving in with Matt, he's initially hesitant to disrupt his workout routine and leave his comfortable surroundings in Alameda. Then he gives the matter some thought and warms to the idea.

"I'm going to go over there and spend some time with him," Cory says. "As long as I can bring girls over there, it's all good."

Cory knows all about Matt's generous side. When Clovis wanted to travel to Utah for Cory's professional opener in June, they knew it would be a stretch financially. Then Matt stepped in and paid for the flight and told Cory to repay him whenever he could. "That tells you a lot about his character," Cory says.

The adrenaline rush of being named Baseball America's number-seven Pioneer League prospect hasn't gone to Cory's head. He spends $25,000 on a used Lincoln Navigator with massive hubcaps, but he plans to save the rest of his bonus money in the event that he never gets to the big leagues. Cory is also committed to keeping his weight in check, working to improve the weaker elements of his game, and sticking with people that he trusts for the duration.

"I don't have no plans to change agents," Cory Dunlap says. "It's a loyalty thing. Matt's loyal to me, I'm loyal to him. I'm cool. I made my decision on who I picked and I'm gonna go with him. I'm gonna stick with him."

It is with a sense of déjà vu and anticipation that Matt Sosnick hands Cory a spare key to the duplex in Burlingame. Déjà vu because it was only a year ago that Dontrelle Willis called from the shoulder of Route 101 with a tremor in his voice and a prelude to the ultimate agent-player bonding moment. Anticipation because in this crazy business, you never know what tomorrow will bring.

"Help yourself to anything in the refrigerator," Matt Sosnick tells Dodgers minor-minor Cory Dunlap, his new off-season roommate.

"And please, drive safely."

ACKNOWLEDGMENTS

The acknowledgments section of a book should be the easy part because it marks the end of the research grind, the solitary hours in front of a computer screen, and the obsessing over every comma. But in some ways, it's the most daunting because it's the repository for feelings and emotions that words can only partially convey.

This book never would have been written without the wisdom and faith of David Black, who coaxed a 13,000-word proposal out of a wannabe author, then refused to take no for an answer in finding a publisher. As a literary agent, he belongs in a higher league. I would also like to extend my thanks to Jason Sacher and Gary Morris of David's agency for being so helpful and attentive to my every question and concern along the way.

I'm forever indebted to Jeremy Katz at Rodale for seeing potential in this project and throwing his energy and resources behind it, and for giving me two editors—Pete Fornatale and Dan Listwa—with extraordinary patience, good judgment, and the sensitivity to embrace what I was trying to accomplish. Lou Schuler of Rodale was instrumental in the early formulation of the book, and Drew Frantzen, Nancy N. Bailey, and Susannah Hogendorn took painstaking care in smoothing out the rough edges at the finish.

My sportswriting colleagues were always there with a recollection or a detail. Thanks go out to Mike Berardino, Mark Fainaru-Wada, Peter Gammons, Richard Justice, Ron Kroichick, Kevin Kernan, Liz Mullen, Ross Newhan, Ed Price, Jason Reid, Ken Rosenthal, Jim Salisbury, Allan Simpson, and Jayson Stark for their input. And Gil Pagovich, a walking agents encyclopedia, was always quick to provide updates on the latest news developments in the business.

Neal Scarbrough of ESPN.com was my personal savior, giving me a spot on his staff and a place to pursue my book-writing ambition during a period of career transition. I'm also grateful to John Walsh, Patrick Stiegman, and David Kraft of ESPN, and to Jim Loftus, Scott Ridge, and Matt Szefc for making sports journalism fun and sticking with me during a challenging year. Editors just don't come any better.

Steve Fainaru, a role model for all journalists, helped out with encouragement, advice, and a place to crash on my trips to San Francisco. David Himmelstein and Curtis Eichelberger provided welcome suggestions on my initial proposal, and Jon Scher, Allen Lessels, Ken Rosenthal, Jim Callis, and John Manuel read portions of the manuscript and flagged errors while providing positive reinforcement. Alan Schwarz, Jim Caple, Buster Olney, and Darren Rovell gave me a place to think aloud and commiserate on the challenges of the book-writing process, and Nick Fortuna, the pride of Teaneck, New Jersey, continually bailed me out in times of panic or distress.

You find that some people just go the extra mile. Marvin Miller, a giant in the baseball business, was gracious enough to give me nearly 3 hours of his time on a September afternoon in Manhattan, and Gene Orza of the Players Association sat down for an interview 2 days after getting out of the hospital. Chris Dahl and Greg Bouris of the players union were, as always, quick to assist. So was Christian Oliver of the California Highway Patrol, who was courteous and professional in helping me reconstruct the details of Dontrelle Willis's car accident.

This book never would have been possible if not for the cooperation of Matt Sosnick, an American original, who gave me entrée to his life and had the courage to consent to a candid portrayal even when it wasn't easy. He is a *mensch* in the truest sense of the word. The same goes for Matt's partner, Paul Cobbe, whose patience and enthusiasm for the project never waned. I owe both of them in a very big way.

My final thank-you is the most heartfelt and gratifying one of all because it hits so close to home. It goes to my daughters, Emily and Caroline, for making each day a joy to behold, and to Deb, my best friend, voice of reason, and the woman who puts up with me for better or worse. I couldn't have done it without you.

SOURCES AND INTERVIEWS

The sports agent business is a relatively new phe-
nomenon, and the catalog of books on the topic is sparse, but several
provided insight and helpful background in the course of my research.
The list includes: John Helyar's *Lords of the Realm*, Marvin Miller's *A
Whole Different Ballgame*, Bob Woolf's *Behind Closed Doors*, Ron
Shapiro's *The Power of Nice*, Randal A. Hendricks's *Inside the Strike
Zone*, and Kenneth L. Shropshire and Timothy Davis's *The Business of
Sports Agents*.

I relied more heavily on the coverage of newspapers, periodicals, and
assorted baseball Web sites. The *Hayward Daily Review*, *Alameda Times-
Star*, *Contra Costa Times*, and *San Francisco Chronicle* provided bountiful
details of Dontrelle Willis's youth in Alameda, while the *Miami Herald*,
Fort Lauderdale Sun-Sentinel, and *Palm Beach Post* were founts of information on his rookie season with the Marlins.

Among the other sources consulted were the *Akron Beacon Journal*,
Arizona Republic, *Arkansas Democrat-Gazette*, *Atlanta Journal*, *Baseball
America*, *Boston Globe*, *Chicago Tribune*, *Denver Post*, *ESPN the Magazine*,

Houston Chronicle, New York Post, Newsday, New York Times, Omaha World-Herald, Orange County Register, Philadelphia Inquirer, Seattle Times, Sports Illustrated, Street & Smith's SportsBusiness Journal, Sporting News, and *USA Today.*

More than 150 people consented to be interviewed for the book. Several baseball officials, agents, and players spoke on background and preferred anonymity, but the following individuals all gave generously of their time and have my utmost appreciation. My sincere apologies to anyone I might have missed.

Agents: Tony Attanasio, Barry Axelrod, Joe Bick, John Boggs, Scott Boras, Casey Close, Paul Cobbe, Jay Franklin, Jeff Frye, Dennis Gilbert, Jeremy Kapstein, Mark Levin, Jim Lindell, Andrew Lowenthal, Miles McAfee, Mike McCann, Keith Miller, Jeff Moorad, Michael Moye, David Pasti, Rob Plummer, Ron Shapiro, Matt Sosnick, Tommy Tanzer, Toby Trotter, Joe Urbon, Ryan Ware

Baseball executives and scouts: Chris Antonetti, Mike Arbuckle, Chuck Armstrong, Billy Beane, Josh Boyd, Chris Buckley, Josh Byrnes, Frank Cashen, Frank Coonelly, Tony DeMacio, Jerry DiPoto, Pat Gillick, Lou Gorman, Roland Hemond, Gary Hughes, Jim Hendry, Dan Jennings, Stan Kasten, Walt Jocketty, Larry Lucchino, Rob Manfred, Tim Mead, Stan Meek, Omar Minaya, John Mirabelli, Doug Melvin, Dan O'Dowd, Gene Orza, Gus Quattlebaum, Tim Purpura, Mike Radcliff, David Rawnsley, J. P. Ricciardi, John Schuerholz, Mark Shapiro, Tony Siegle, Paul Snyder, Michael Weiner, Logan White, Frank Wren

Players, coaches, and managers (minor leagues): Dusty Bergman, Cory Dunlap, Jesse Foppert, Matt Ford, Chris Gruler, Travis Hanson, Mike Hinckley, Bobby Jenks, Bob Keppel, Steve Nelson, Scott Olsen, Jason Pridie, Jon Pridie, Chris Rojas, Rex Rundgren, Troy Schader, Corey Shafer, Andy Sisco, John Scheschuk, Zach Sorensen, Adam Stern, Josh Willingham, Tracy Woodson

Players, coaches, and managers (major leagues): Sandy Alomar Jr., Don Baylor, Tim Belcher, Phil Garner, Tom Glavine, Goose Gossage, Clint Hurdle, Reggie Jackson, Chipper Jones, Al Leiter,

Curtis Leskanic, Brandon Lyon, Tom McCraw, Matt Morris, Joe Oliver, Jake Peavy, Chad Qualls, Mark Redman, Jim Riggleman, Jimmy Rollins, Joe Rudi, Gary Sheffield, Dontrelle Willis

Friends and relatives of Matt Sosnick and Paul Cobbe: Ron Abta, Ellen Cobbe, George Cobbe, Jill Cohen, John Devincenzi, Rochelle Eskenas, Brad Galinson, Andrea Glick, Eric and Chelsea Karp, Alisa Law, Jeff Lubow, Mark Mintz, Pat O'Brien, Eric Polis, Josh Rittenberg, Ron Sosnick, Isabella Sikaffy, Cynthia Werts, Victoria Zackheim

Other voices: Julie Bradley, Clovis Burton, Tim Davis, Ed DeBenedetti, the Richard Dodson family, Mazonie Franklin, Joyce Guy-Harris, David and Lyn Hinckley, Charlie Juhl, Perry Keith, Wally Lubanski, Rommie Maxey, Bobby Mintz, David Morway, Jerry Prior, Steve Reed, Jeff Rosenberg, the Gerald Russell family, Kenneth Shropshire, Jim Saunders, Tom Stubbs, David Taylor, Manny and Yvonne Upton, Andrew Zimbalist

INDEX